KELSI BOOCOCK

Healthy Kelsi

**SIMPLE, VIBRANT
PLANT-BASED FOOD**

BATEMAN BOOKS

To my amazing mum and dad. You've always taught me to live a life full of fun, laughter, travel and adventure. Thank you for your continuous encouragement and support in every aspect of my life. This book would be nothing without you both!

Contents

Welcome   7

Staple Ingredients   14

Ingredient Substitutes   17

Be Flexible in the Kitchen   18

Rise and Shine!   23

Cheers!   61

Snack Time   79

Sun-kissed Salads   105

Mouth-watering Mains   133

Sweet Treats   177

Back to Basics   209

Thank yous   219

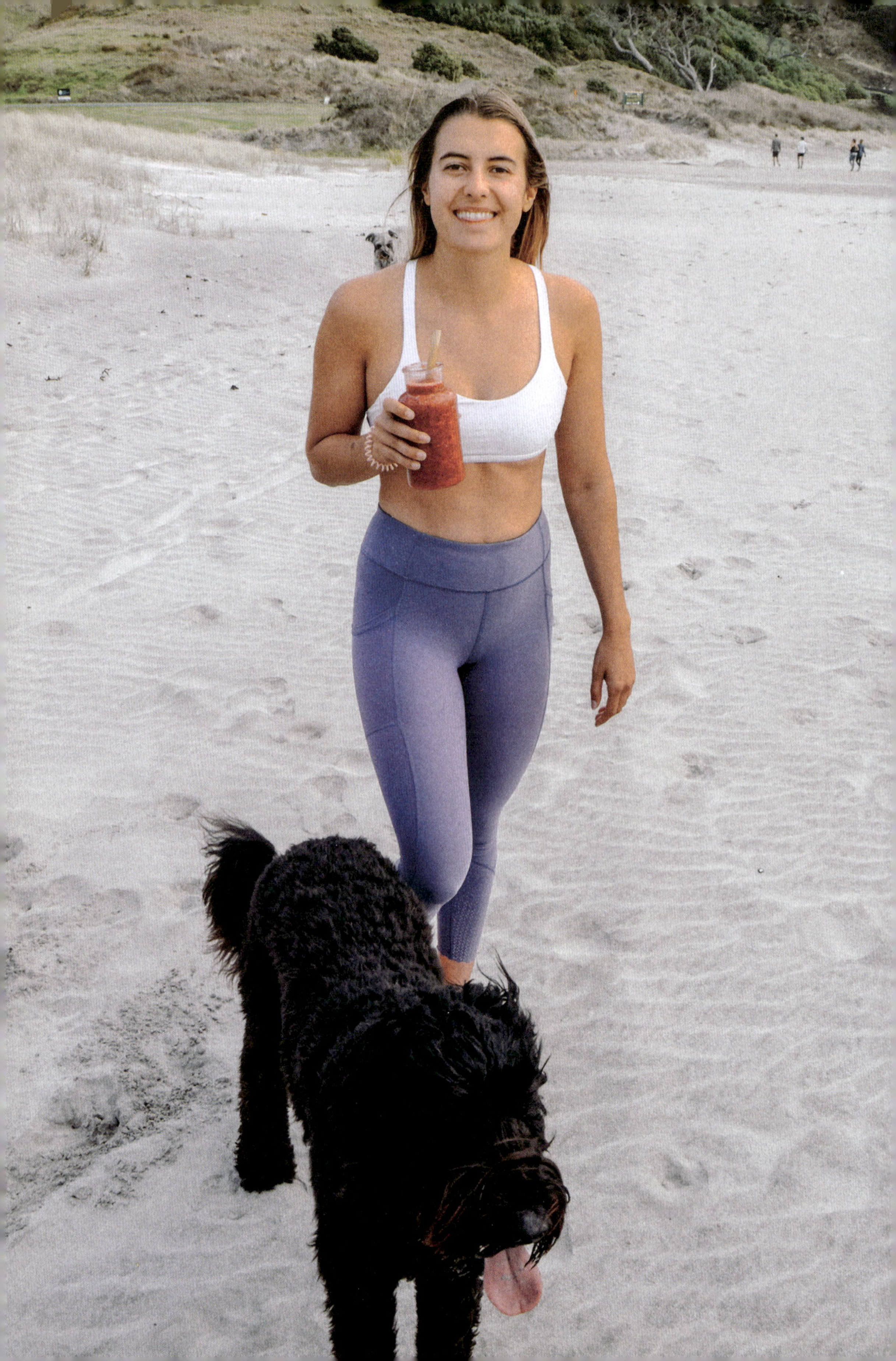

Welcome

ABOUT ME

Hi, my name is Kelsi Boocock. I grew up just north of Auckland in New Zealand. I've had a passion for healthy, nutritious food since I was a competitive swimmer during my school years. Some of you might know me from my blog and Instagram page Healthy Kelsi, where I love to share new recipes and photos as well as my travels and adventures.

I've dreamt of putting my own cookbook together for the longest time. It turns out it is no easy task, but with a bit of determination, luck and support, I created something that I am genuinely proud of. Throughout this project I have mastered so many new tricks in the kitchen as well as brand-new skills like food photography and food writing. I've spent days in the kitchen testing recipes (my family happily volunteered their services for the taste-testing part). I had the pleasure of 'veganising' a lot of the dishes and sweet treats that were my favourites growing up, such as the Custard Tarts on page 191 and the Self-saucing Sticky Date Pudding on page 204.

I was born into a family that loves not only eating but eating food that is nourishing and natural. When I finished high school, I decided to study a Bachelor of Retail Business Management as it worked in well with being an athlete. It wasn't long after I finished my degree that I realised my passion was actually cooking and making people happy through creating and sharing food. This was about the time I decided to start eating a wholefood plant-based diet, due to developing some digestive issues. I dedicated myself to creating amazing flavours with plants. I soon learnt that it is easy to create flavourful food using less-processed, whole ingredients. Since changing my diet I've honestly never felt better and eating this way has helped me to develop such a positive relationship with food. My approach to food has changed over time and I'm sure it will continue to do so. However, my philosophy is quite simple:

'Eat colourful foods in their natural form and try not to think too much about it.'

Over the last few years, I believe I have developed a healthy, balanced lifestyle around food and exercise. Researchers have found definite links between what we eat and our mental health. It is my belief that making certain positive changes in your diet can reduce stress, lift your mood, and improve your confidence, self-esteem and general wellbeing. Fruit, vegetables and wholegrains help maintain your energy levels for longer, which is why I love to use them in my recipes.

WHAT INSPIRES ME IN THE KITCHEN?

I had a pretty amazing childhood, which included visiting some unique countries — my mum and dad were always organising the next family adventure. When I was eight years old we moved to Nadi, Fiji for just over a year, where I attended an international school. This allowed me to experience different cultures at a young age. Most Sundays we would take the boat out, doing all kinds of activities, including waterskiing, wakeboarding and surfing.

When we returned to New Zealand, we were lucky enough to live by the ocean and — as you can probably tell by the images in this book — that is where I have always felt happiest. I love to mix up flavours, textures and colours from places I've travelled to with the more familiar flavours of home, and develop them into simple, tasty recipes — like speedy breakfasts and colourful salads, to burgers, curries and stews, as well as sweet treats and desserts.

WHY PLANT-BASED?

Nowadays there is a massive disconnect between what we eat and how it makes us feel — food is meant to sustain our bodies and help us feel our best. When I first changed my diet to mostly wholefood and plant-based, I noticed such positive changes, including in my energy levels, skin and mental wellness. I became fascinated with learning about the optimal diet for our health. I found that fruit, vegetables, nuts, seeds, grains and legumes are the best source of nutrients for my body. I became obsessed with turning produce that most people dislike into something delicious. I want *Healthy Kelsi* to be a resource for anyone who wants to improve both their mental and physical well-being and eat some divine food along the way.

FOR THE PLANET

To be honest, I didn't start eating a plant-based diet because of the benefits for the planet but now it's something I think about often. It's no secret the world is facing a climate emergency. Thousands of acres of rainforest are cut down every day to make way for cattle farming. Going vegan even one day a week can free up land for more energy-efficient food production and help reduce greenhouse gas emissions. A Meatless Monday can be a great place to start!

FOR THE ANIMALS

Factory farming is practiced all around the world and is the leading cause of animal cruelty. Billions of animals a year are born and bred for consumption. I'm not saying the entire world should go plant-based overnight, that's not realistic. However, being conscious of what we're consuming can have a huge impact on animal welfare.

FOR OUR HEALTH

This book is free of refined sugar and caters to many people with dietary requirements, including those who are gluten-free. I've also offered options to substitute where it may be needed. I really do believe that my way of eating is, in many cases, a positive lifestyle

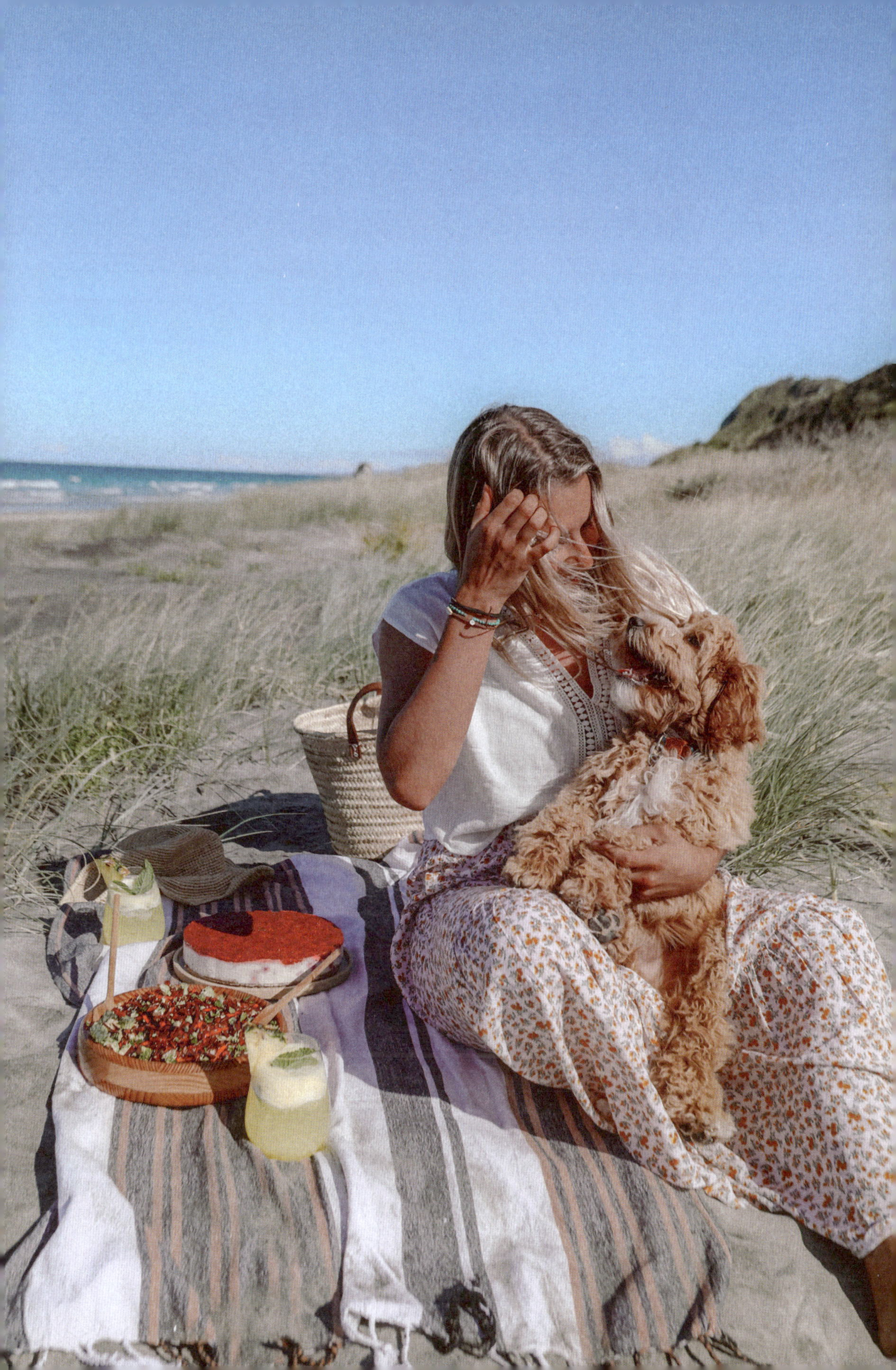

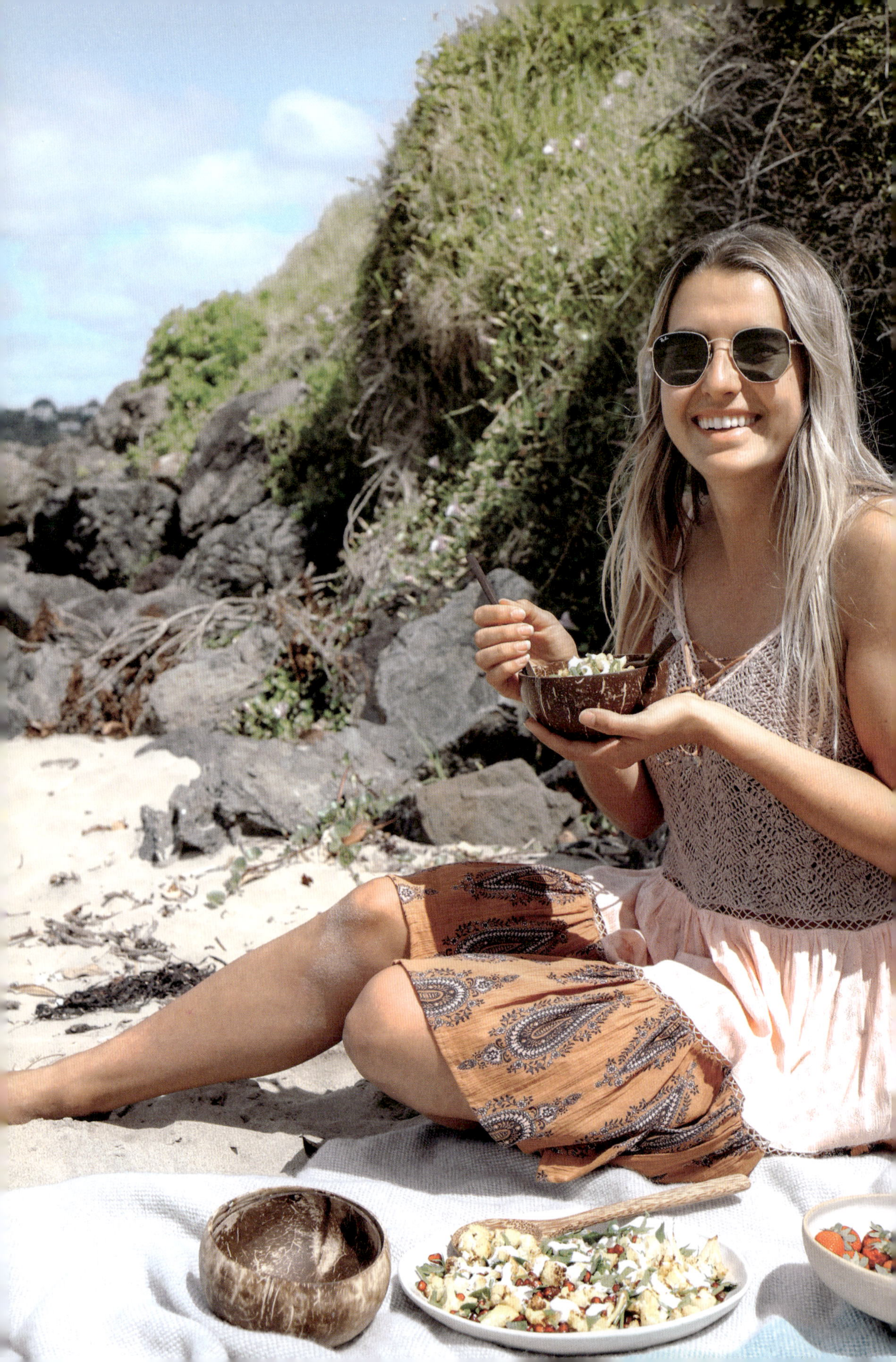

choice and not just a 'fad diet'. However, I am the last one to dictate what anyone should or shouldn't eat. So, please, just take whatever you want from this book. No pressure here! Everyone has different needs and foods that make them happy, but I do strongly believe that by adding more natural colours and more plants to your diet, it's hard not to feel better, inside and out. I wanted to create a book that can be used by everyone, so feel free to add or change ingredients depending on your lifestyle. If you want meat with your salad, add meat; if you feel the need for a sugar hit, add sugar. On the other hand, if you or your family are wanting to cut down on animal products and refined sugars then this book is the perfect way to start.

KNOW YOUR FOOD SOURCES

No doubt you will be familiar with the saying 'You are what you eat.' It seems crazy to me that so many people have no idea where their food actually comes from. If you are eating highly processed food and too much protein from animals that have been raised in a stressful environment and given food they weren't meant to eat, it seems logical to me that it may impact you in negative ways. Try visiting your neighbourhood market, getting to know your local farmers and learning how they look after their crops and animals.

If you do your shopping at the supermarket, try to opt for organic produce where affordable. Organic produce means its free from chemicals, pesticides and other contaminants. Try to choose fresh, and if you do have to go for the packet option, watch out for dodgy labels and marketing tricks. Just because it says 'natural', doesn't mean it really is. Look for labels such as 'certified organic'.

Always make a point of knowing where your food comes from. This way you can make a conscious decision about what goes into your body

CONNECT WITH ME

I post new recipes regularly on my social media channels @healthykelsii and blog www.healthykelsi.co.nz as well as updates from my life, including travel photography and surfing adventures. I would love to see your food creations, too, so be sure to tag me on Instagram and Facebook, or flick me a message with any questions you may have.

My mission is to share with people how easy it is to cook healthy, delicious food and to encourage people to eat more plants. I poured my heart into this project and I hope you enjoy making (and eating) these recipes as much as I enjoyed creating them. For me, being healthy isn't about being on some fancy diet, but about nourishing your body and fuelling it with a variety of colourful, whole, plant-based foods. So why not give it a go? It's worth making the small changes. It's easier and more rewarding than you think.

I am so passionate about food and beyond grateful to have you along on my food journey. So, let's dig in!

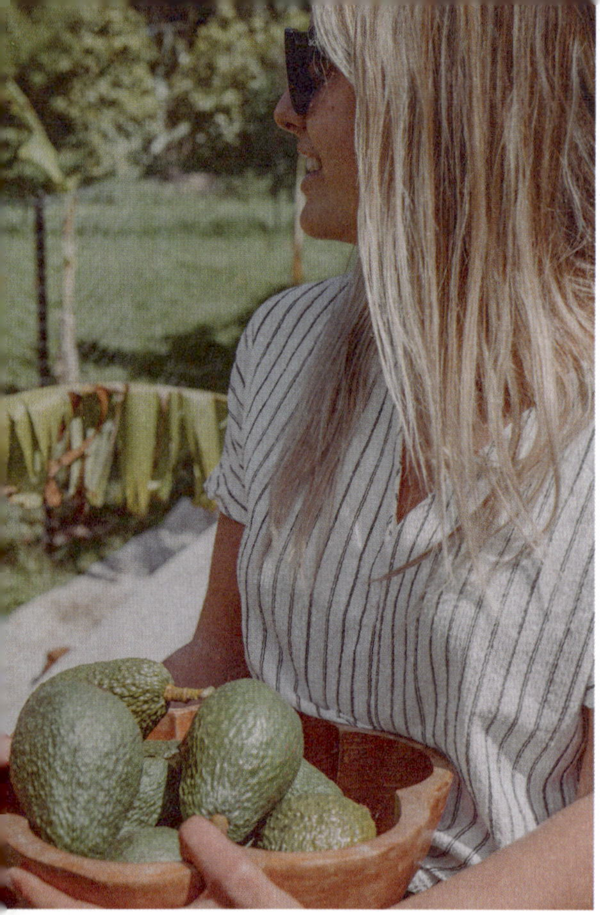
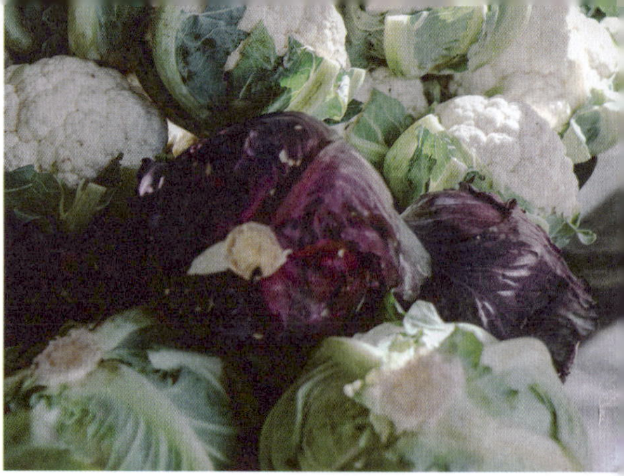
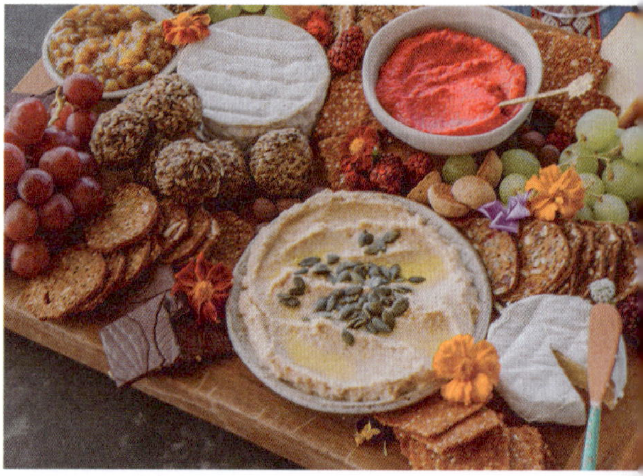
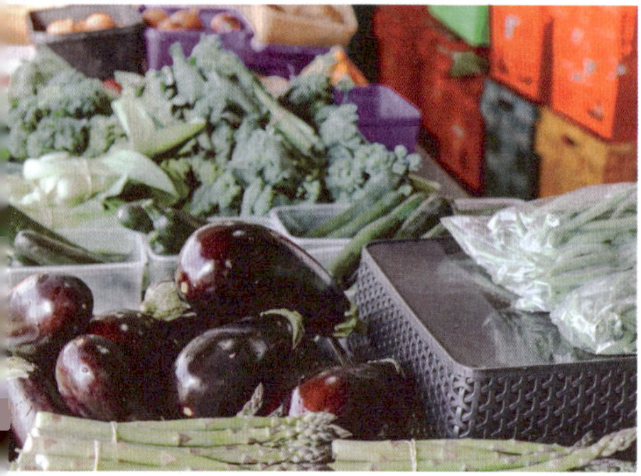
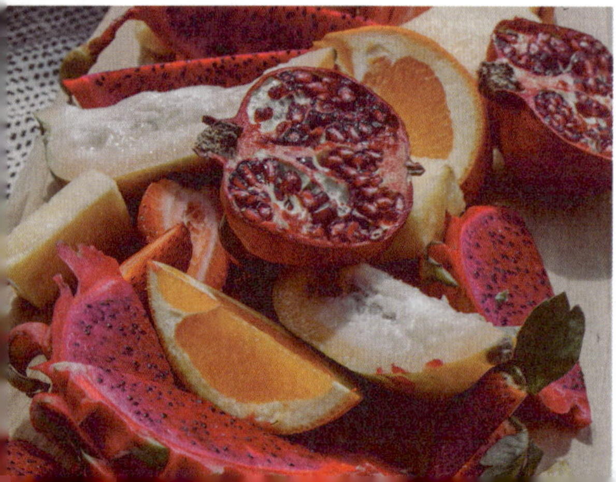
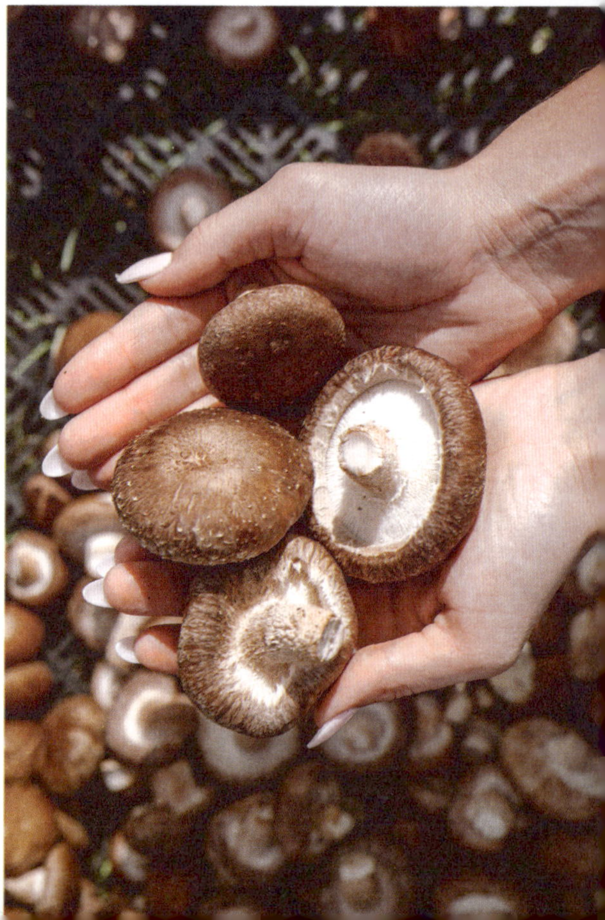

Q1.50

Staple Ingredients

I always try to keep certain staple ingredients in my pantry. It's amazing the variety of flavoursome meals you can make out of a little bit of fruit or a couple of vegetables, some grains and a sprinkle of herbs or spices.

ALMONDS
Almonds are among my favourite nuts and can be used to make butter, flour or milk, and are also perfect whole as a nutritious snack. Almond meal is a great gluten-free alternative when paired with other flours.

BUCKWHEAT FLOUR
My favourite alternative flour is buckwheat: a highly nutritious wholegrain that many people consider to be a superfood. Perfect for adding extra protein to things like pancakes and muffins as well as being a great gluten-free option.

CASHEWS
Soaked cashews are great for raw treats, ice cream, frostings and even dressings and cheese sauces. They can be used to create a creamy-textured base for a lot of dishes, while also being high in vitamins like potassium and B6.

CHIA SEEDS AND FLAXMEAL
For anyone who doesn't yet incorporate chia seeds or flaxmeal regularly into their diet, I highly recommend changing that. Nutritious and high in Omega-3s, adding a spoonful to smoothies or sprinkling over your morning cereal offers an instant boost. Both improve digestion and help you absorb nutrients. They are perfect egg replacements and can be added to almost any sort of baking.

CHICKPEA FLOUR
I love chickpea flour for savoury goods such as corn fritters and falafels. Low in calories, it is rich in a ton of vitamins and minerals including iron and magnesium.

COCONUT CREAM/MILK
I like to keep canned coconut milk and cream in the pantry as both are perfect for raw treats, curries and sauces. They are a superb source of healthy fats.

COCONUT SUGAR
Coconut sugar is one of my favourite sweeteners as it is less processed than table sugar and includes many more nutrients. However, this doesn't mean it's good for you to have in large quantities. Any sweetener is still sugar after all.

FRUITS AND VEGETABLES

I like to 'eat the rainbow' and try to eat seasonally due to the nutritional benefits of plants growing in their natural outdoor climates. It's also more affordable, and you can purchase frozen fruits and vegetables that are out of season or even freeze them yourself. Bananas are perfect for snacks, smoothies and baking. As are apples, which I love to cook up with a bit of cinnamon for dessert. I always try to ensure I have leafy greens growing in the garden, too, as well as some chopped spinach in the freezer. Canned tomatoes are also great to have on hand for pasta sauces and bolognese.

GRAINS AND PULSES

I recommend always keeping a can or two of beans and chickpeas, as well as packets of rice and quinoa on hand. These fundamentals will allow you to create a meal base easily. An added bonus is that they all keep for a lengthy period.

MAPLE SYRUP

If ever someone I know goes to Canada, I always ask them to bring me back a large bottle of good-quality maple syrup. It's always been a favourite in my family. Try to buy real maple syrup, rather than the fake stuff full of additives. It's perfect for baking and raw treats as well as adding to pancakes and porridge.

NUTRITIONAL YEAST

I'm a little obsessed with nutritional yeast. It's super high in B12 and creates an amazing cheesy flavour when added to savoury dishes. Try my Cheese Sauce on page 172.

OATS

It's no secret, I love oats. They are rich in antioxidants and high in fibre, zinc and magnesium, and improve blood sugar control and keep you full for hours. Plus, I love turning oats into flour by blitzing them in a blender to make pancakes and muffins. You can find a recipe for oat milk on page 215.

SPICES

Possibly one of the most essential pantry staples is a well-stocked spice collection. With only a few simple spices you can turn a regular meal into something extraordinary. My top spice picks to keep on hand would have to be cumin, coriander, turmeric, paprika, cinnamon and a good-quality curry powder. In fact, there's a game-changing recipe to make your own curry powder in this book (see p. 211).

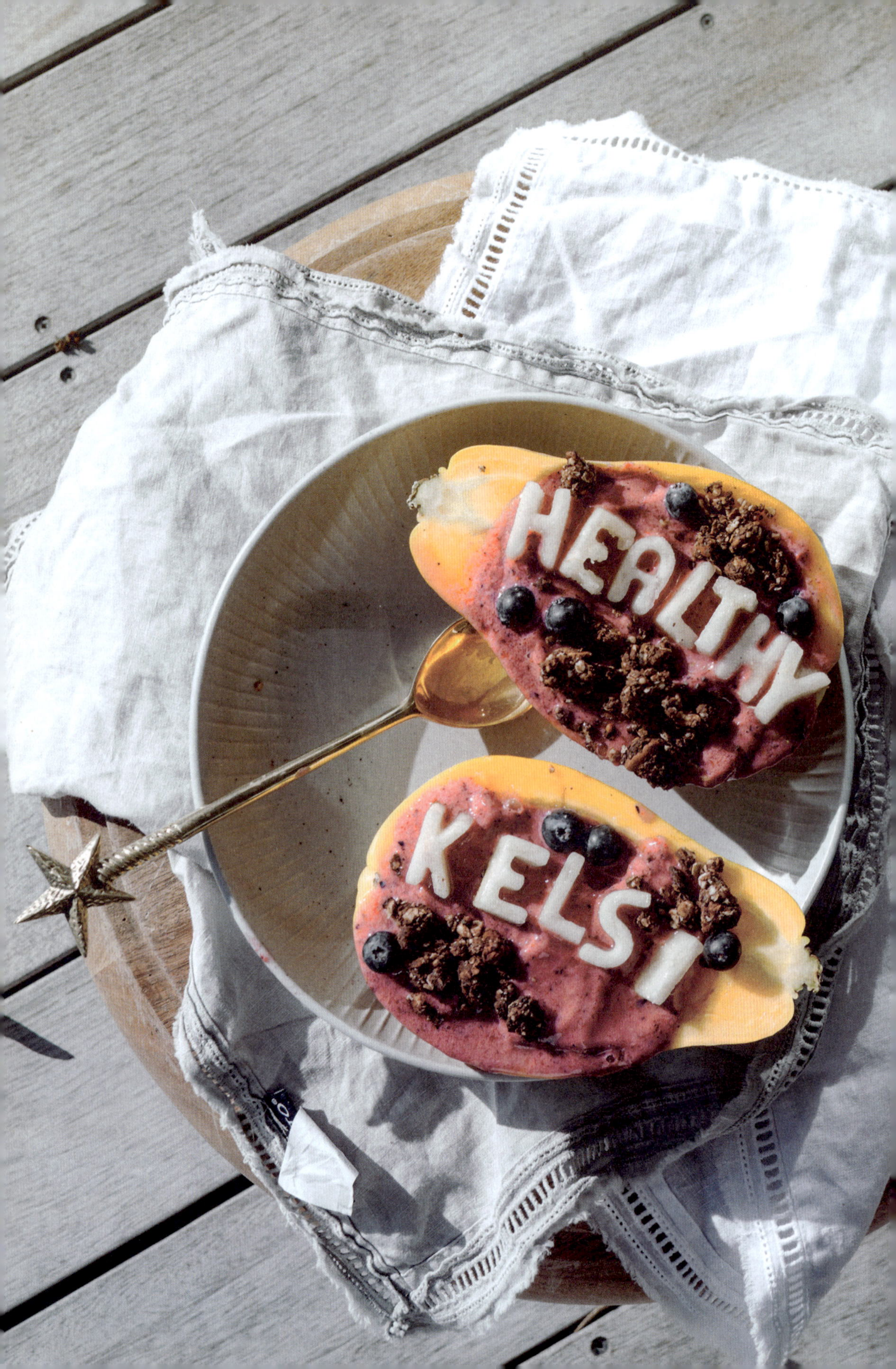
HEALTHY
KELSI

Ingredient Substitutes

Often when I decide I want to make a certain recipe, I realise that I don't have one of the ingredients in my pantry. So, I thought I'd give you a little rundown of my go-to substitutes for some of the common ingredients in this book. Please bear in mind, these are just general tips and tricks — I haven't trialled every recipe with these substitutions.

EGGS
I personally don't eat eggs, so there are no eggs in my recipes. However, you can substitute my 'egg replacements' with eggs if you prefer. I get a lot of questions on how to bake without eggs. My favourite egg replacements are flaxmeal, chia seeds, mashed banana, nut butters and aquafaba (the liquid from canned chickpeas).

FLOURS
I use a lot of alternative flours because I am conscious of different food allergies and intolerances. However, if the only thing in your pantry is plain flour, that usually subs in just fine. If the recipe calls for wholemeal or spelt flour and you are using a gluten-free flour, I recommend mixing it with an alternative, such as almond meal or buckwheat.

NUTS
I absolutely love using nuts and nut butters in my cooking. However, if you can't eat nuts, seeds are a great substitute. I also love using tahini as a nut butter substitute, it's beyond delicious in sweet and savoury food.

OATS
If you have coeliac disease or are gluten intolerant, you can find gluten-free oats at most supermarkets. Alternatively, you can substitute oats 1:1 with quinoa flakes, buckwheat flakes or millet.

OILS
I tend to pick what oil to use depending on the recipe flavours and how hot the oil will get during cooking or baking. Each type of oil has its own chemical composition and once an oil reaches a certain temperature, beneficial nutrients found in some oils are destroyed. Cooking oils with a higher smoke point retain their nutrients at higher temperatures. Some of those include avocado oil and grapeseed oil. For those who prefer to avoid using oils, nut butters have a delicious taste and a high fat content and are perfect in pancakes and brownies. Apple sauce is a nutritious alternative for adding moisture to baking mixes, as well as keeping goods fresh for a longer period of time. Yoghurt is another great alternative that makes baking light and fluffy, especially coconut yoghurt due to its high fat content. Almond and soy yoghurt work well also.

SWEETENERS
My sweet recipes all have a low sugar content (yet still taste divine!). I try to avoid refined sugars — however, if you prefer a little more sweetness, swap my unrefined sweetener with whatever sugar you have in your pantry. I also use maple syrup a lot in my recipes which can be replaced with date syrup, golden syrup, agave and rice malt syrup.

Be Flexible in the Kitchen!

I create all my recipes by throwing ingredients together, testing and refining, and using flavour as the measure of a dish's success. I really want people to enjoy the cooking process, rather than feeling confined by the 'rules' of a recipe. Trust your instincts, your cravings, your taste buds and work with what's available, what's in season and what's on special at the market. The majority of my recipes serve between 2–6 people but you can definitely adjust the recipes up or down.

I encourage you to get creative and put your own stamp on things. If this is your first time cooking plant-based food, some of the ingredients may seem unfamiliar to start with, but I promise that, like anything, the more you cook with whole plants the easier it gets.

EQUIPMENT
There are a few pieces of equipment that are helpful for creating some of the recipes in this book. However, if you don't have the equipment listed, you can of course make do with what you have. If there is just one essential piece of equipment I would recommend investing in, it would be a good-quality food processor or blender. A food processor with all the different attachments is always handy, but a trusty stick blender or small food blender can usually do the job just as well.

KEY
When you see the following symbols in my recipes, this is what they stand for:

GF	GLUTEN-FREE	**GFO**	GLUTEN-FREE OPTION
NF	NUT-FREE	**NFO**	NUT-FREE OPTION

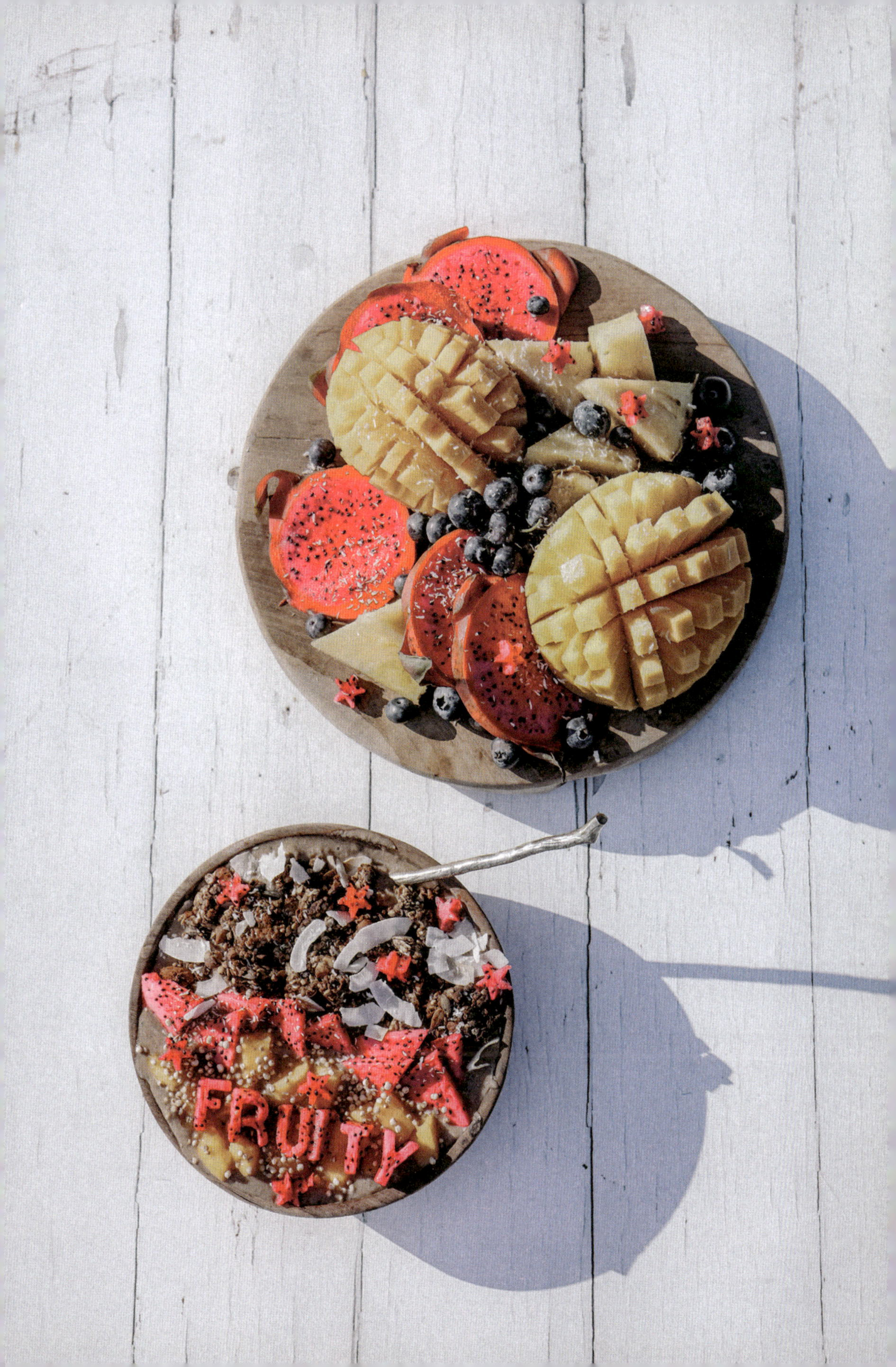
FRUITY

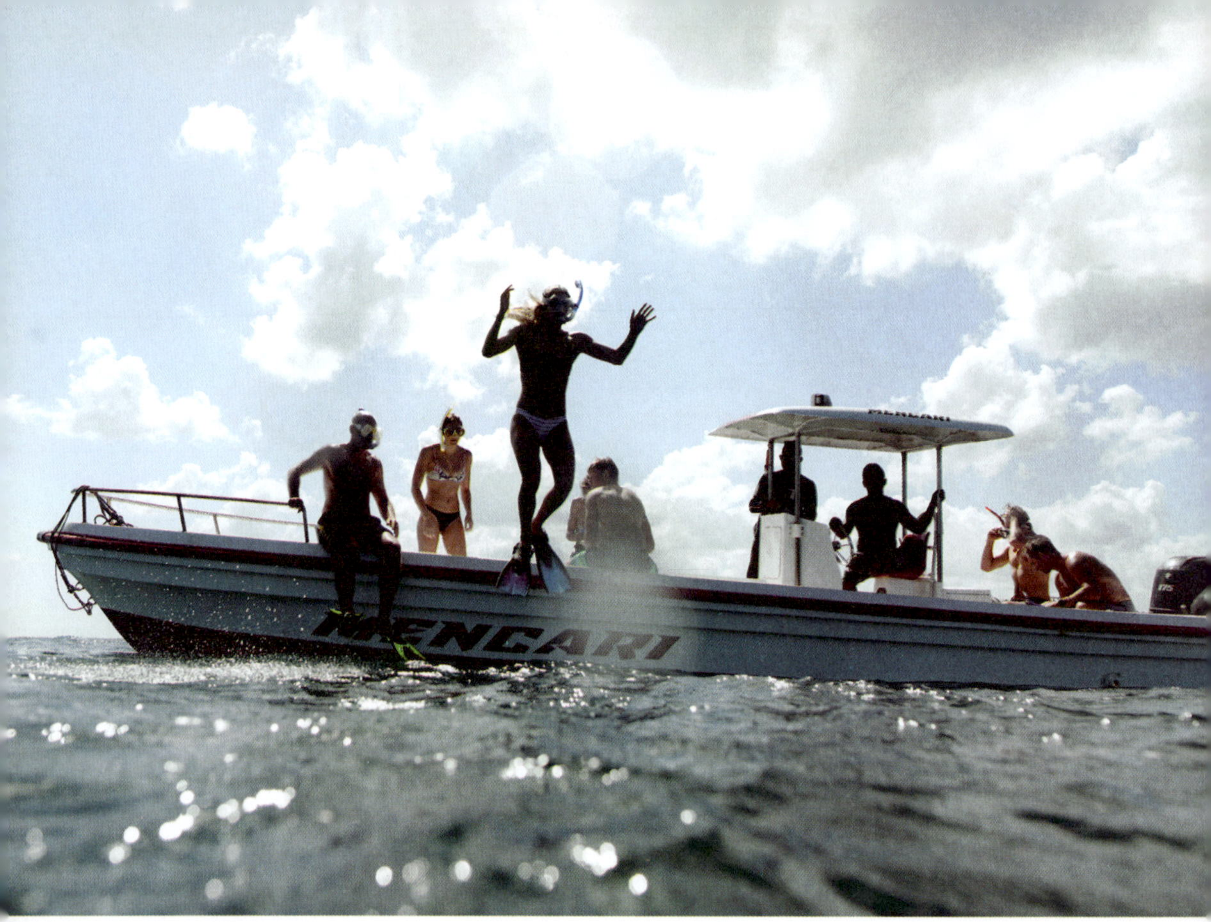
MENCARI

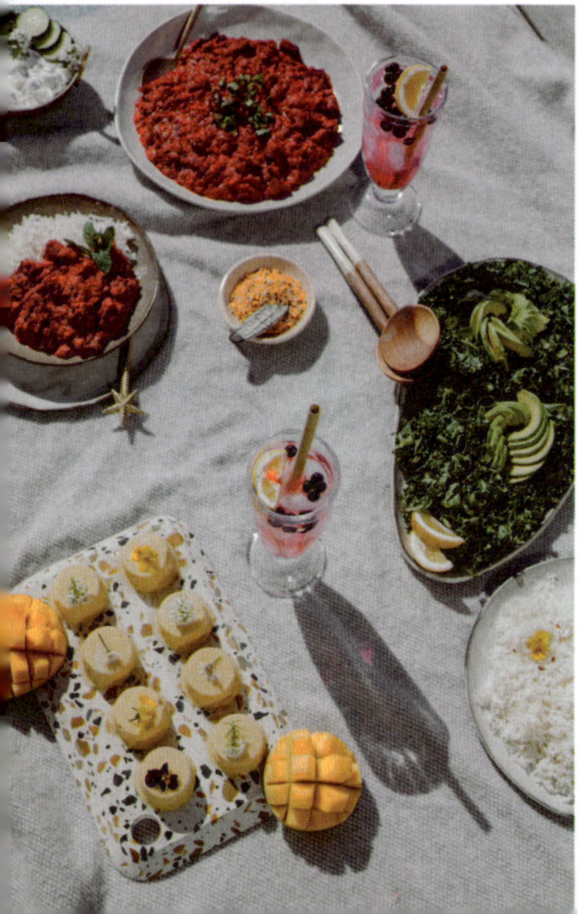

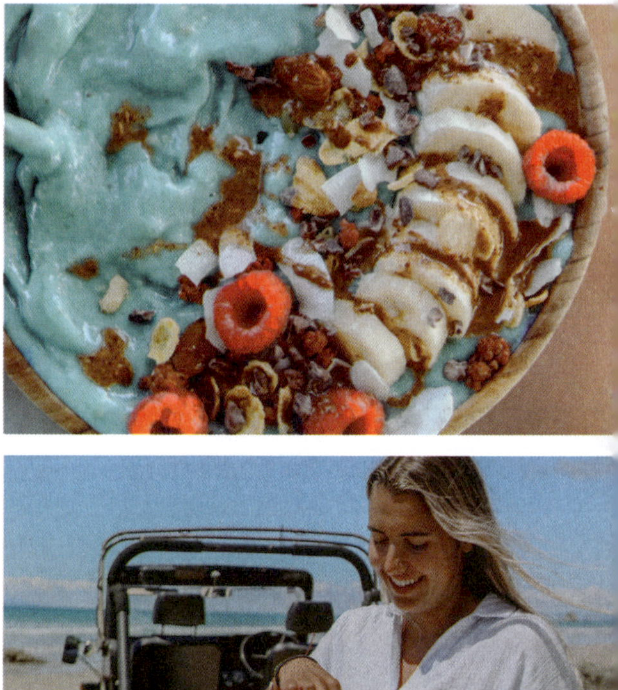

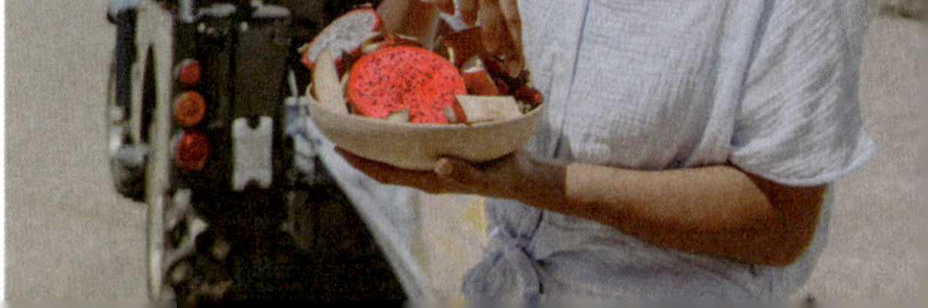

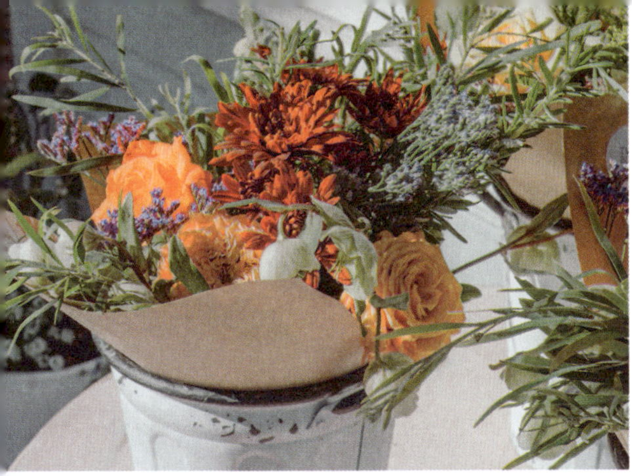
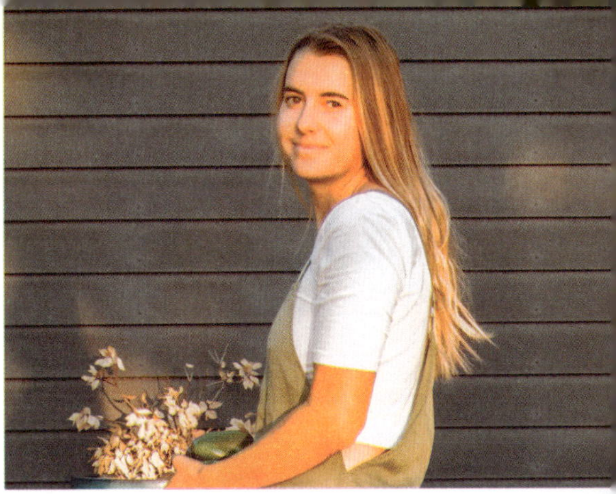
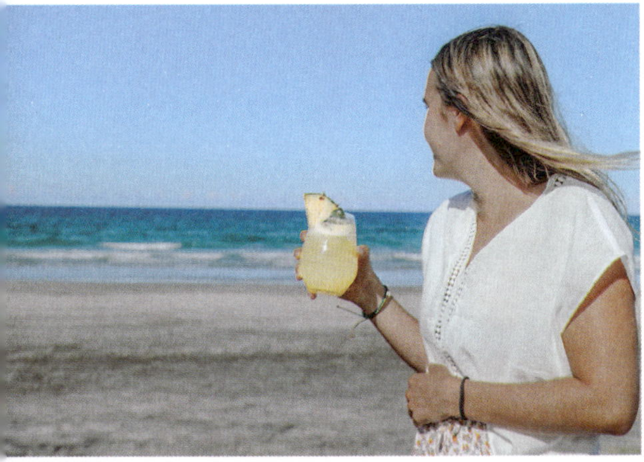
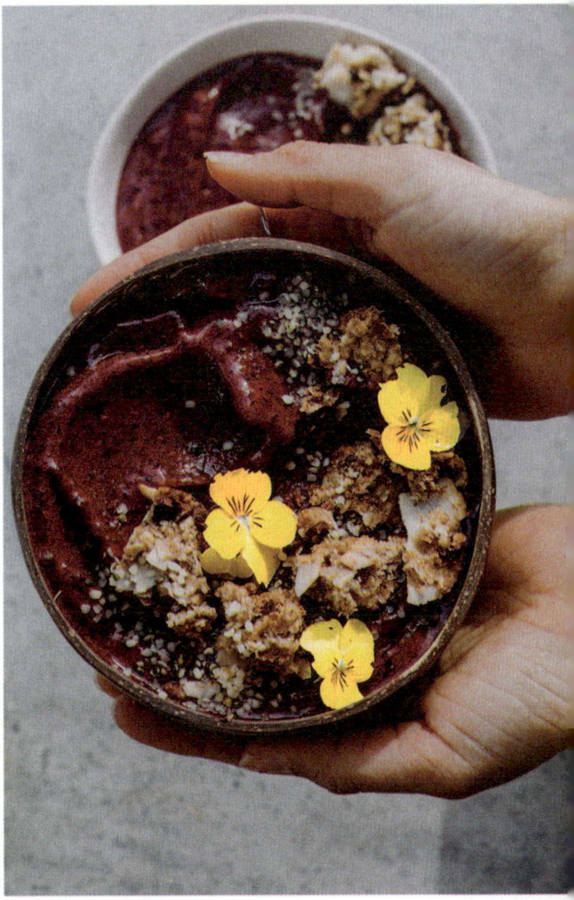
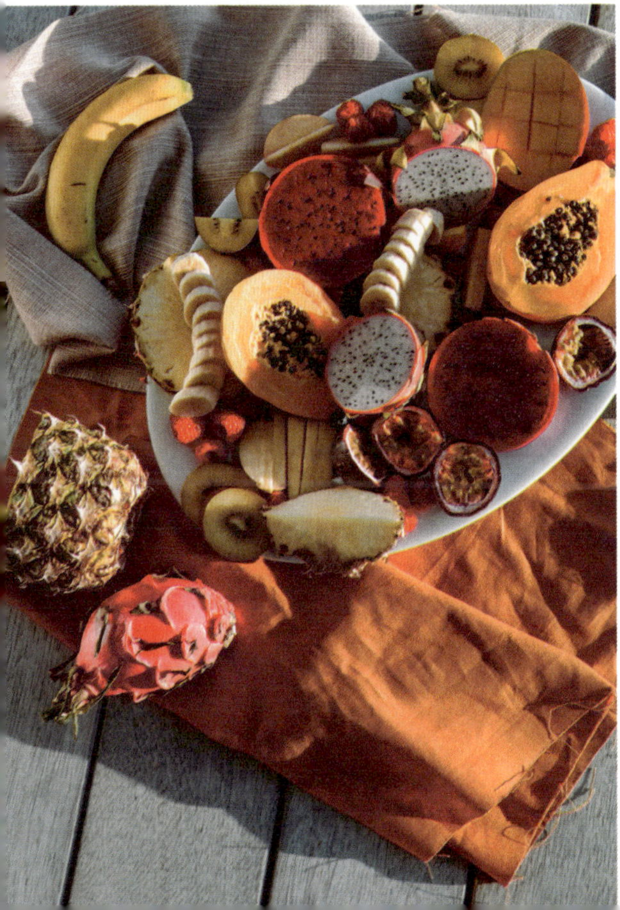
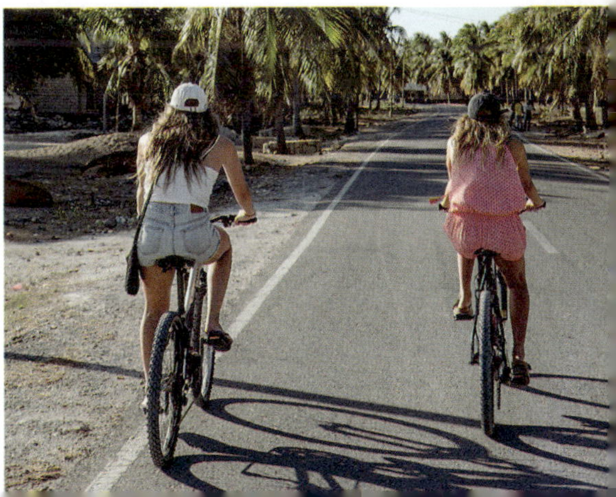

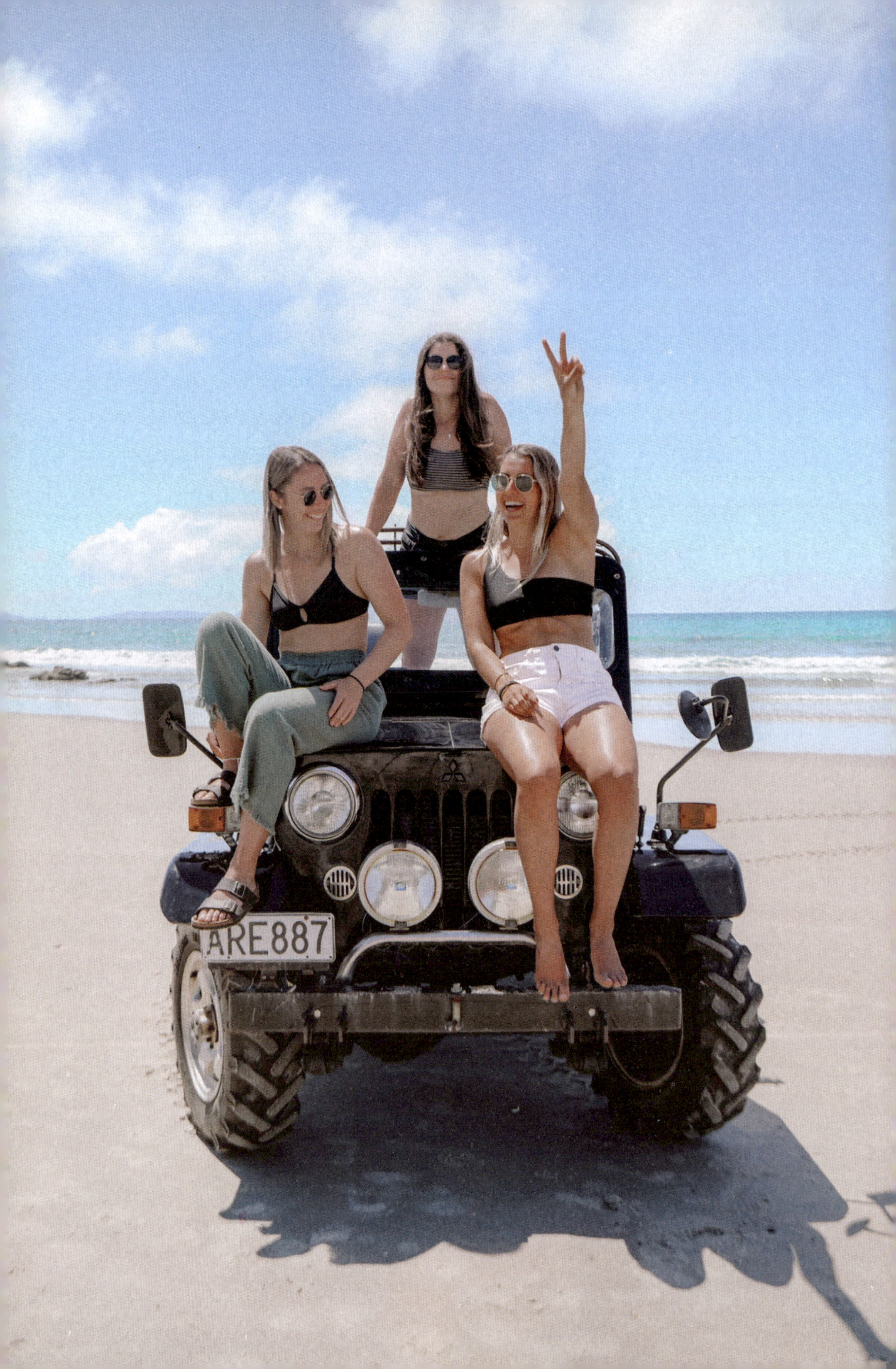
ARE887

Rise and Shine!

I believe that the choices you make in the morning can really affect the rest of your day, which is why I absolutely love breakfast! Hydration is one of the most important things when you first wake up — I try to leave a large glass of water next to my bed and make sure I finish it in the morning before I've reached the kitchen. I love to incorporate good fats, protein and carbs into my morning meal to ensure I feel full for a long period of time. I have included a diverse range of breakfast options in this chapter for both sweet and savoury lovers, or if you're always on the run I recommend preparing some breakfast muffins and cookies for your week ahead. Sometimes I even have leftover dinner for breakfast if I'm in a savoury mood!

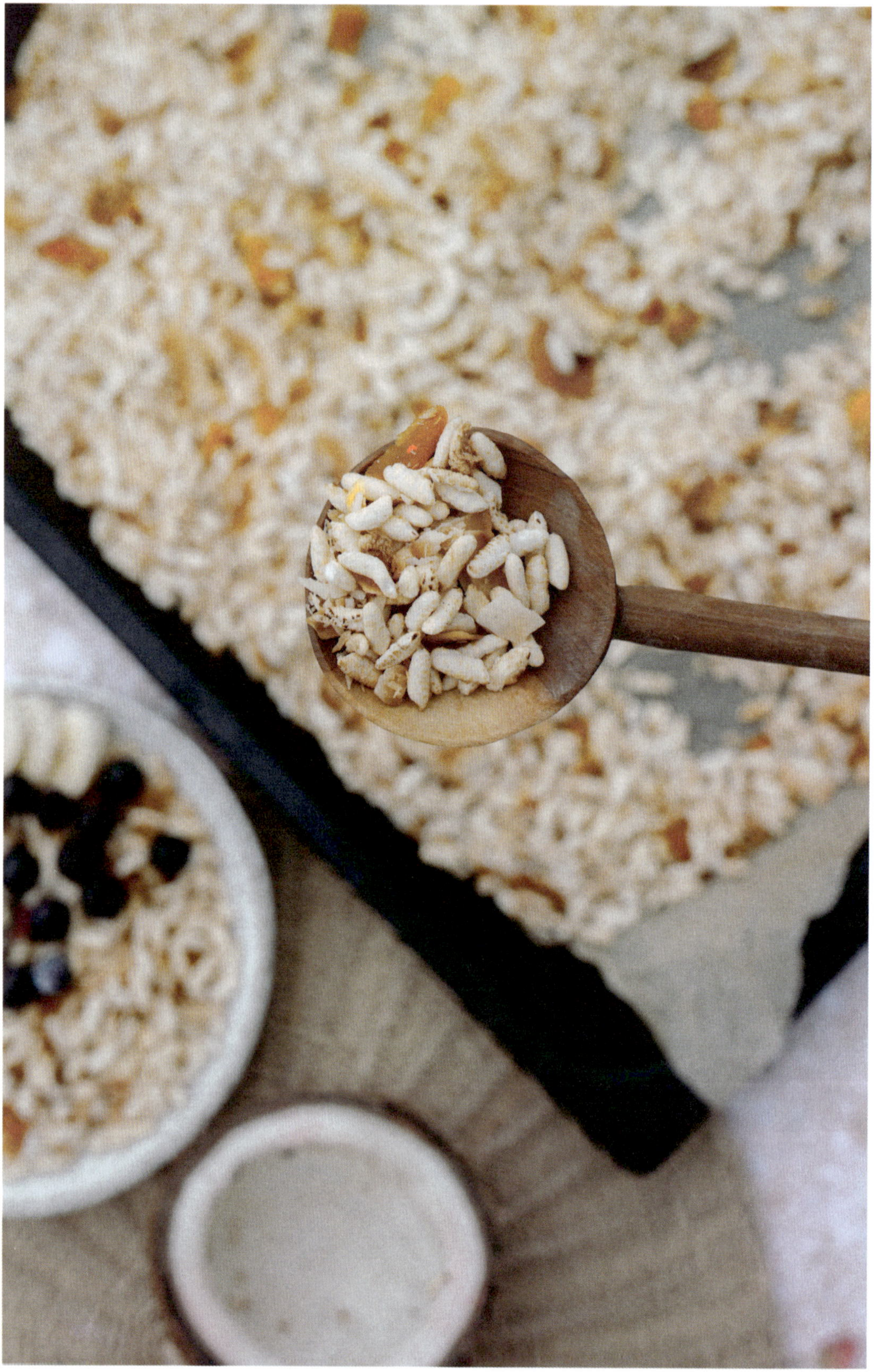

Apricot and Coconut Rice Bubble Muesli

Serves 8 • 20 minutes

Like every other kid, I loved rice bubbles when I was little, but my mum didn't like buying processed cereal for us. However, she did buy plain rice puffs which we loved to have for breakfast or in treats. I tested this recipe on my little cousins and they gave it the big thumbs up!

4 cups gluten-free rice puffs
1 cup coconut chips
½ cup desiccated coconut
1 tsp vanilla extract
2 Tbsp maple syrup
3 Tbsp coconut oil, melted
½ cup dried apricots, chopped

To Serve
Plant milk
Fresh fruit
Coconut yoghurt

Preheat oven to 180°C and line a baking tray with baking paper.

Add the rice puffs, coconut chips, desiccated coconut, vanilla, maple syrup and coconut oil to a large bowl and mix thoroughly. Tip the mixture onto the baking tray and toast in the oven for 10 minutes, tossing halfway through. Keep an eye on the coconut chips to ensure they don't burn.

Remove from the oven, add the chopped apricots and mix through. I like to serve mine with my homemade Oat Milk (see p. 215), fresh fruit and coconut yoghurt.

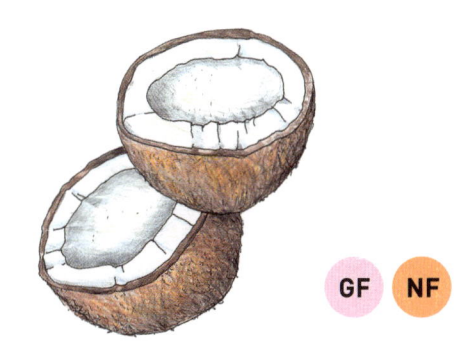

GF NF

Rise and Shine! • 25

Bircher Bowls

Serves 2 • 10 minutes (and overnight)

Bircher muesli is the perfect breakfast to take to work. It's also great for when you feel like porridge but it's a hot day. Prepare the bircher the night before and in the morning it becomes deliciously creamy and keeps you going until lunchtime.

1 cup gluten-free rolled oats
1 apple, grated
1 Tbsp chia seeds
1 Tbsp apple cider vinegar
1 Tbsp maple syrup
1 tsp ground cinnamon
½ tsp ground nutmeg
2 cups plant milk

To Serve
Fresh fruit
Coconut yoghurt
Hemp seeds
Pumpkin seeds

Combine all of the ingredients in a bowl or container, cover and leave in the fridge overnight. I like to top mine with fresh fruit, coconut yoghurt, hemp seeds and pumpkin seeds.

· · · · · · ·

Hot Tip: Make a batch of this bircher and leave it in the fridge for up to 3 days for breakfast on the go!

· · · · · · ·

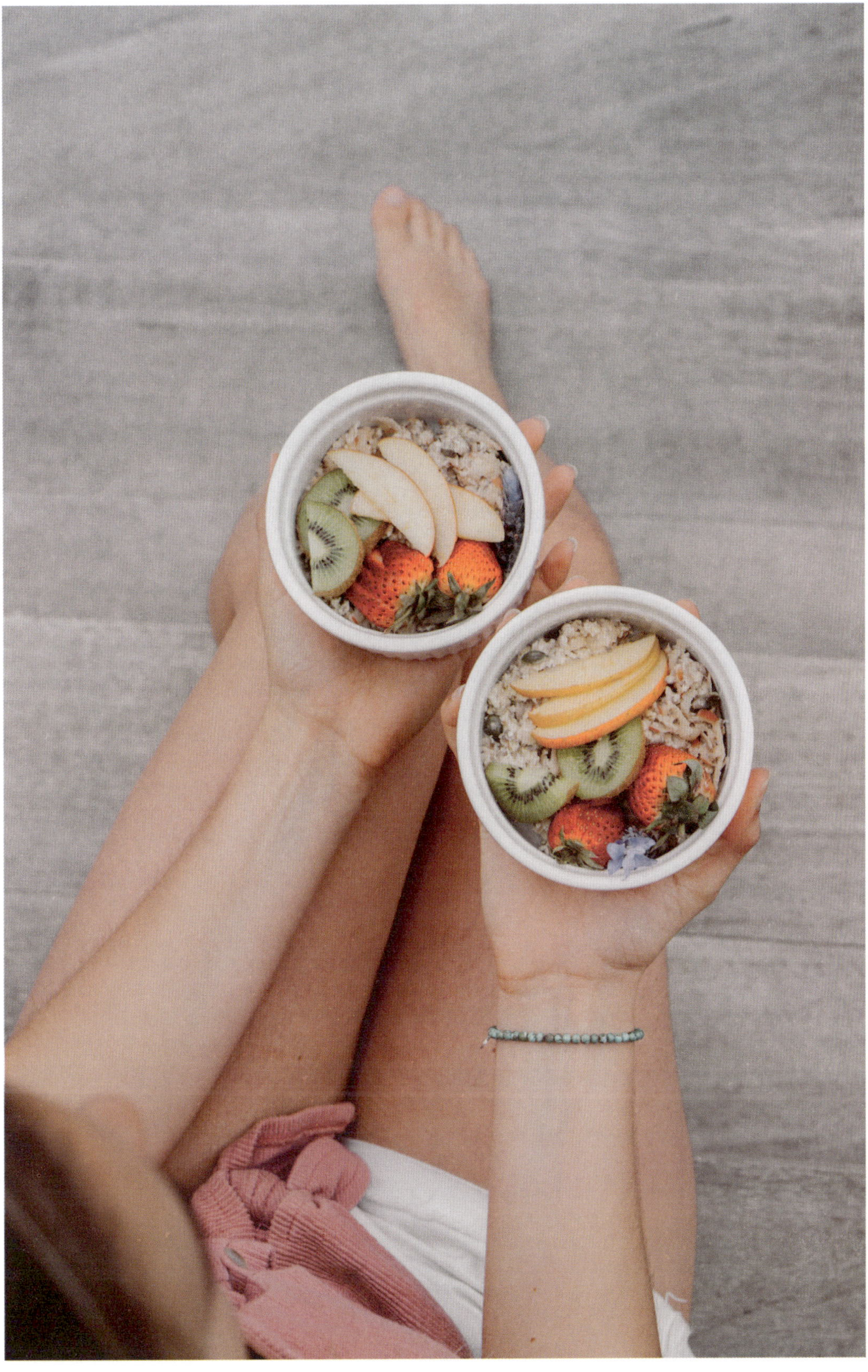

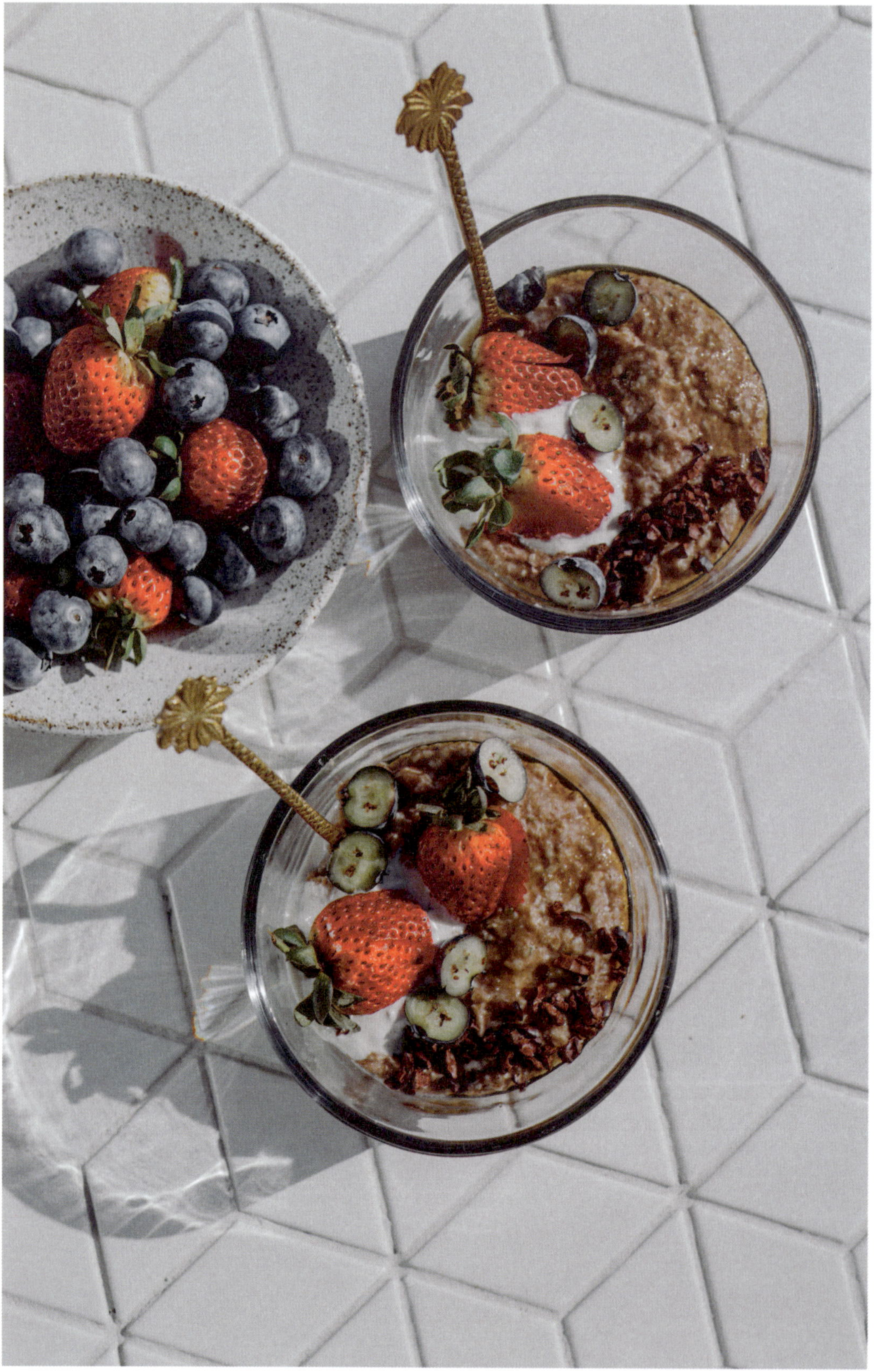

Chocolate Porridge

Serves 2 • 15 minutes

Chocolate is one of my favourite things to eat for breakfast — well, anytime of the day really. But I feel like it's even more exciting for breakfast, especially when it's good for you! Raw cacao is packed with antioxidants as well as being high in magnesium and protein.

1 cup gluten-free rolled oats
2 cups water
½ cup plant milk
1 Tbsp hemp seeds
1 Tbsp cacao powder

To Serve
1 Tbsp maple syrup
2 Tbsp coconut yoghurt
1 Tbsp cacao nibs
Fresh berries

Add oats and water to a small pot and place over a medium heat. Stir continuously and, as the liquid absorbs, add your plant milk ¼ cup at a time. When it almost reaches the consistency you like, add the hemp seeds and cacao powder and mix through.

Tip into two bowls and top with the maple syrup, coconut yoghurt, cacao nibs and berries, if desired.

• • • • • • •

Hot Tip: For a little extra protein, you can add chocolate protein powder to the oats while they're cooking!

• • • • • • •

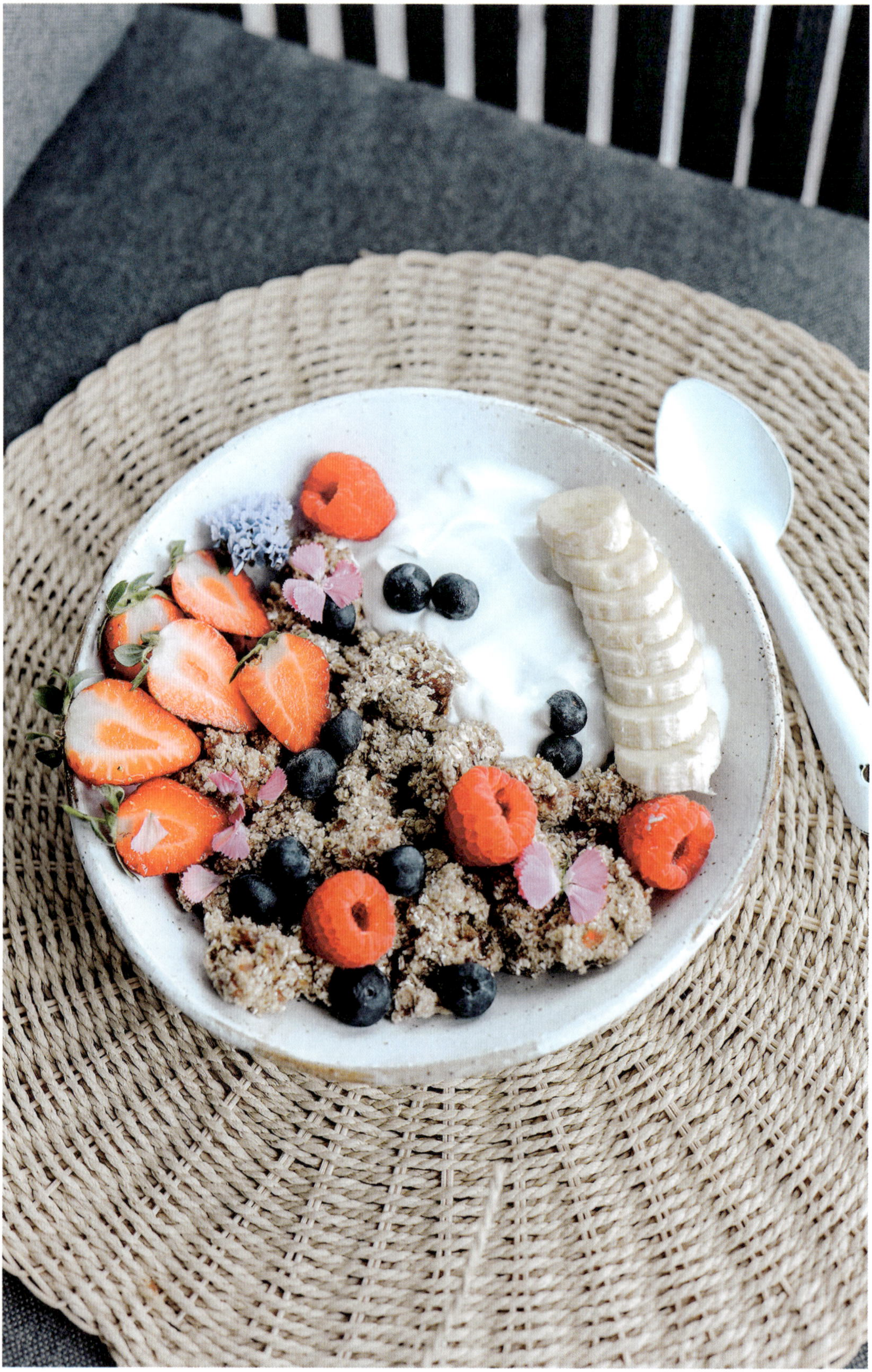

Banoffee Pie Rawnola Bowl

Serves 4 • 10 minutes

I almost always have a banana with my breakfast, I think because of all my years swimming. It was such an easy snack to grab on the go. This is a super healthy, wholesome recipe that I've been making for a long time — it's also a great afternoon snack.

2 ½ cups gluten-free rolled oats
1 banana
8 medjool dates, pitted
1 tsp ground cinnamon

To Serve
1 cup coconut yoghurt
1 banana, sliced
Fresh berries

Add all ingredients to a food processor and pulse until combined. Divide rawnola between four bowls and top with coconut yoghurt, banana and berries, if desired.

Store in the fridge for up to a week.

GF NF

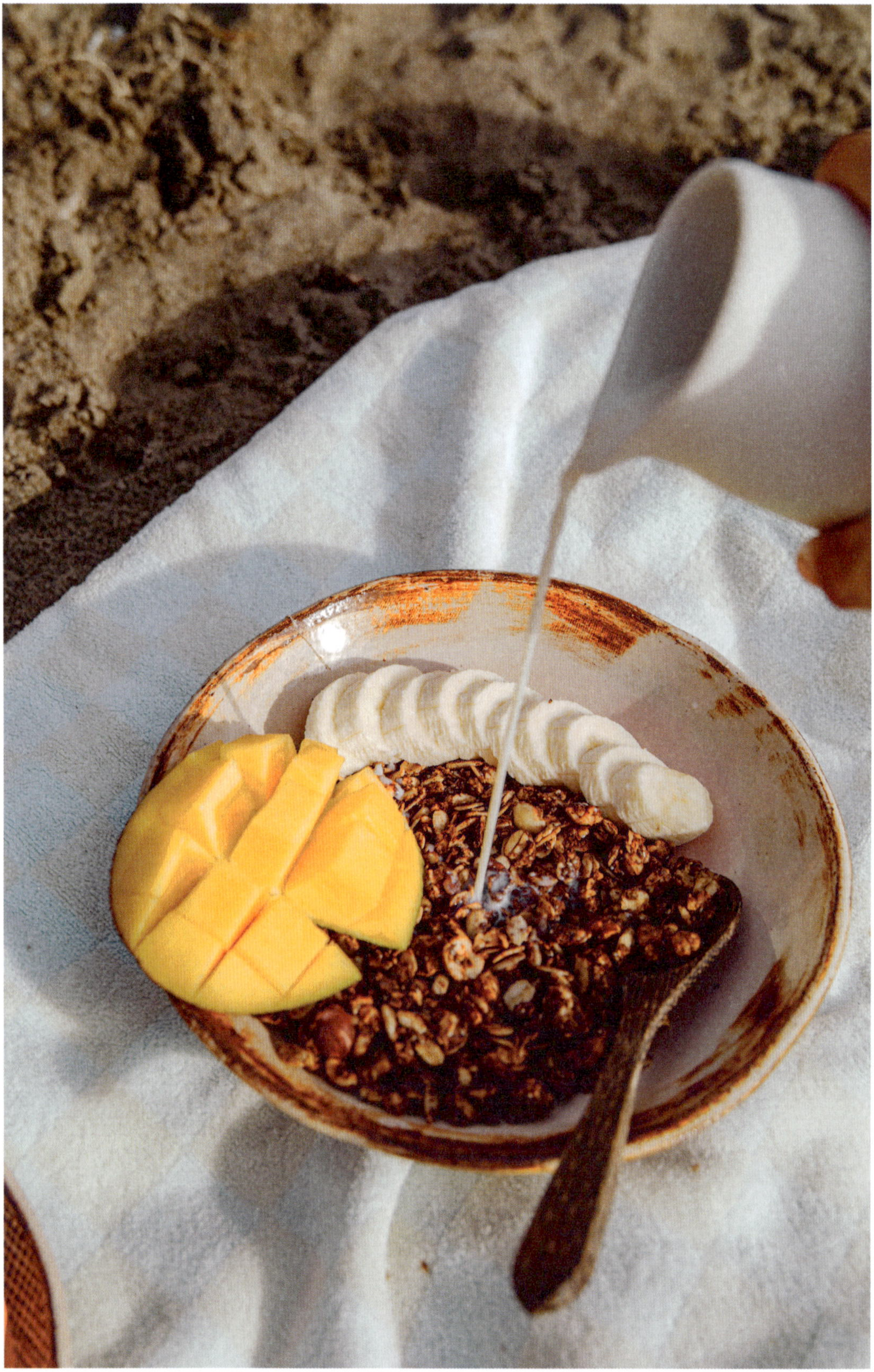

Oat and Nutty Chocolate Granola

Serves 6 • 45 minutes

The majority of the time I'm a sweet breakfast person, and this recipe satisfies those chocolatey cravings early on. This granola is very low in sugars as it only contains a little bit of maple syrup.

1½ cups gluten-free rolled oats

1 cup buckwheat

¼ cup sunflower seeds

¼ cup pumpkin seeds

¼ cup cacao powder

⅓ cup cacao nibs

1 cup nuts, roughly chopped (I use almonds)

⅓ cup water

¼ cup maple syrup

2 Tbsp almond butter

1 cup dried fruit (I like sultanas and goji berries)

To Serve
Plant milk
Fresh fruit

Preheat oven to 180°C and line a baking tray with baking paper.

Combine oats, buckwheat, seeds, cacao powder, cacao nibs and nuts in a large bowl.

In a small bowl, mix together water, maple syrup and almond butter. Tip the wet mixture into the dry and fold through until the dry mixture is completely wet.

Place granola mixture onto lined tray and cook for 25 minutes, tossing every 10 minutes. Remove from oven and stir through dried fruit. Serve with plant milk and fresh fruit.

GF

Fruit Salad Breakfast Muffins

Makes 10 • 40 minutes

These are a really good to grab on the go if you're heading to work or as a post-gym snack. The fruity flavours add that sweetness and the oats keep you full for hours.

1 Tbsp coconut oil, melted
1 apple, grated
2 bananas, chopped
10 medjool dates, pitted and chopped
⅓ cup maple syrup or honey
2 cups gluten-free oat flour
1½ cups almond meal
1 tsp ground cinnamon
1 tsp baking soda
½ tsp baking powder
Pinch of salt
½ cup water

Preheat oven to 180°C and grease 10 holes of a muffin tray with coconut oil.

In a medium-sized bowl, combine apple, bananas, dates and maple syrup or honey, and mix thoroughly.

Place the oat flour, almond meal, cinnamon, baking soda, baking powder and salt in a bowl, and mix together.

Add the wet ingredients to the dry, slowly adding the water and mixing until combined. Spoon the mixture into the muffin tray and bake for 25 minutes until golden.

• • • • • • •

Hot Tip: Substitute whatever fruit you have handy or whatever is in season, e.g. pear instead of apple, berries instead of dates, etc.

• • • • • • •

GF

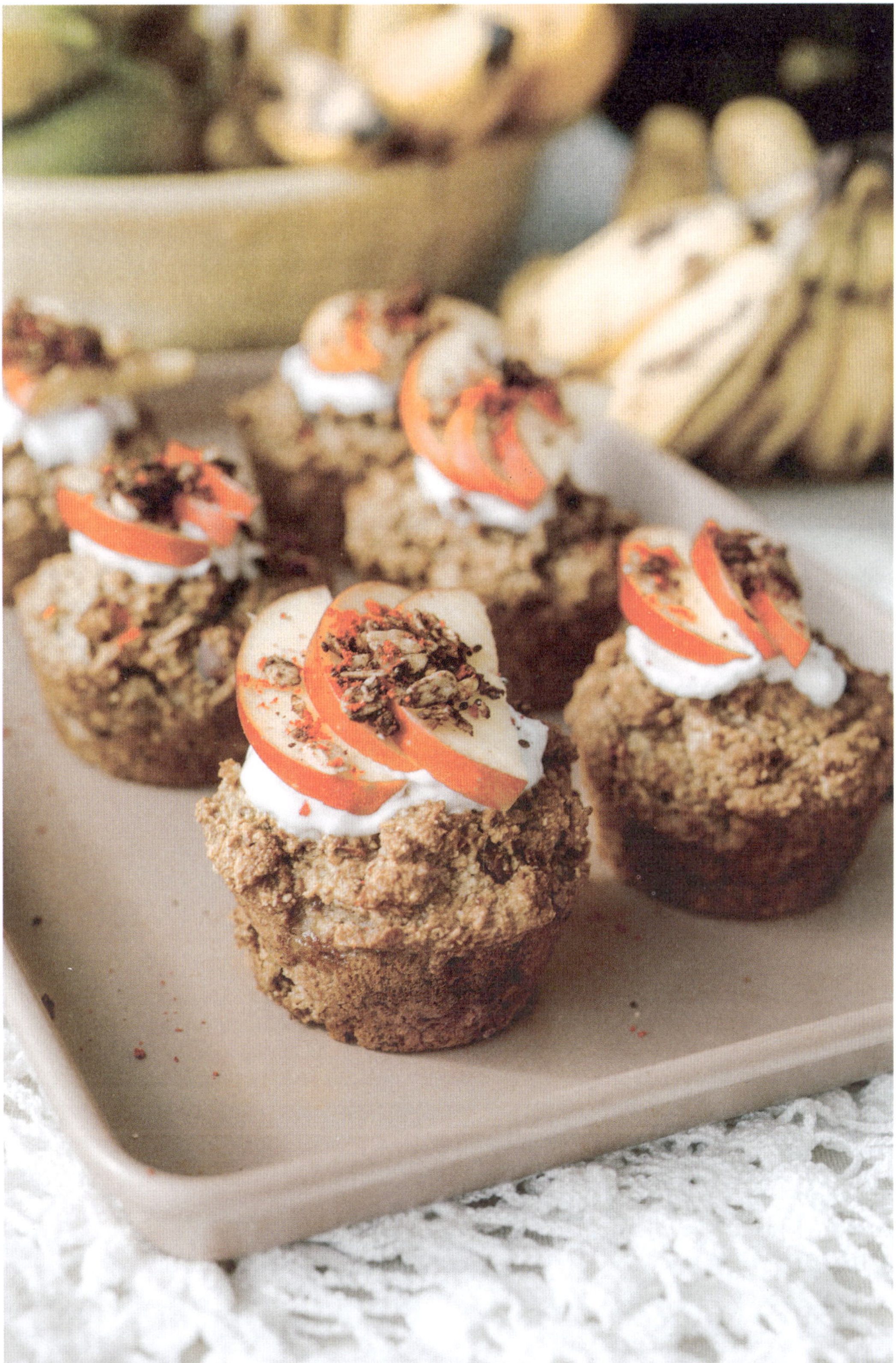

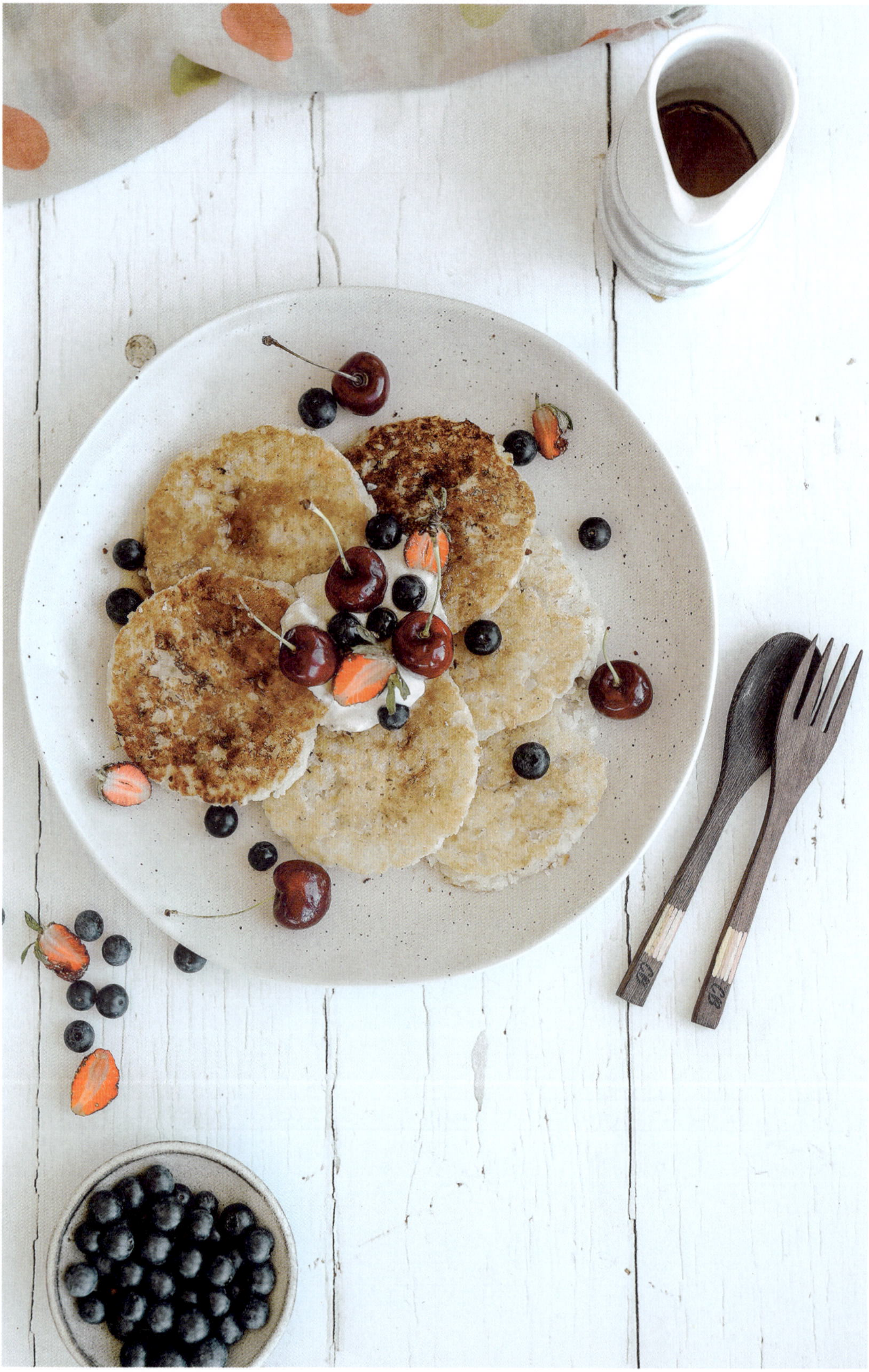

Coconut Cakes

Serves 2 • 35 minutes

This is my interpretation of a traditional Javanese sweet snack. I had these cakes for the first time in Bali when I was 12 and I've been hooked ever since! This recipe is even easier than making pancakes, with the added bonus of it being gluten- and nut-free.

1½ cups rice flour
1½ cups desiccated coconut
2 Tbsp coconut sugar
¼ tsp baking soda
400 ml can coconut milk
Pinch of salt
1 Tbsp coconut oil

To Serve
Fresh fruit
Maple syrup
Coconut yoghurt

In a medium-sized bowl, mix together rice flour, coconut, coconut sugar, baking soda, coconut milk and salt. The mixture should be quite thick and sticky.

Add coconut oil to a pan over a medium heat.
Add spoonfuls of mixture to the pan to create small pancakes. Use a round cookie cutter in the pan to create perfect circles, if you prefer, by placing around 1 heaped tablespoon of mixture inside.

Cook for around 2 minutes each side. Serve with fresh fruit, maple syrup and coconut yoghurt.

• • • • • • •

Hot Tip: These make the best leftovers or afternoon snack. I like to pop them in the toaster and top them with nut butter and sliced bananas.

• • • • • • •

GF NF

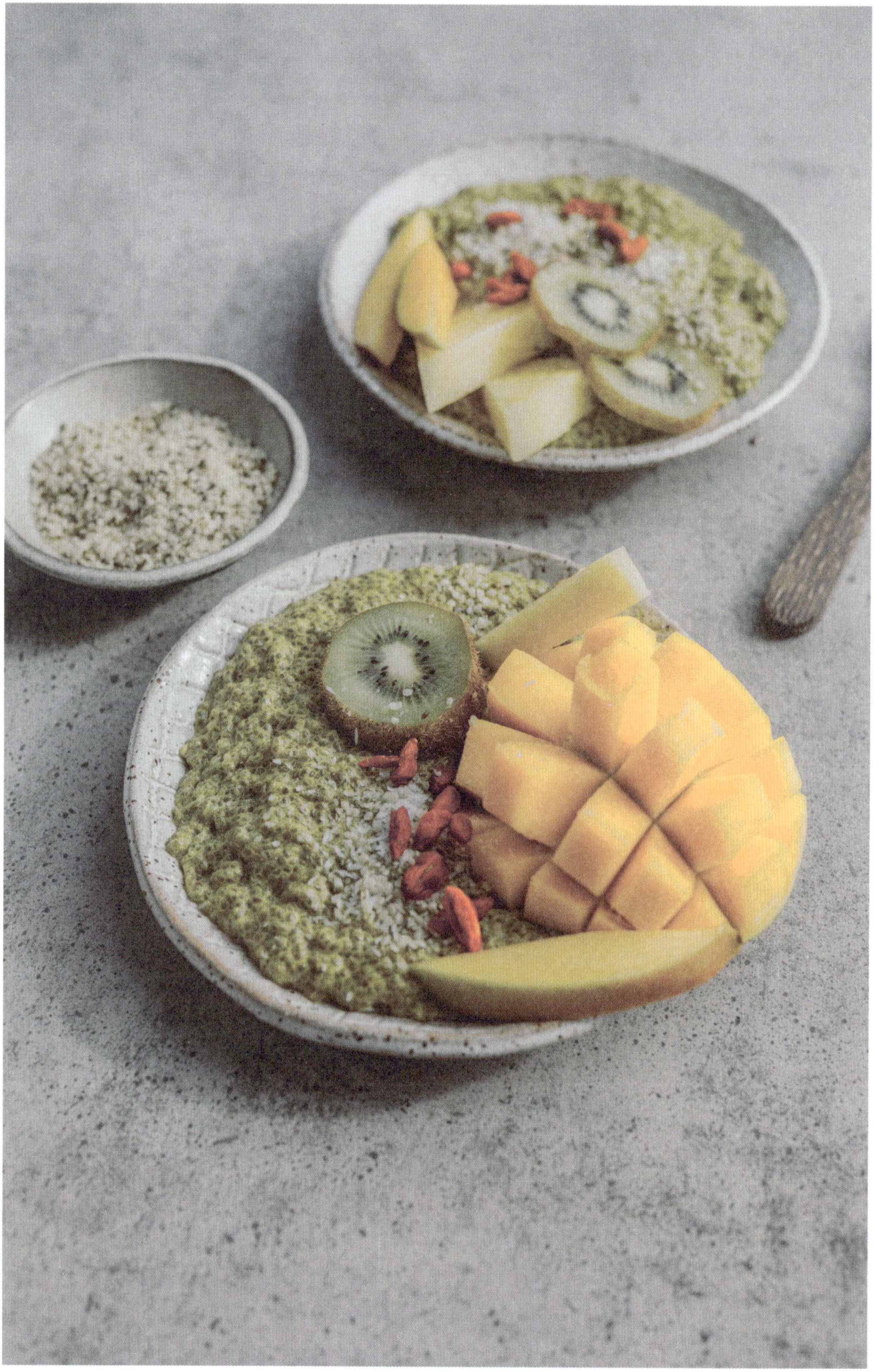

Sunrise Chia Pudding

Serves 2 • 10 minutes (and overnight)

Ever thought of adding turmeric to your sweet breakfasts? This is my favourite way to do it. Turmeric is known for its antioxidant and anti-inflammatory properties. I add it to most of my curries, soups and stews, but it also tastes delicious in sweet meals. Chia seeds are high in fibre, protein, Omega-3s and magnesium. This nourishing breakfast is a fantastic start to the day.

½ cup chia seeds
1½ cups plant milk
2 Tbsp maple syrup
½ tsp ground turmeric
½ tsp ground cinnamon
¼ tsp ground nutmeg
Pinch of cracked pepper

To Serve
Fresh fruit
Hemp seeds
Goji berries

Combine all the ingredients in a bowl and place in the fridge overnight.

Remove from the fridge the next morning and top with fresh fruit, hemp seeds and goji berries.

. . . .

Hot Tip: You can also make this breakfast warm — just combine all the ingredients in a pot and simmer for 15 minutes.

. . . .

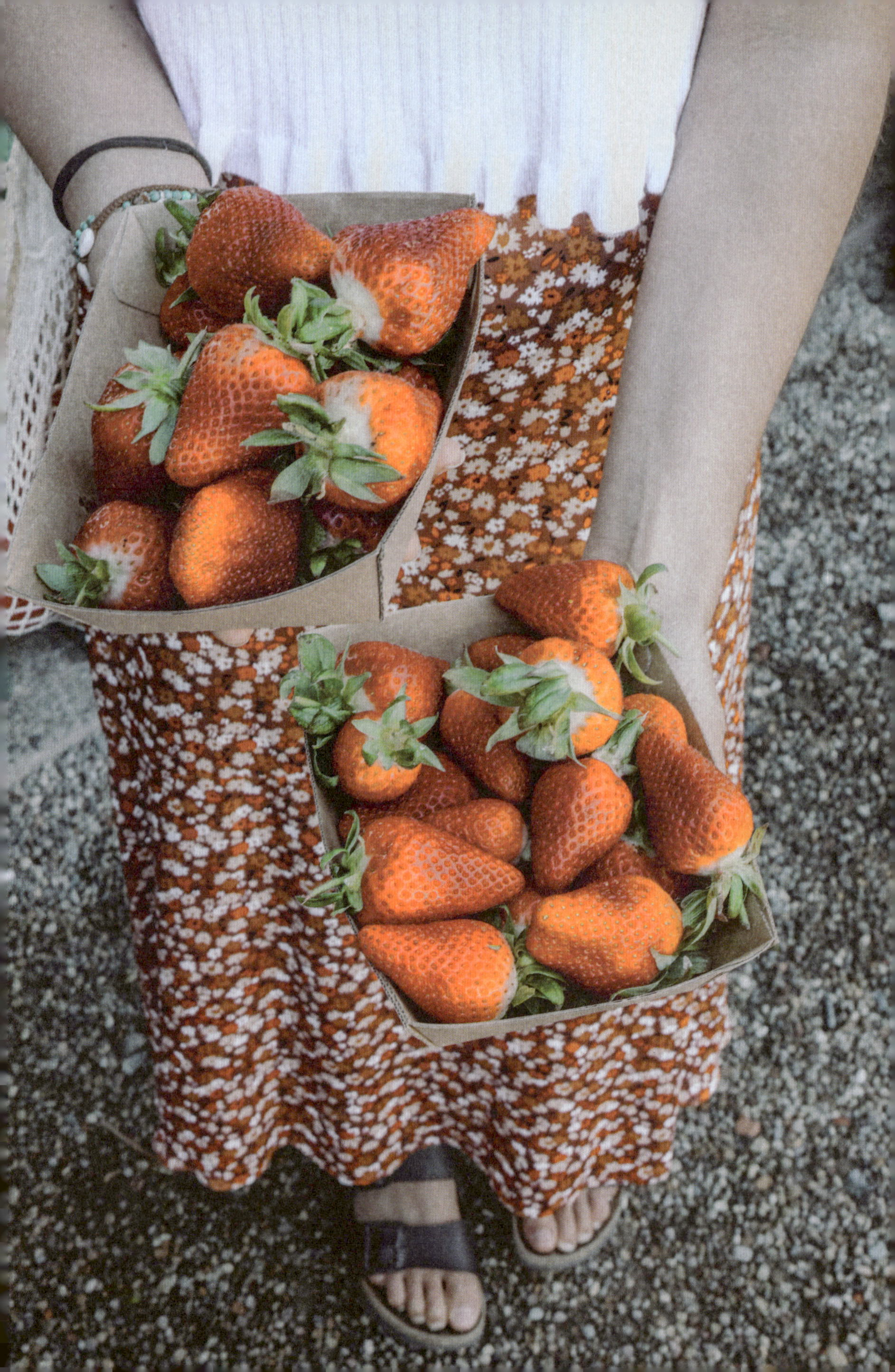

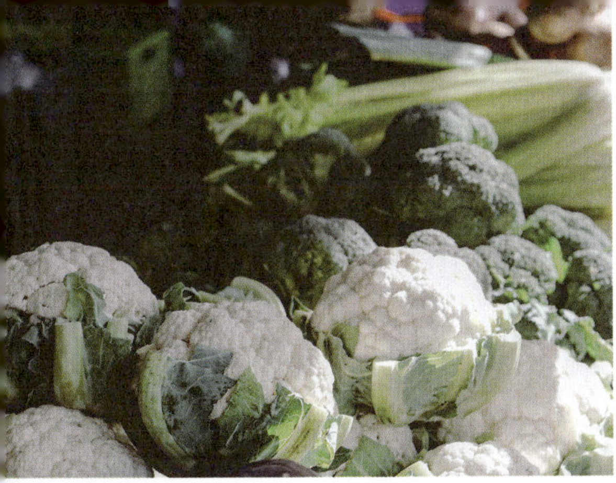

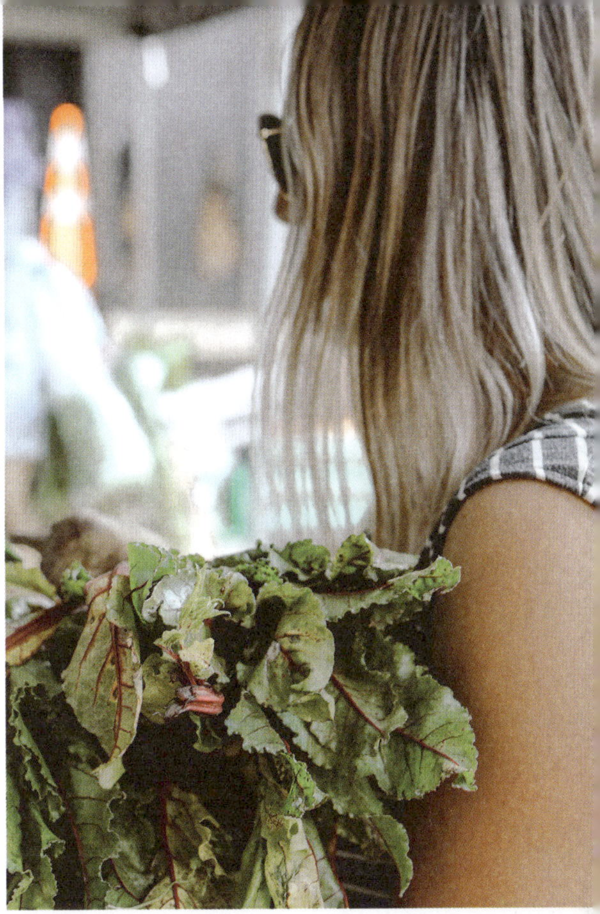

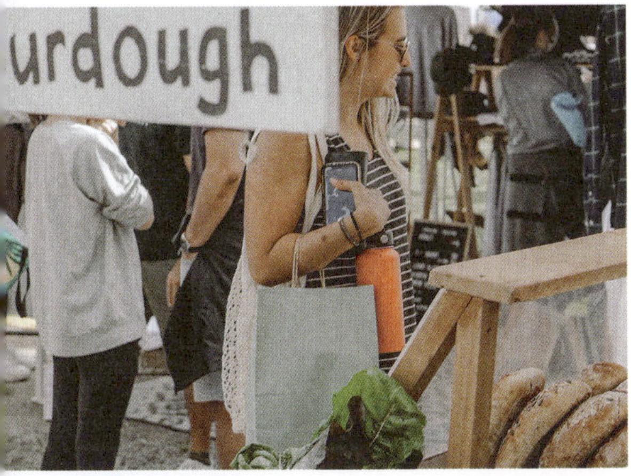
urdough

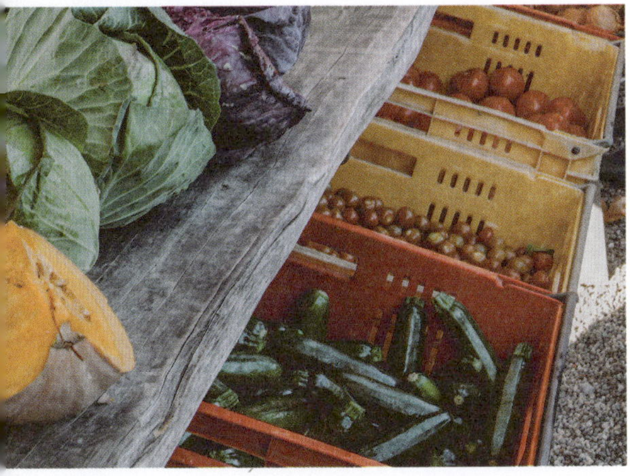

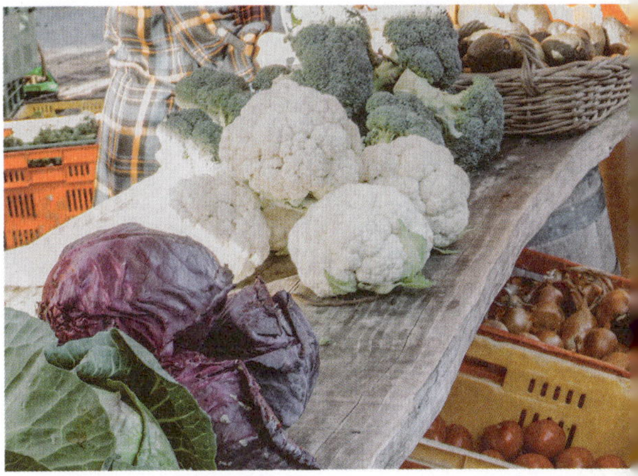

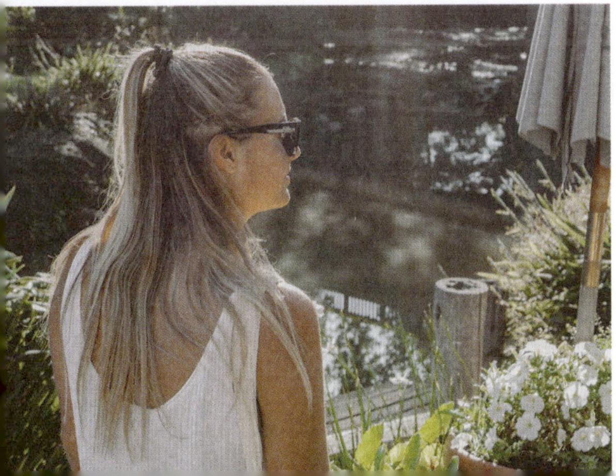

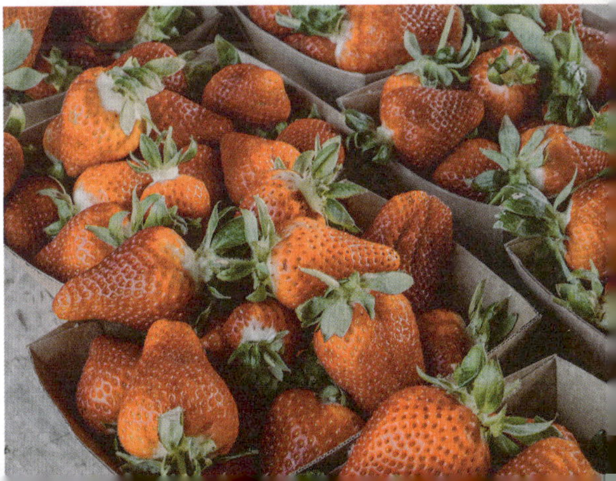

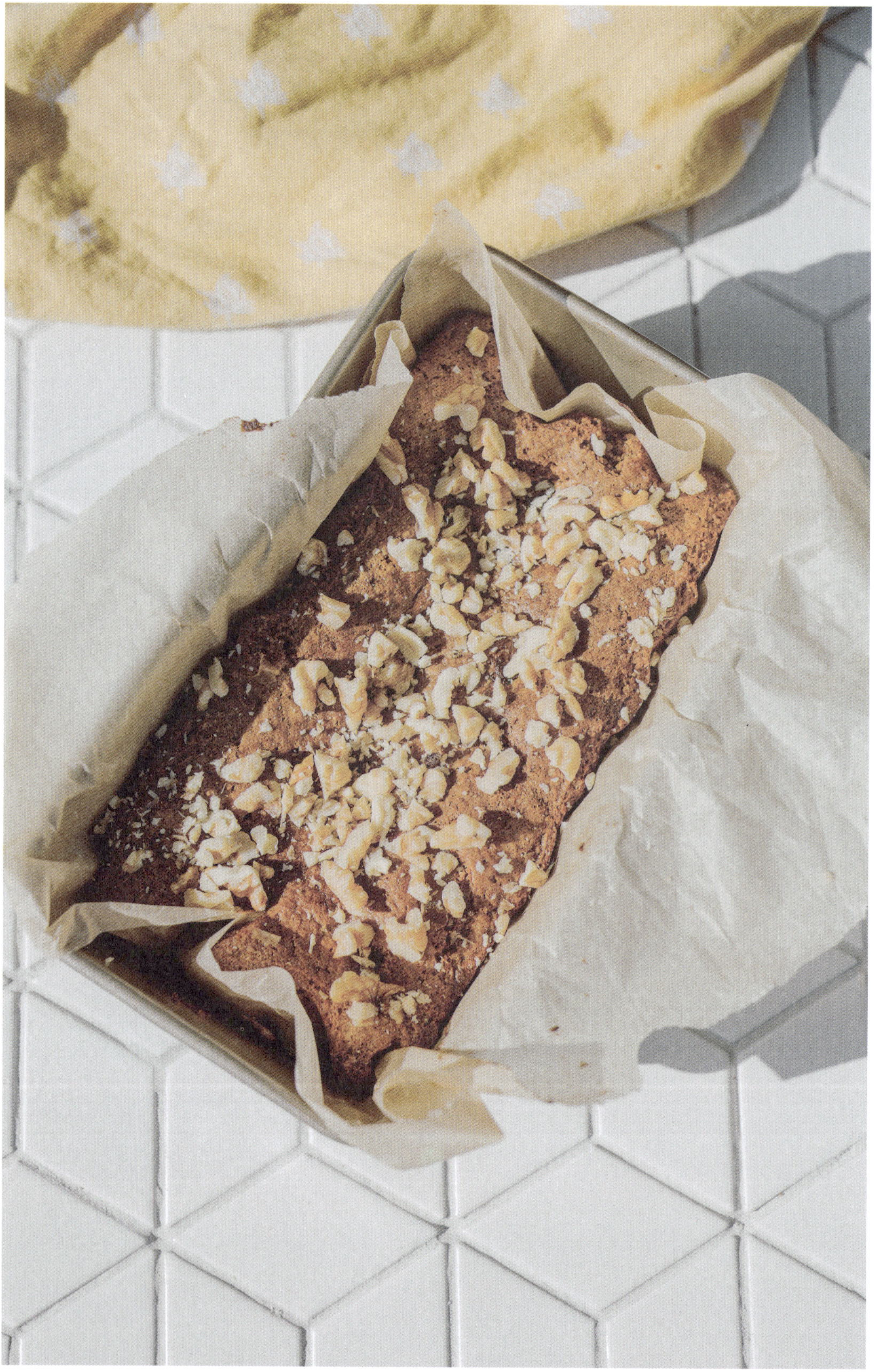

Gingerbread Breakfast Loaf

Makes 1 loaf • 60 minutes

Ginger is one of my favourite ingredients in baking — I find it so comforting, especially straight out of the oven. My mum loves this as a simple breakfast topped with a little almond butter, banana and the Berry Chia Jam from page 213.

2 cups wholemeal flour
1 tsp baking powder
½ tsp baking soda
½ cup coconut sugar
Pinch of salt
1 Tbsp ground cinnamon
2 Tbsp ground ginger
½ cup olive oil
3 Tbsp maple syrup
½ cup plant milk

Topping
⅓ cup chopped crystallised ginger
¼ cup chopped walnuts
1 Tbsp pumpkin seeds

Preheat oven to 180°C and line a 10 x 20 cm loaf tin with baking paper.

In a medium-sized bowl, combine flour, baking powder, baking soda, coconut sugar, salt, cinnamon and ground ginger and mix through.

In a separate bowl, mix together olive oil, maple syrup and plant milk. Tip the wet mixture into the dry and fold through until combined.

Pour mixture into loaf tin and top with crystallised ginger, walnuts and pumpkin seeds, and place in the oven for 40 minutes or until golden and a skewer inserted into the middle comes out clean.

Seedy Buckwheat Bread

Makes 1 loaf • 60 minutes

I've always been obsessed with seedy bread. It requires no yeast, kneading or proofing and contains a bunch of nutrients to get you through the day. Psyllium is a type of fibre made from the husks of *Plantago ovata* seeds that helps with digestive health. It also works really well as a moisture retainer in bread. I often top my bread with almond butter and homemade Berry Chia Jam (see p. 213). It also tastes great with savoury toppings such as hummus, avocado and tomato.

3 Tbsp psyllium husk
1¼ cups water
¾ cup sunflower seeds
½ cup pumpkin seeds
2 Tbsp chia seeds
½ cup buckwheat flour
½ cup almond meal (or gluten-free oats for nut-free)
1 tsp baking powder
½ tsp baking soda
¼ tsp salt
2 Tbsp olive oil
2 Tbsp maple syrup

Topping
1 Tbsp sunflower seeds
1 Tbsp pumpkin seeds
1 Tbsp sesame seeds

Preheat oven to 170°C and line a 10 x 20 cm loaf tin with baking paper.

In a medium-sized bowl, combine psyllium husk and water, and set aside.

In a separate bowl, combine sunflower seeds, pumpkin seeds, chia seeds, buckwheat flour, almond meal or gluten-free oats, baking powder, baking soda and salt.

Fold the dry ingredients through the psyllium husk mixture. Add the olive oil and maple syrup until you have a wet, doughy consistency.

Pour mixture into loaf tin and top with extra seeds. Place in the oven for 45 minutes or until a skewer inserted into the middle comes out clean.

GF NFO

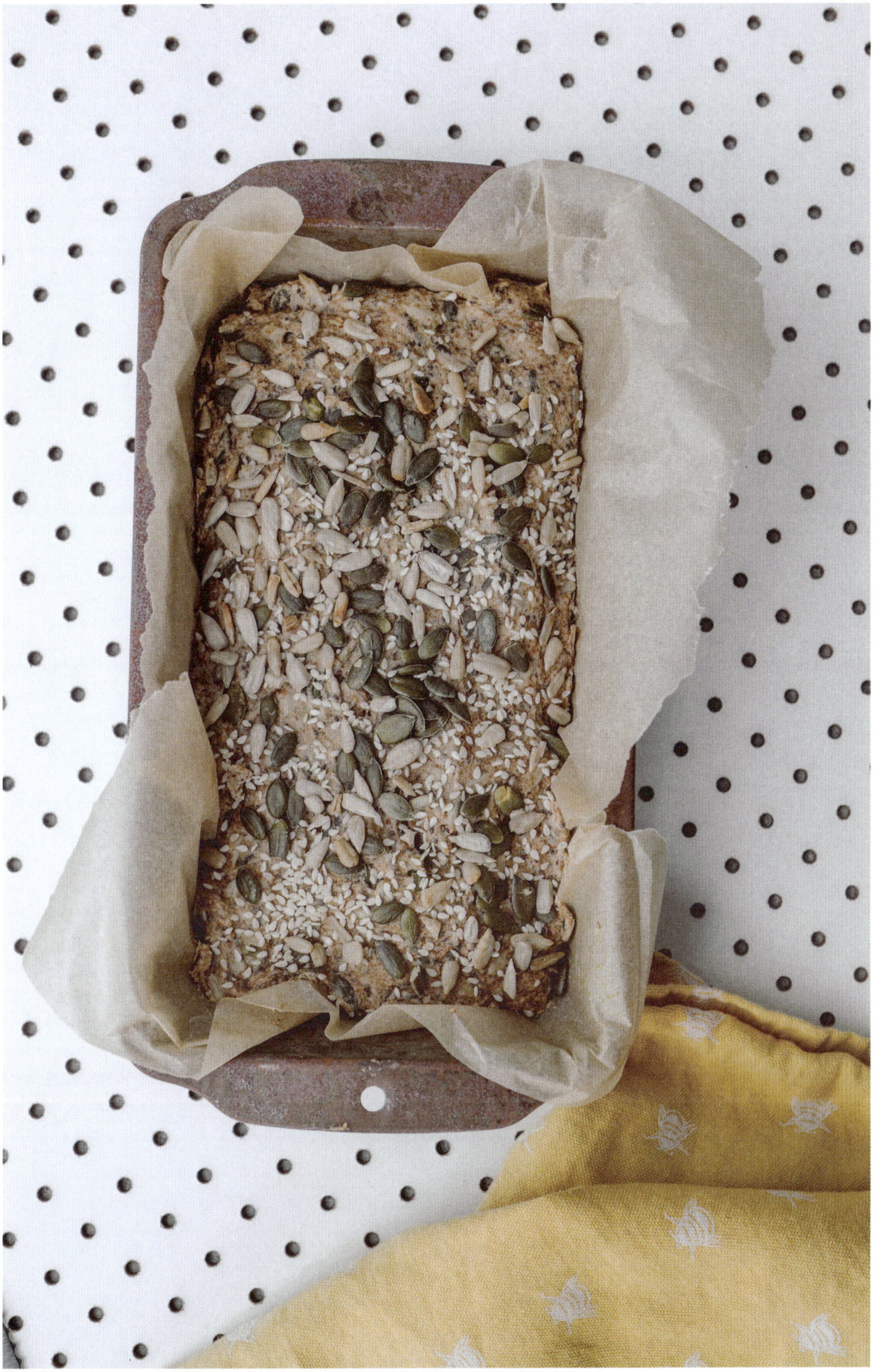

Omega-3 French Toast

Serves 2 • 20 minutes

French toast has been a favourite in my family for a long time. When I was swimming competitively on a Saturday morning, I'd pick up fresh brioche from the local French bakery so we could make homemade French toast when I got home. This particular recipe requires flaxmeal, which is another name for ground flax seeds. These seeds are loaded with nutrients, rich in dietary fibre and high in Omega-3 fatty acids.

4 Tbsp flaxmeal
1 cup plant milk
1 tsp ground cinnamon
1 tsp ground nutmeg
1 Tbsp coconut sugar
1 Tbsp coconut oil
4 slices brioche (or use gluten-free bread)

To Serve
Nut butter (replace with tahini if nut-free)
Fresh fruit
Maple syrup

In a medium-sized bowl, combine flaxmeal, milk, cinnamon, nutmeg and coconut sugar.

Heat up a pan and add coconut oil. Place a slice of bread in the milk mixture. Once bread is coated, add to the pan and cook for around 2 minutes each side. You want to make sure all of the moisture has been absorbed so be sure to wait until each side is brown before flipping.

Serve with nut butter, fresh fruit and maple syrup.

GF NF

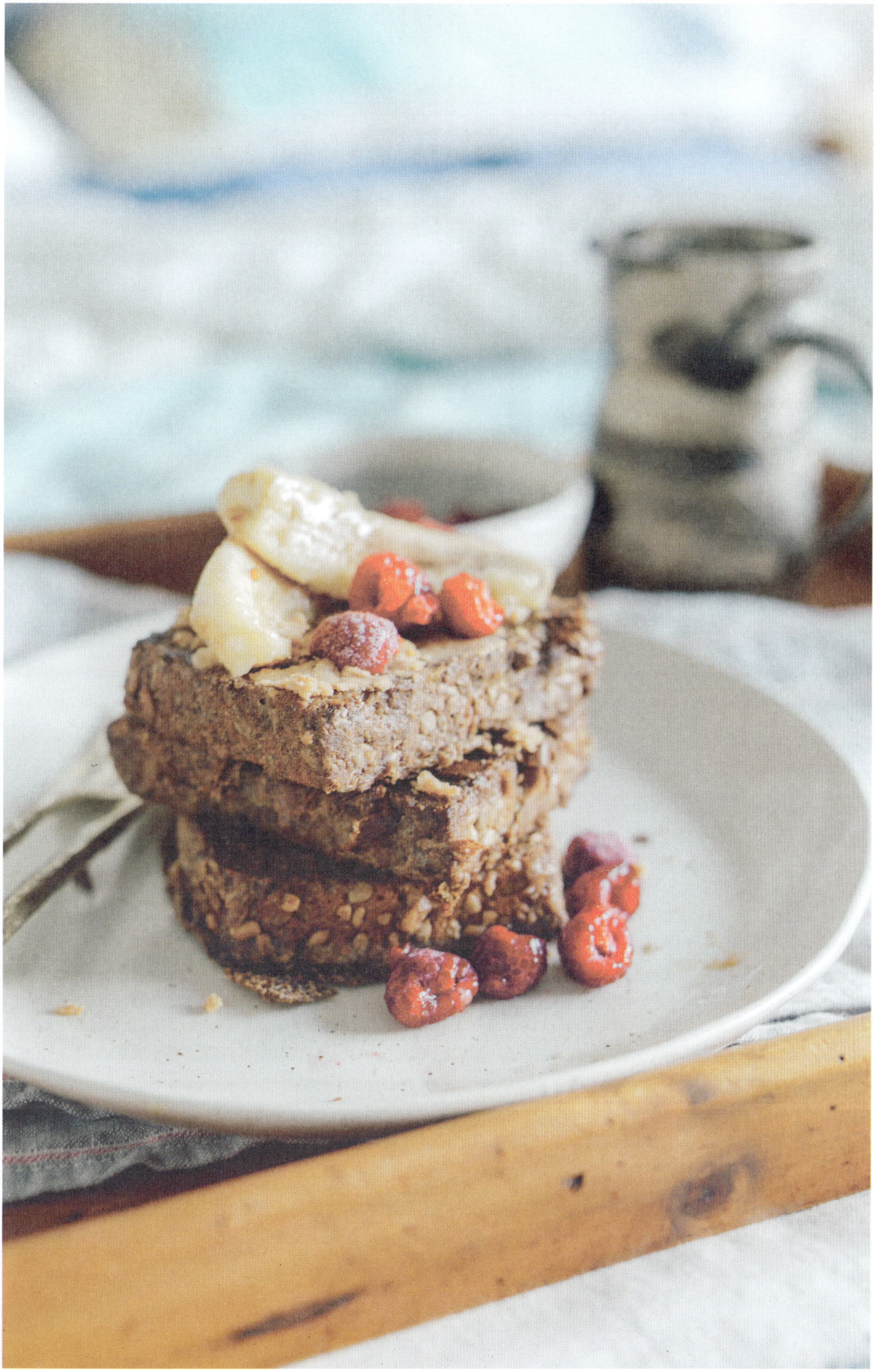

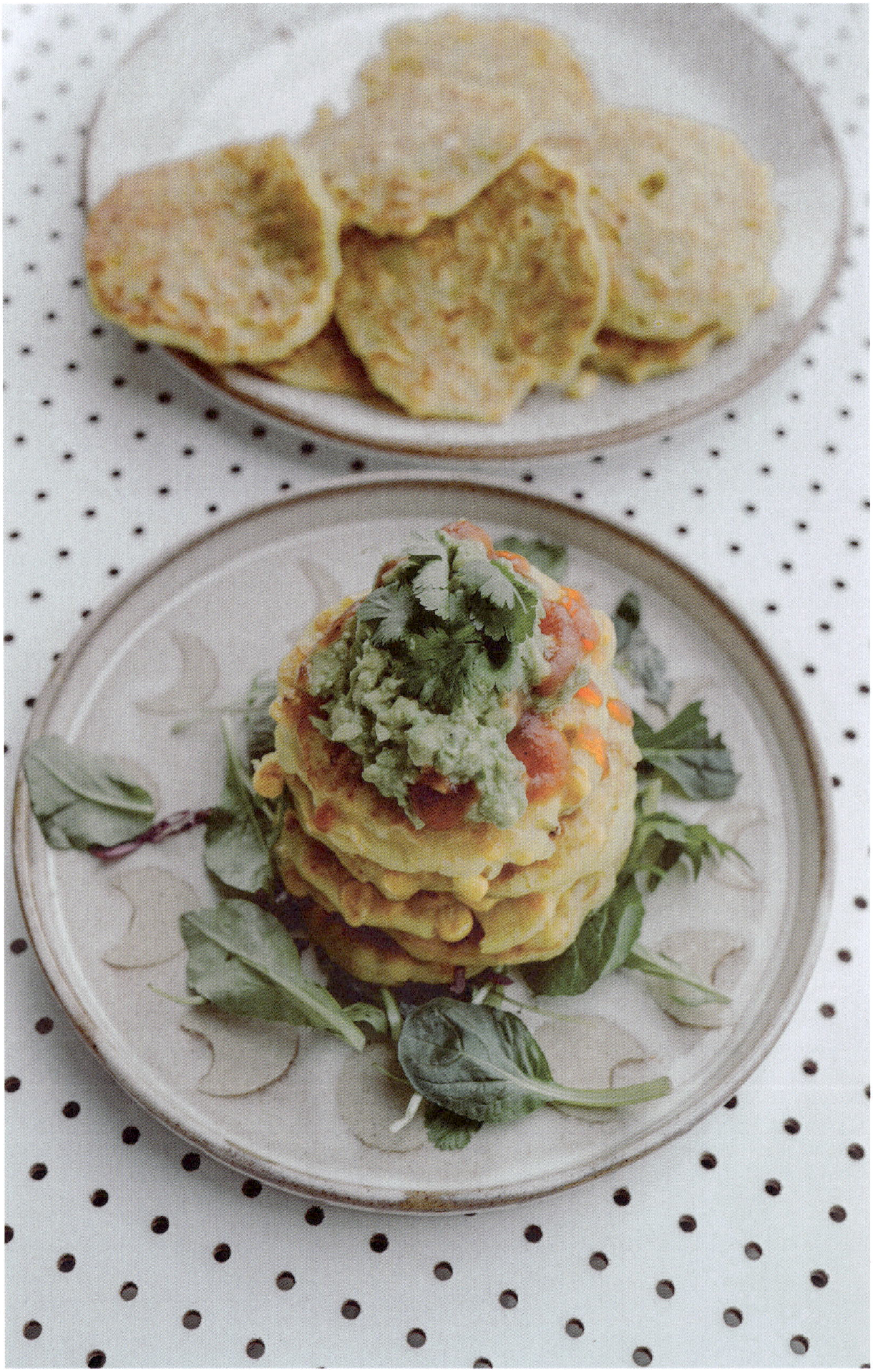

Coconut Corn Fritters

Makes 15 • 45 minutes

My partner requests these corn fritters almost every weekend. They were inspired by Halo, one of my favourite cafés in Queenstown. The wet ingredients are actually similar to how I make a curry. Sounds weird, but I promise they taste divine!

1 onion, roughly chopped
2 cloves garlic
1 tsp ground turmeric
400 ml can coconut milk
1 tsp vegetable stock powder
1 tsp ground coriander
½ cup water
1 cup sweetcorn kernels
2½ cups wholemeal flour
1 tsp baking powder
Pinch of salt
Olive oil for frying fritters

To Serve
1 cup mixed lettuce leaves
Coconut yoghurt
Sweet chilli sauce
1 avocado, mashed
Fresh coriander

Add the onion, garlic, turmeric, coconut milk, vegetable stock, ground coriander and water to a blender and blend until smooth.

In a medium-sized bowl, combine corn, flour, baking powder and salt then stir into the blended mixture.

Heat up a dash of olive oil in a pan, and add ¼ cupfuls of mixture. Cook on one side for around 2–3 minutes. Flip and cook until golden.

Serve your corn fritters topped with lettuce, coconut yoghurt, sweet chilli sauce, avocado and coriander.

NF

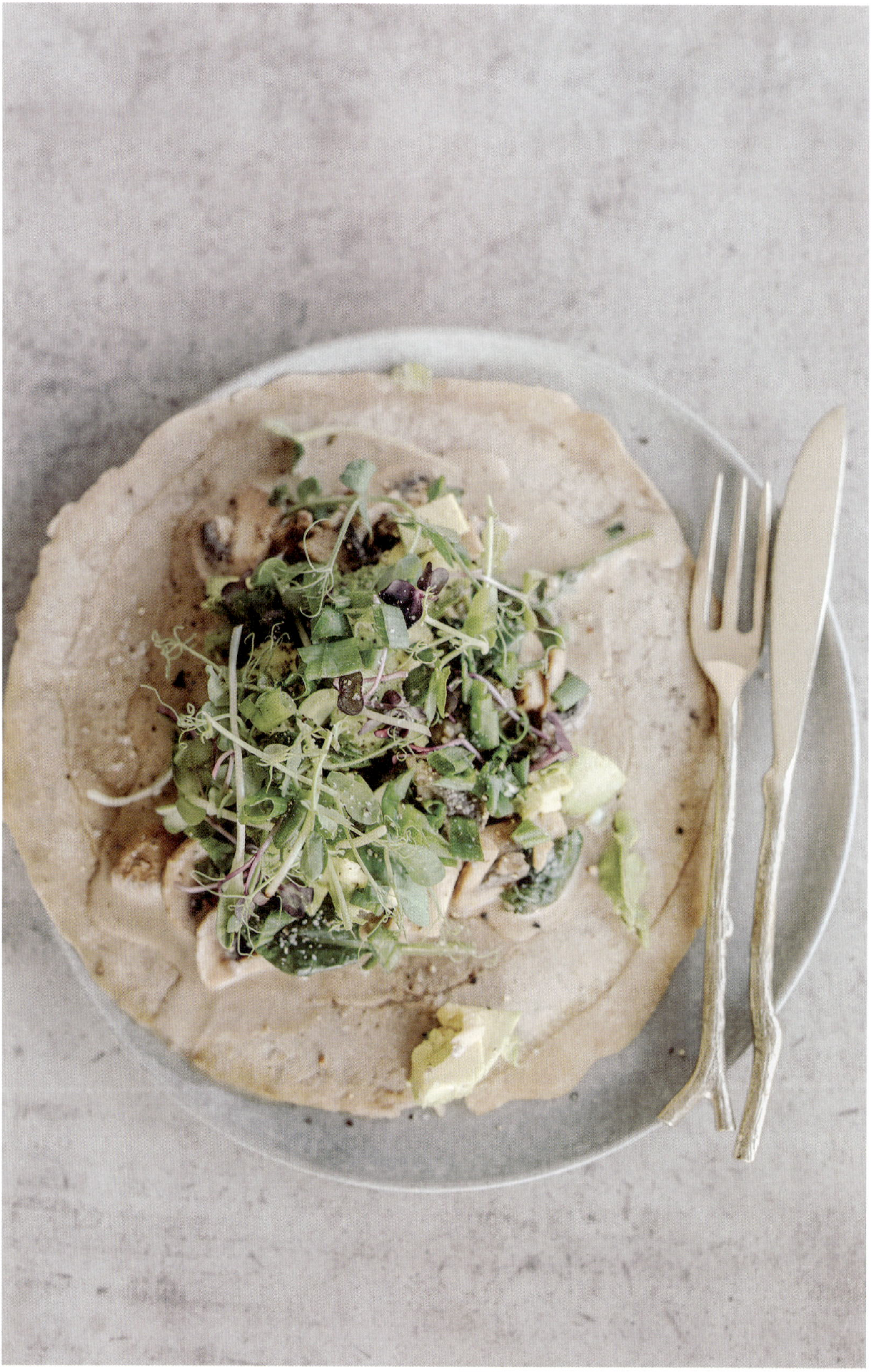

Buckwheat Crêpes with Creamy Mushrooms

Makes 2 crêpes • 20 minutes

This is probably my all-time favourite savoury breakfast. I absolutely love creamy mushrooms and this buckwheat crêpe is possibly the easiest crêpe variation you'll ever make. I make them almost every week.

¾ cup buckwheat flour
1 cup plant milk
1 tsp baking powder
300 g mixed mushrooms, chopped
½ cup coconut yoghurt
3 cloves garlic, crushed
1 Tbsp soy sauce or tamari

To Serve
Fresh herbs, chopped
Avocado, sliced
Chilli flakes

Combine buckwheat, plant milk and baking powder in a bowl and mix well. Add half the mixture to a hot pan and cook for 1–2 minutes on each side. Repeat with remaining batter to make 2 crêpes.

Combine remaining ingredients in a bowl then add to a separate pan over medium heat and sauté until mushrooms are soft.

Serve crêpes topped with mushroom mixture and scattered with fresh herbs, avocado and chilli flakes. Roll up or eat with knife and fork if preferred.

. . . .

Hot Tip: These crêpes taste great with both sweet and savoury fillings. Other filling ideas include peanut butter and banana or the Berry Chia Jam on page 213.

. . . .

GF NF

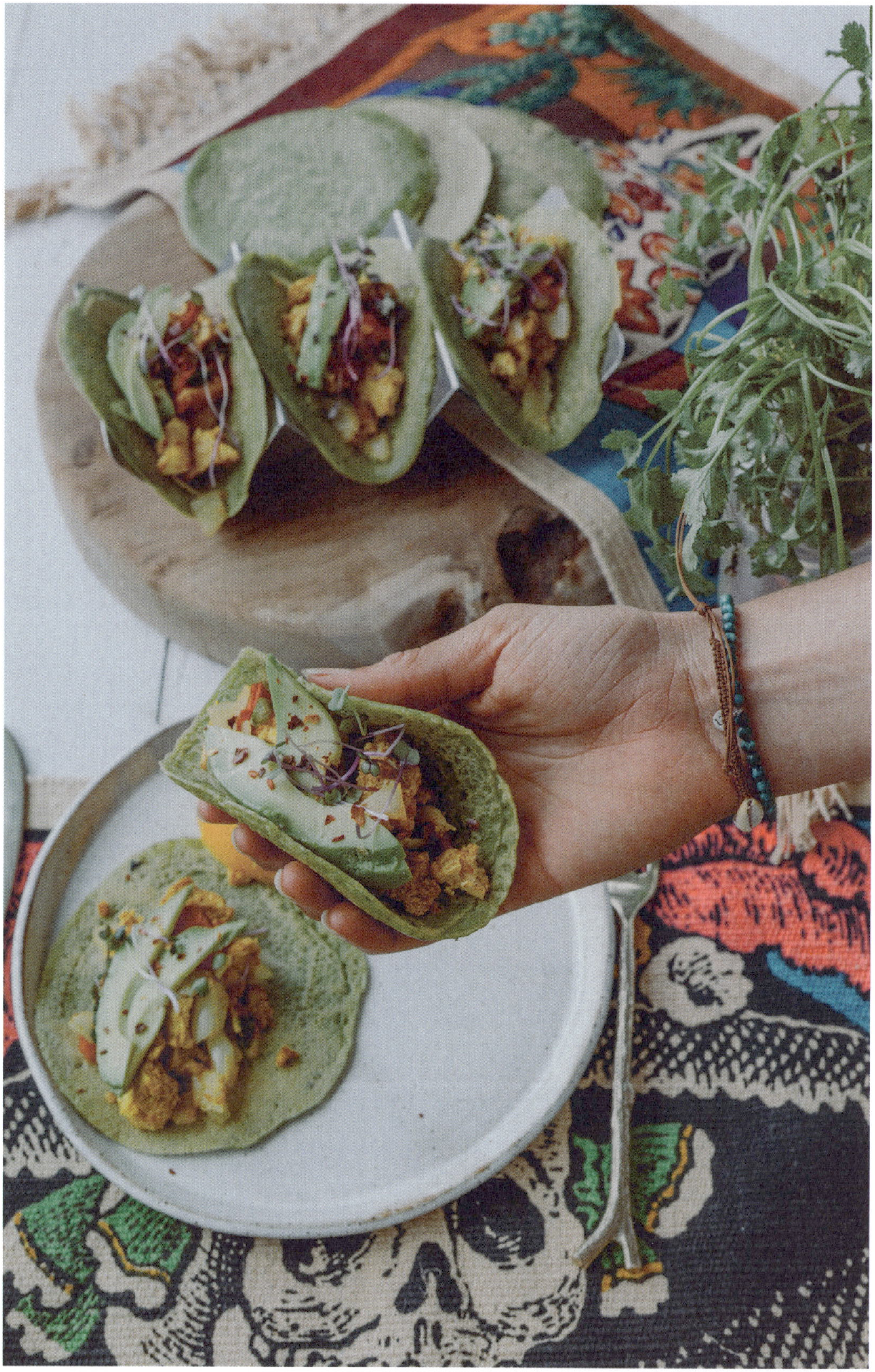

Breakfast Tacos

Serves 4 • 30 minutes

These tacos are perfect for a big family breakfast. I can almost guarantee that if you don't like tofu, you will like it after you make this recipe!

Taco Wraps
1 cup spinach
1½ cups chickpea flour
½ cup tapioca flour
1½ cups water
Pinch of salt

Tofu Scramble
300 g soft tofu
1 onion, finely chopped
1 tsp ground coriander
1 tsp ground cumin
½ tsp ground cinnamon
½ tsp ground turmeric
2 Tbsp plant milk
Large handful of fresh coriander, chopped
2 medium-sized tomatoes, sliced

To Serve
1 avocado, sliced
Handful of fresh coriander
Juice from 1 lime

Place all taco wrap ingredients in a blender and blend until smooth. Place a pan over a medium heat with a bit of olive oil and begin to cook your tacos by adding ¼ cup of the mixture into the pan. Leave to cook for 1 minute until bubbling then flip and cook for another minute on the other side. Repeat with the remaining mixture.

Use your fingers to crumble tofu into small pieces, then add to a separate pan. Add remaining ingredients and stir for 5–10 minutes until cooked.

Add a scoop of tofu mixture to the middle of each taco wrap. Top with sliced avocado, fresh coriander and lime juice then fold in half or roll into a wrap, as per your preference.

GF NF

Kumara Pancake Stack

Serves 4 (makes 10–12 pancakes) • 30 minutes

These pancakes have a crispy, caramelised outside and a fluffy, sweet interior. There's even a sneaky vegetable in there which makes them the perfect healthy start to your day.

1 small kumara (sweet potato), around 150g, peeled and roughly chopped
1 Tbsp flaxmeal
1 Tbsp apple cider vinegar
1½ cups plant milk
1 cup wholemeal flour (buckwheat flour for GF option)
1 tsp baking powder
½ tsp baking soda

To Serve
Rich Chocolate Sauce (see p. 212)
Fresh berries

Precook kumara either by steaming or boiling it.

In a bowl, add the flaxmeal and apple cider vinegar to milk and leave for 5 minutes until it curdles.

Once the kumara is soft, transfer to a bowl and mash until combined. Add the milk mixture along with the wholemeal flour, baking powder and baking soda and mix together.

Heat a pan over medium–high heat and add 2–3 Tbsp of the pancake mixture. Cook until bubbles form, then flip. Once pancakes are done, transfer to the oven to keep warm.

Top with Rich Chocolate Sauce and fresh berries.

. . . .

Hot Tip: If you don't have kumara on hand, banana is a great substitute.

. . . .

GF NF

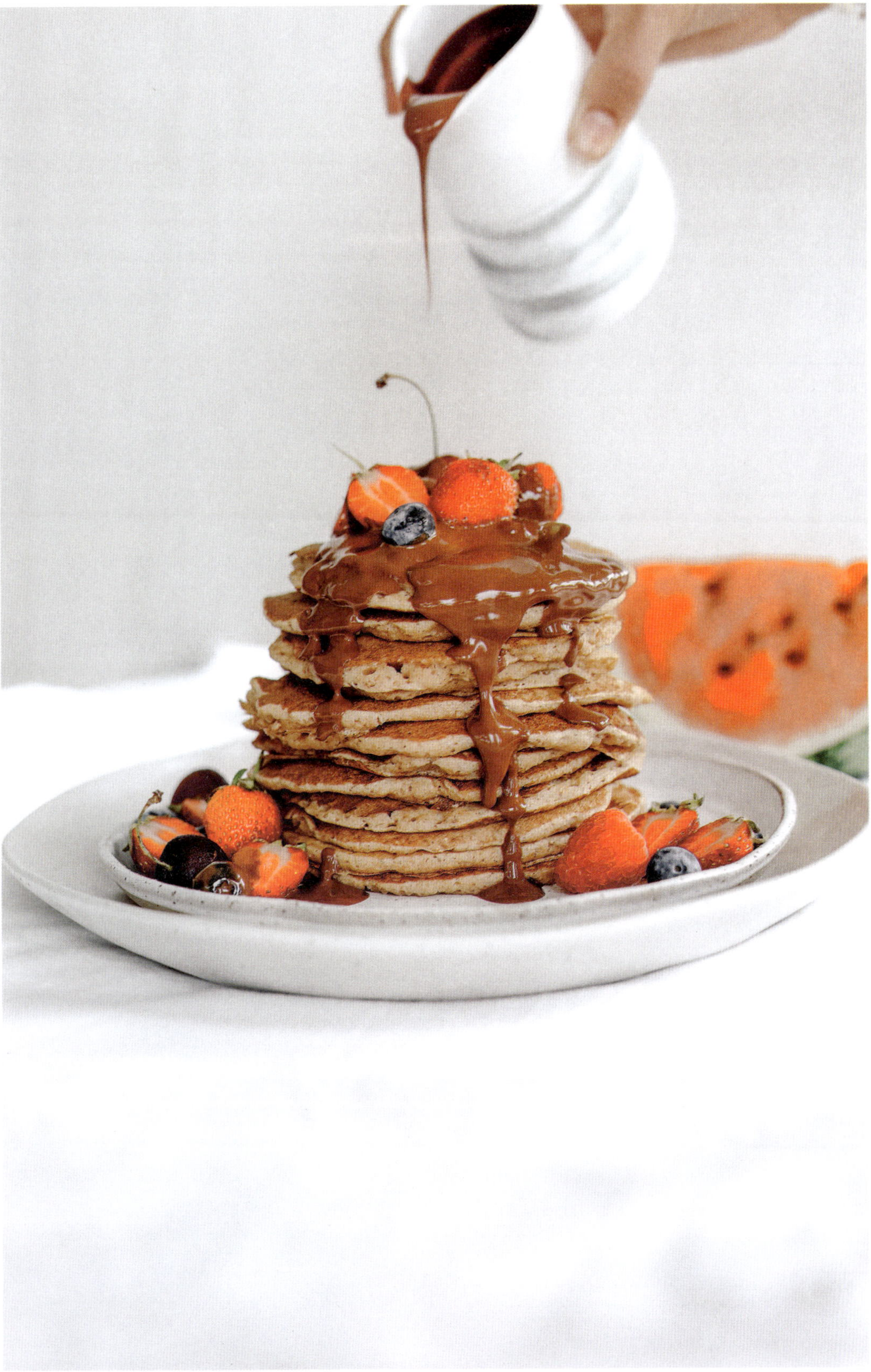

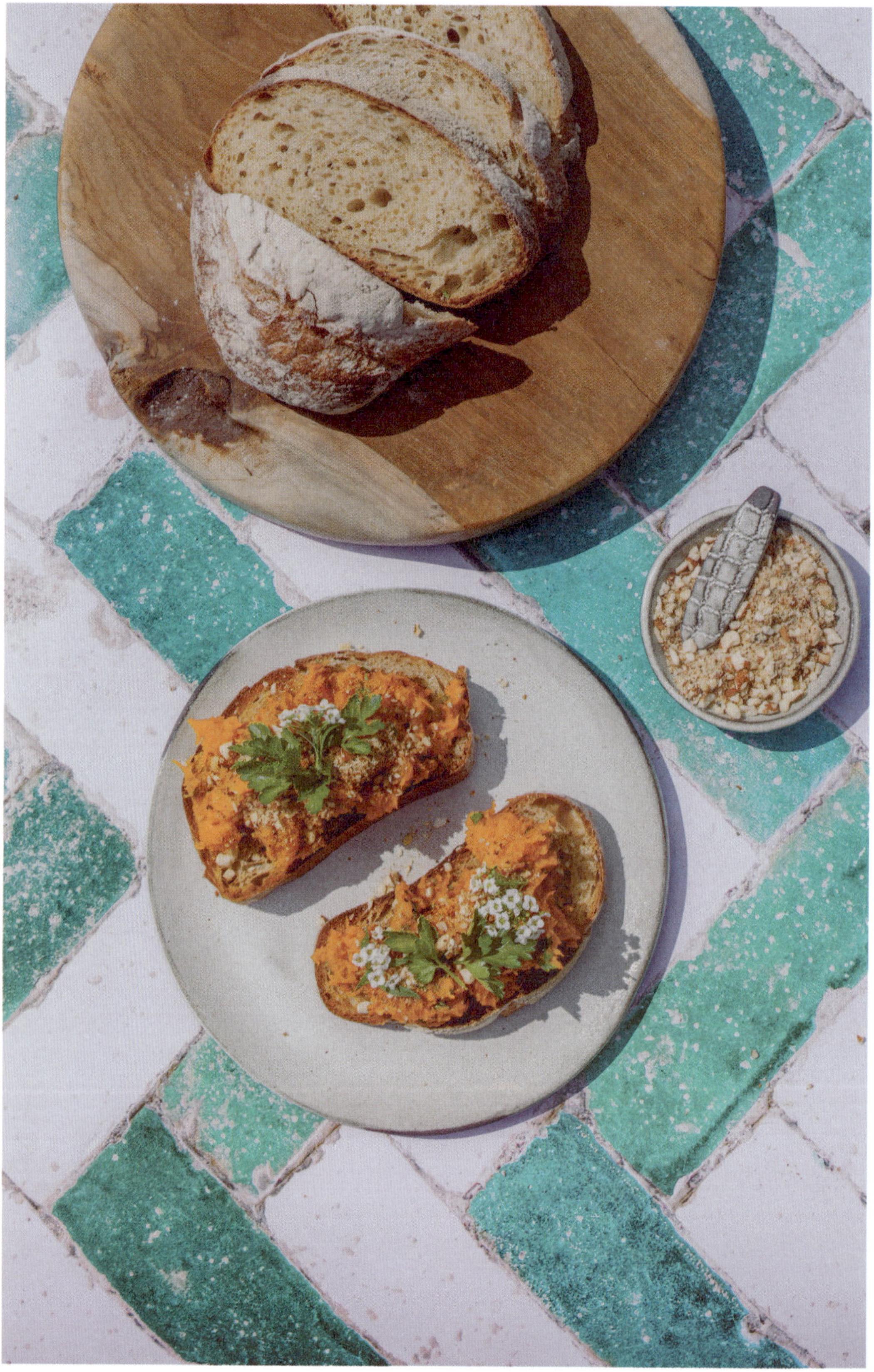

Miso Smashed Pumpkin with Herbs and Dukkah

Serves 5 • 30 minutes

Try this for a unique twist on smashed avo. I love how versatile pumpkin is and it carries such a sweet, delicious flavour. As a kid I never liked pumpkin and now it's probably one of my favourite foods. It may sound a little strange but it really is the perfect toast topping.

1 medium-sized pumpkin, peeled, deseeded and chopped into cubes
1 tsp miso paste
¼ cup chopped parsley
¼ cup chopped mint
1 clove garlic, crushed

To Serve
1 loaf sourdough (or use gluten-free bread), sliced and toasted
Fresh parsley
¼ cup Homemade Dukkah (see p. 211) (leave out if nut free)

Begin by steaming pumpkin. While pumpkin is cooking, combine miso paste, parsley, mint and garlic in a medium-sized bowl.

Once pumpkin is cooked and cooled, add it to the bowl with the other ingredients and mash with a fork — it doesn't have to be smooth.

Scoop pumpkin mixture onto a slice of toast and top with extra parsley and dukkah.

. . . .

Hot Tip: My Seedy Buckwheat Bread (see p. 44) tastes absolutely delicious when paired with this dish.

. . . .

GFO NFO

Rise and Shine! • 57

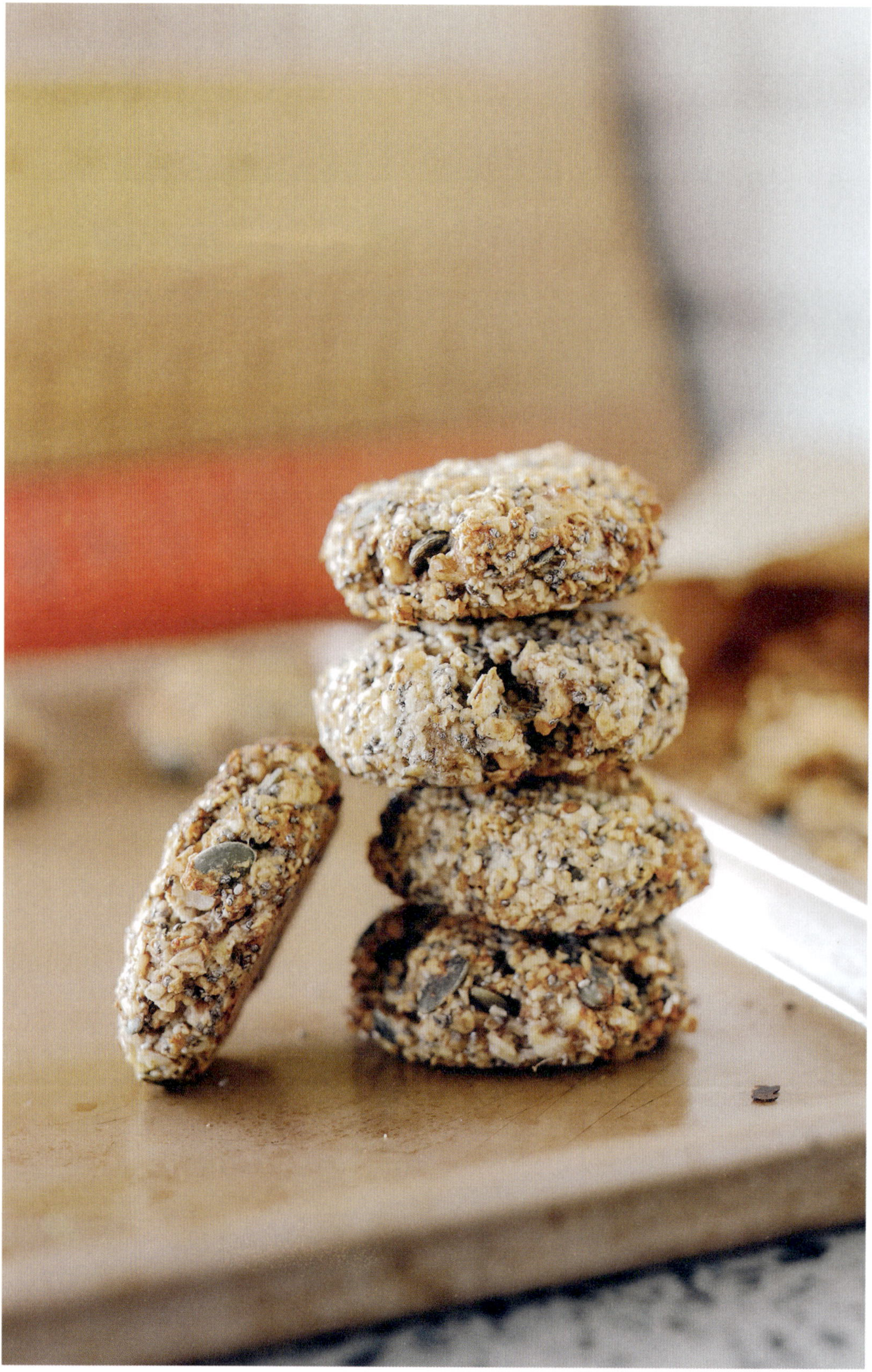

Walnut Breakfast Cookies

Serves 8–10 • 30 minutes

Not that you need an excuse to eat cookies for breakfast, but these ones are packed with wholesome nutrients and also taste sensational. I'm obsessed with the combo of wholesome oats and gooey banana — so delicious, especially straight out of the oven. These are made in one bowl and are ready in 30 minutes.

2 ripe bananas, mashed
1 Tbsp coconut oil, melted
1 Tbsp maple syrup or honey
1 cup gluten-free rolled oats
½ cup gluten-free oat flour
¼ cup pumpkin seeds
½ cup chopped walnuts (could substitute for other nuts)
¼ cup chia seeds
1 tsp ground cinnamon
½ tsp ground nutmeg
1 tsp ground ginger
1 tsp baking powder
½ tsp baking soda

Preheat oven to 180°C and line a tray with baking paper.

In a bowl, combine bananas, coconut oil and maple syrup or honey.

In a separate bowl, combine oats, oat flour, pumpkin seeds, walnuts, chia seeds, cinnamon, nutmeg, ginger, baking powder and baking soda and mix through. Tip banana mixture into dry ingredients and mix until just combined.

Place tablespoonfuls of mixture onto tray and cook for 15–20 minutes or until golden.

. . . .

Hot Tip: You can use apple sauce in place of the bananas for a different flavour combination.

. . . .

GF

Rise and Shine!

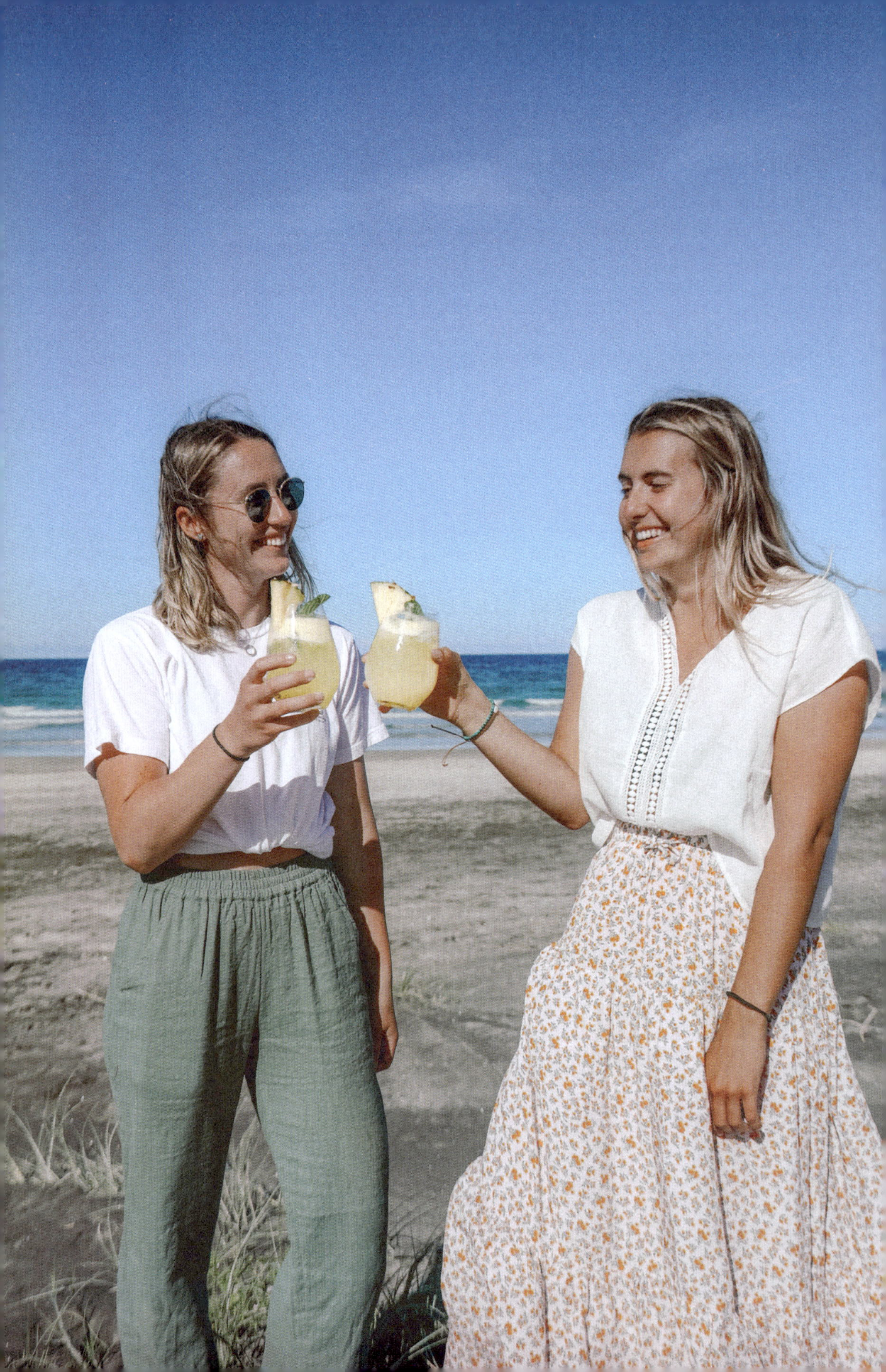

Cheers!

Whether it's a refreshing smoothie, warm hot chocolate or zingy strawberry margarita you're craving, this chapter has got you covered for beverages. I often start my day with a big smoothie or smoothie bowl and finish with something like the Lemon and Blueberry Fizz (see p. 64). I have to confess that I consider myself a bit of a smoothie expert. I'm lucky enough to have a super-efficient blender (that I use almost every day). This means I can make nice thick creams, smoothie bowls and even some frozen mocktails super easily. But if you don't have a powerful blender, feel free to use a food processor instead.

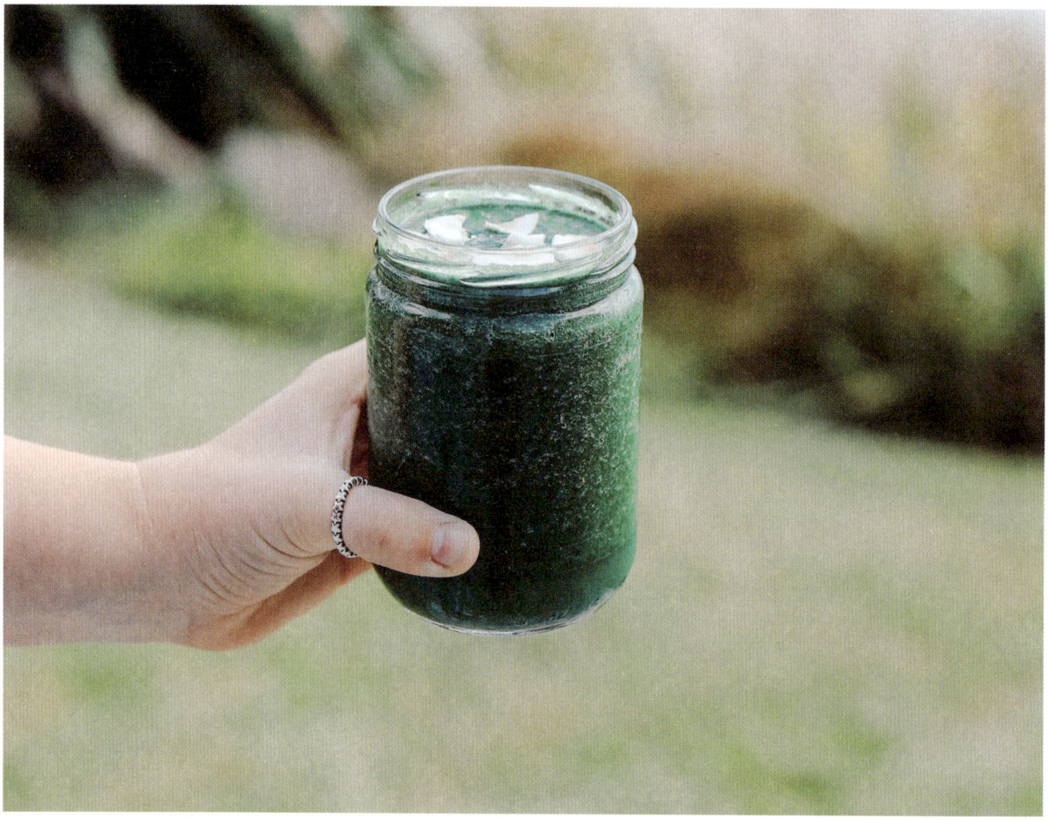

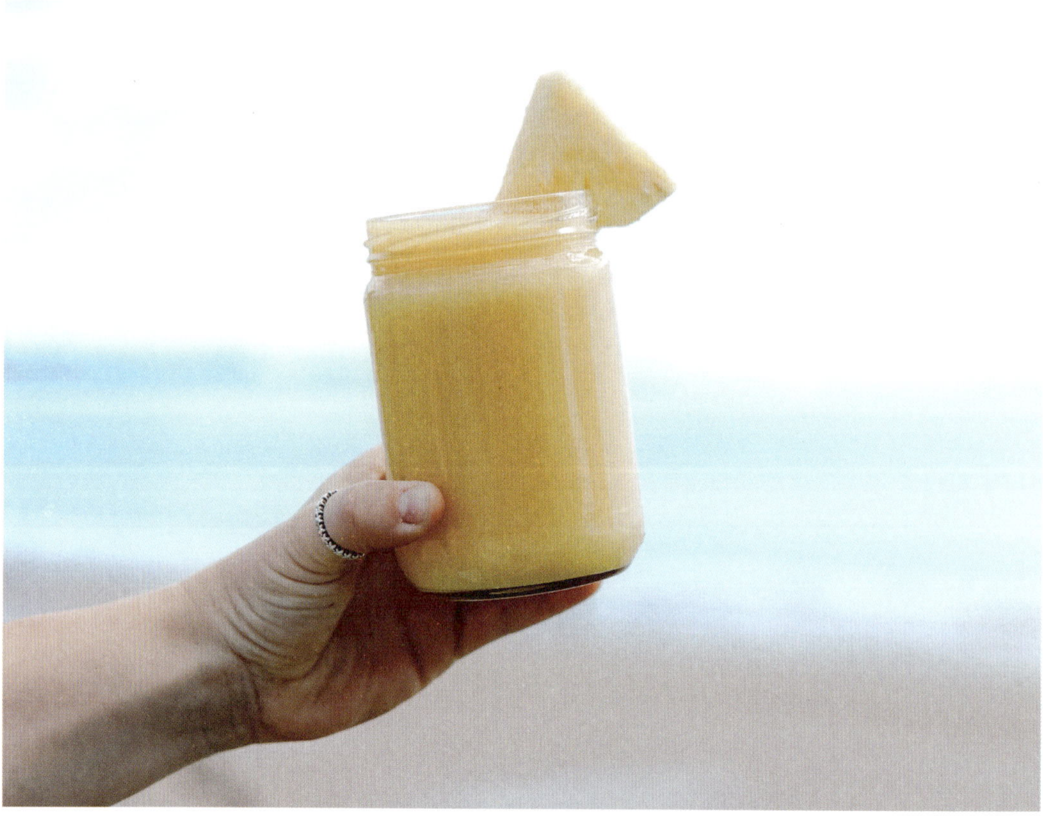

Green Goodness

Serves 1 • 5 minutes • GF

I am a sucker for a green smoothie. This is a great way to rehydrate in the morning, and it gets your digestive system in full swing.

½ cup frozen mango
1 Tbsp almond butter
2 cups spinach
1 Tbsp chia seeds
1 tsp spirulina powder
1 cup plant milk or coconut water

Combine all ingredients in a blender and process until smooth.

• • • • • • • •

Hot Tip: Try adding frozen zucchini. It's an amazing way to make your smoothie extra creamy while sneaking in some additional nutrients.

• • • • • • • •

Hempy Tropical Vibes

Serves 1 • 5 minutes • GF, NF

I absolutely adore this thick smoothie. The sweet pineapple reminds me of my childhood living in Fiji. Add a little spinach to get those extra greens in.

1 cup chopped frozen pineapple
½ cup chopped frozen mango
1 Tbsp hemp seeds
1½ cups coconut water

Place all ingredients in a blender and process until smooth.

Lemon and Blueberry Fizz

Serves 4 • 5 minutes • GF, NF

I originally made this recipe simply to look pretty in the background of a photo and then I became obsessed with the lemon flavour and bright colour of the berries.

4 cups sparkling water
Juice from 4 medium-sized lemons, plus 4 lemon slices
2 cups ice
½ cup frozen blueberries

Add all ingredients to a large jug or divide evenly between four glasses.

Orange Spritzer

Serves 2 • 10 minutes • GF, NF

Such an easy, refreshing drink. The fresh orange juice is so sweet and delicious. It's the perfect mocktail for any occasion.

1 cup freshly squeezed orange juice
1 cup soda water
1 orange, sliced
Handful of ice
Dehydrated fruit to garnish

Divide orange juice, soda water, sliced orange and ice between two medium-sized glasses. Mix and top with the dehydrated fruit.

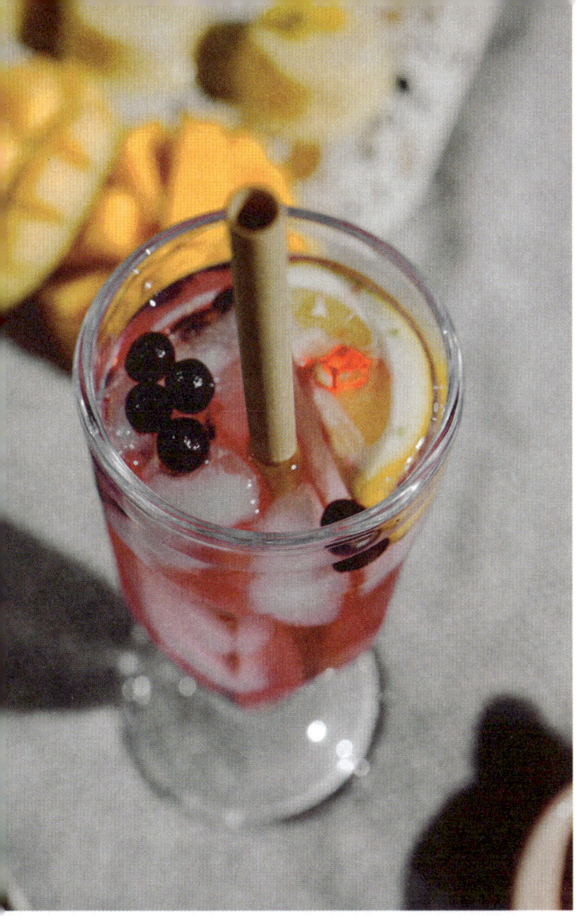
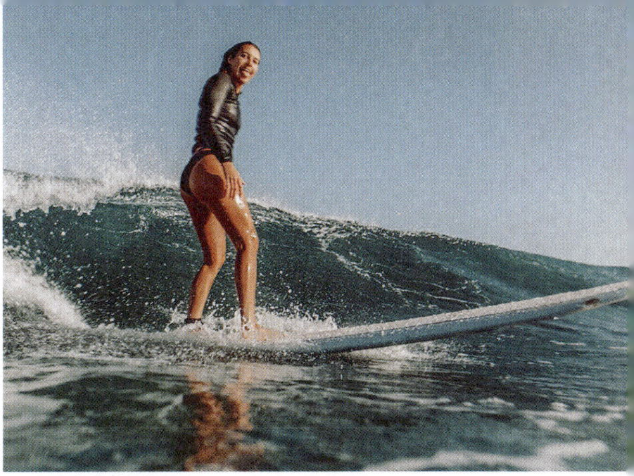
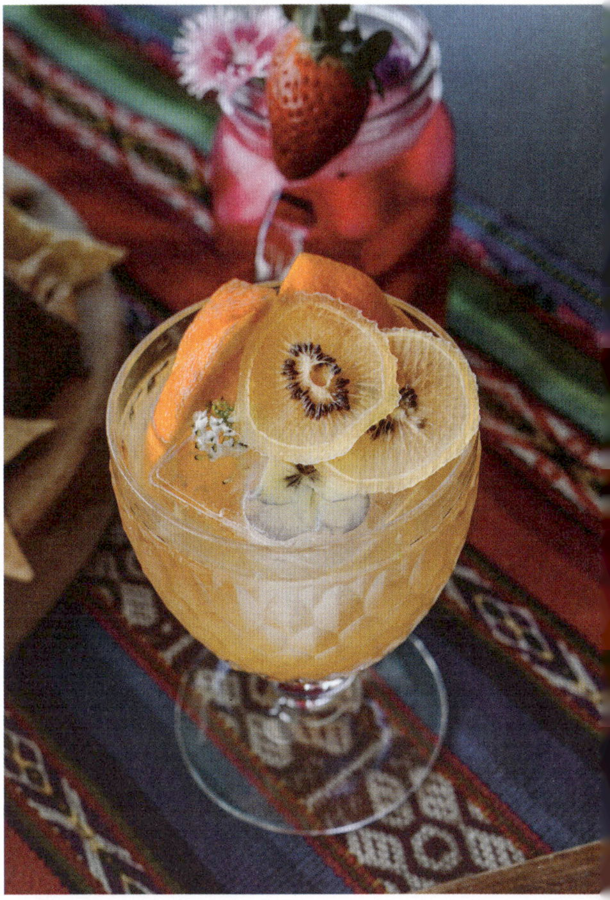
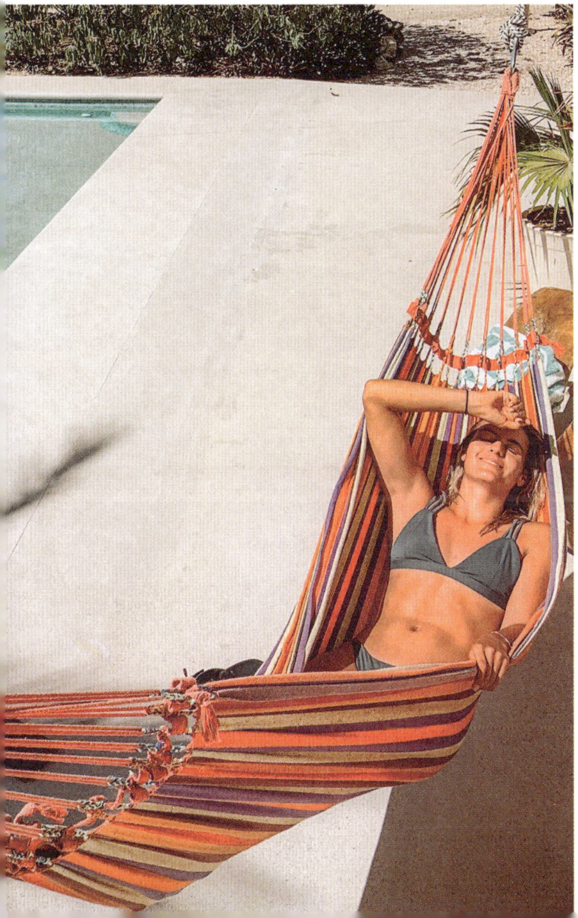
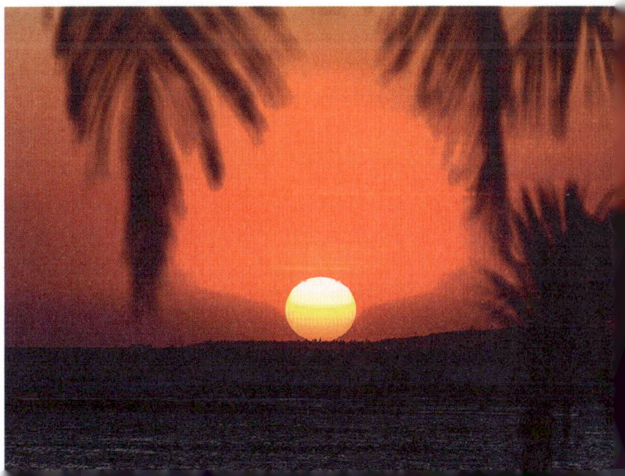

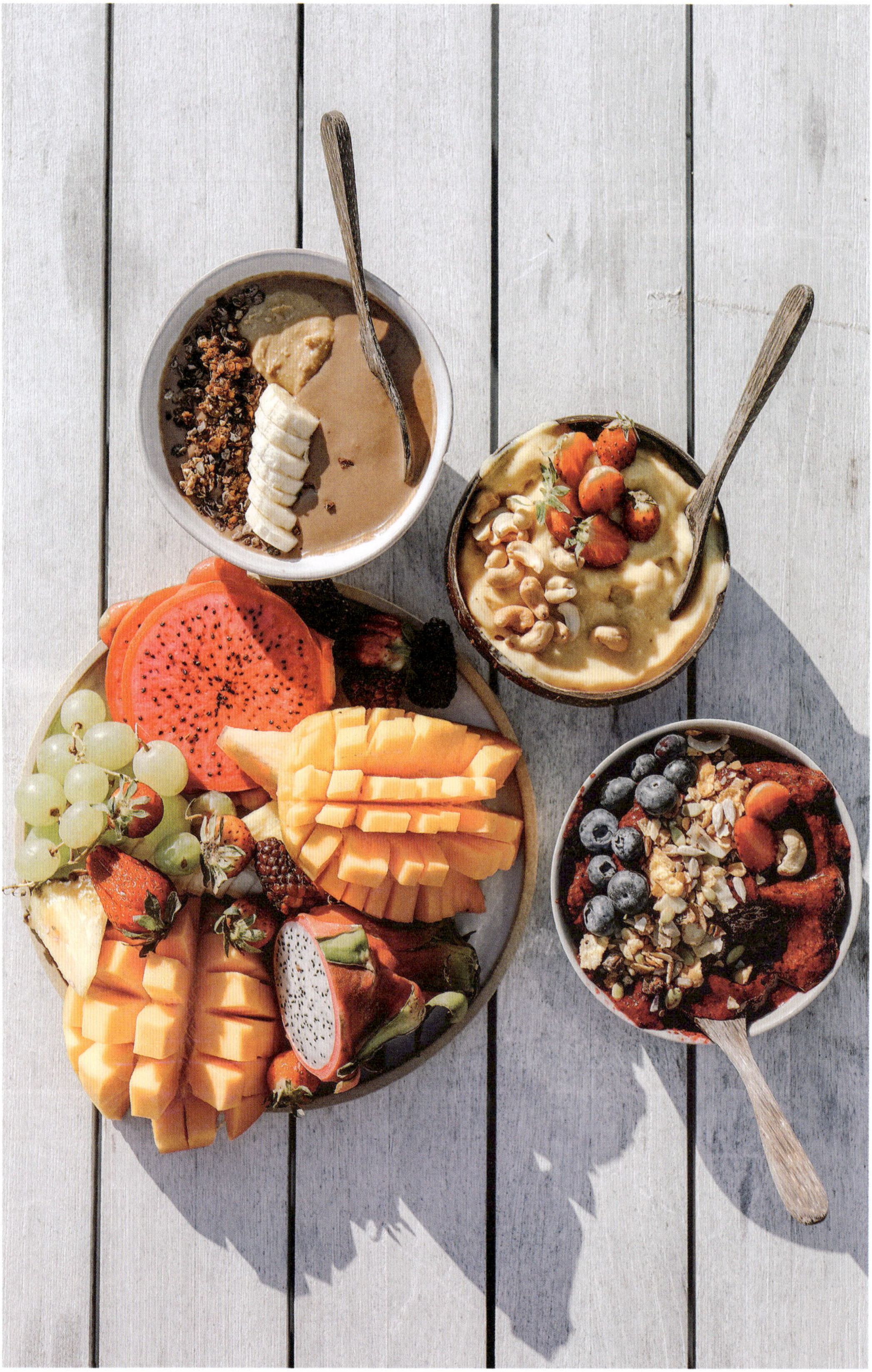

Smoothie Bowl 3 Ways

Serves 1 • 10 minutes

Breakfast, lunch or dinner; summer or winter — smoothies are amongst my favourite meals. The Oat and Nutty Chocolate Granola (see p. 33) makes the perfect topping.

1. **Berry and Beet**
2 cups frozen berries
½ cup chopped beetroot
½–1 cup plant milk
1 Tbsp hemp seeds
1 Tbsp flaxmeal

2. **Sunshine Smoothie Bowl**
1 frozen banana
1 cup frozen mango
½ tsp ground turmeric
½ tsp ground cinnamon
½–1 cup coconut water
Pinch of black pepper

3. **Chunky Monkey**
2 frozen bananas
2 Tbsp peanut butter
1 Tbsp cacao powder
½–1 cup plant milk

Choose your smoothie flavour from the three options on the left. Combine all ingredients in a high-powered blender and process until smooth (you might need to stop a few times to scrape down the sides). Top with granola and fresh fruit.

GF NFO

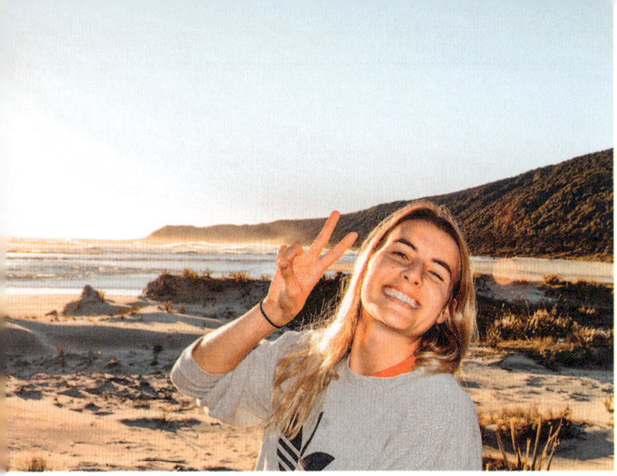
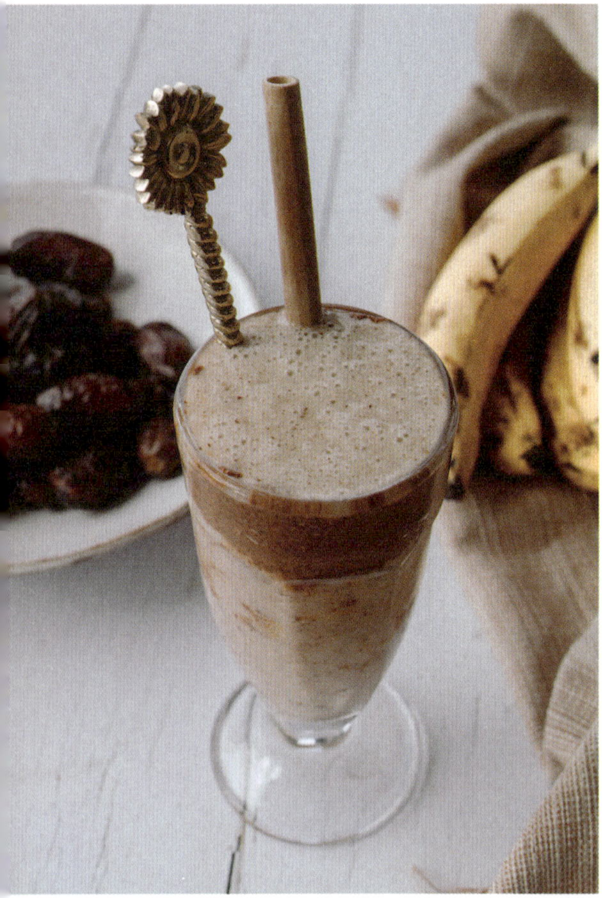
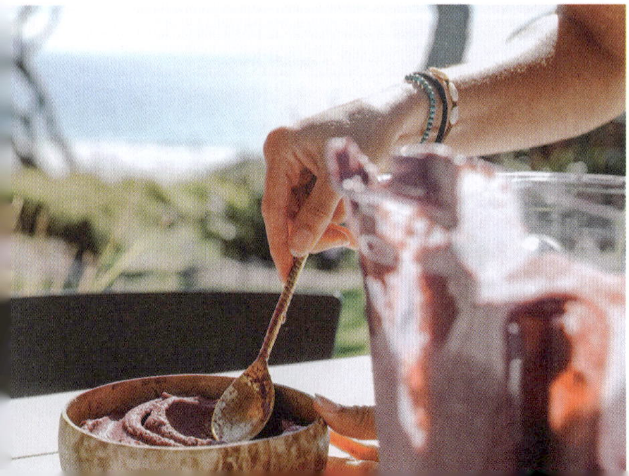
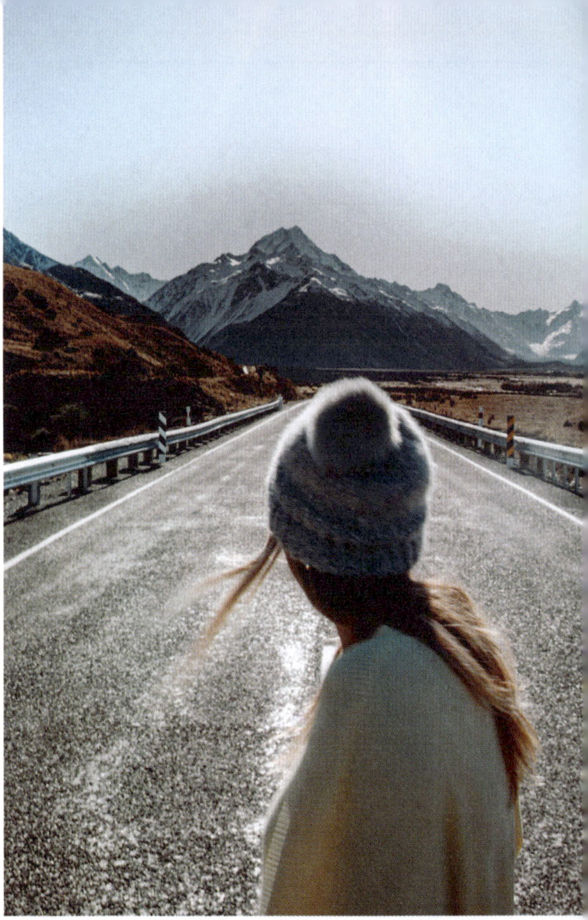
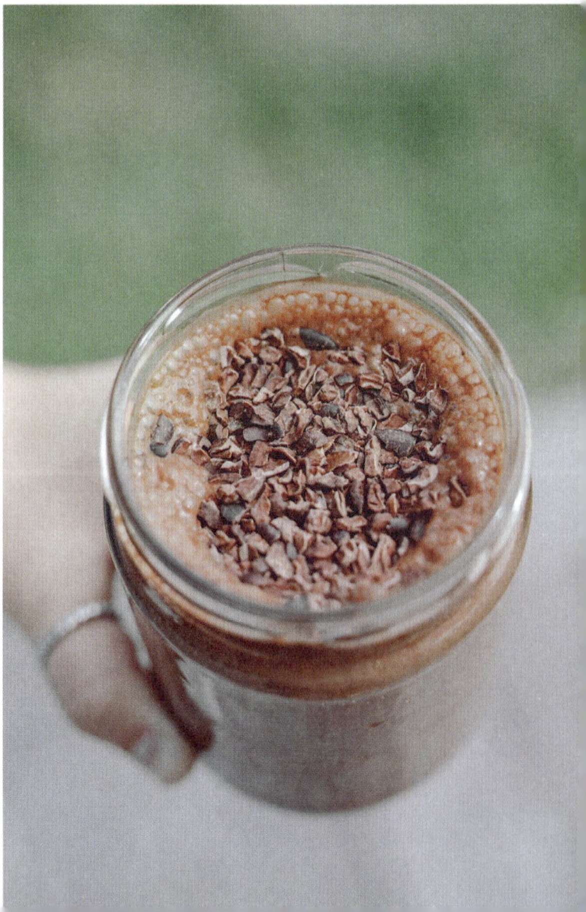

Salted Caramel Blend

Serves 1 • 5 minutes • GF

I've always been a sucker for anything salted caramel and this smoothie really hits the spot. It is high in fibre and Omega-3 fatty acids from the almond butter and flaxmeal.

1 frozen banana
2 medjool dates, pitted
1 Tbsp flaxmeal
1 Tbsp almond butter
½ tsp ground cinnamon
Pinch of salt
1 cup plant milk

Place all ingredients in a blender and process until smooth.

. . . .

Hot Tip: 1 tablespoon of salted caramel protein powder tastes amazing in this smoothie.

. . . .

Chocolate Banana Shake

Serves 1 • 5 minutes • GF, NF

I have been making this smoothie for as long as I can remember. I always let my bananas go spotty before freezing them for an extra-sweet smoothie.

1 frozen banana
1 Tbsp cacao powder
1 Tbsp cacao nibs
1 tsp maca powder
1 Tbsp hemp seeds
1 cup plant milk

Combine all ingredients in a blender and process until smooth.

. . . .

Hot Tip: This recipe is also delicious when you add ½ cup frozen blueberries.

. . . .

Cheers!

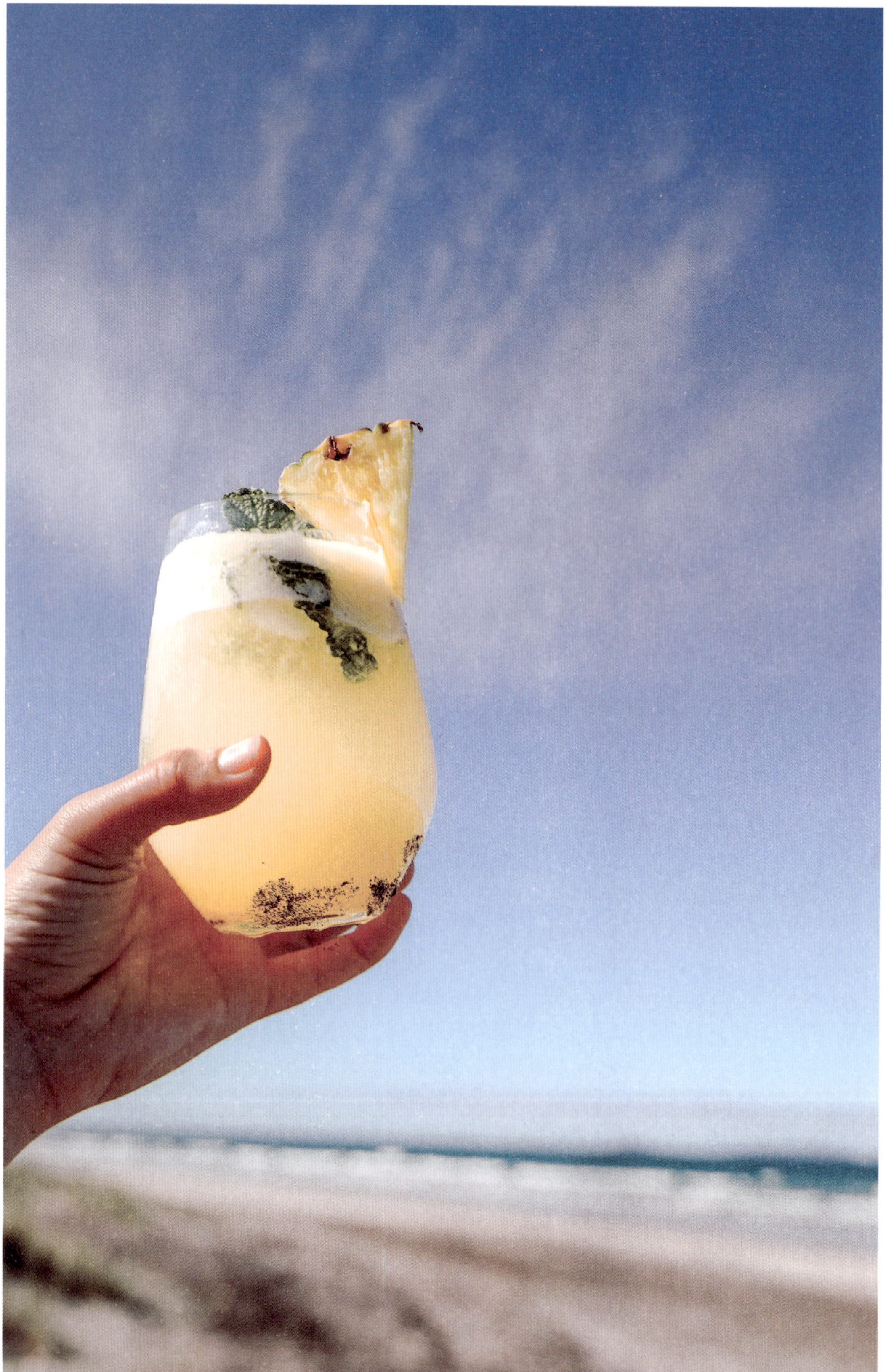

Frozen Pineapple Mojitos

Serves 2 • 10 minutes

Pineapple has always been one of my favourite fruits and it adds a wonderful dimension to this popular summer mocktail (or cocktail, if you prefer).

1 cup roughly chopped frozen pineapple
2 cups ice
2 Tbsp maple syrup
2 cups sparkling water
Juice from 2 fresh limes
½ cup fresh mint, chopped
¼ cup white rum, optional

Add pineapple, ice, maple syrup and sparkling water to a blender and process until combined. Pour into two glasses, along with lime juice, mint and rum (if using). Stir to combine.

GF NF

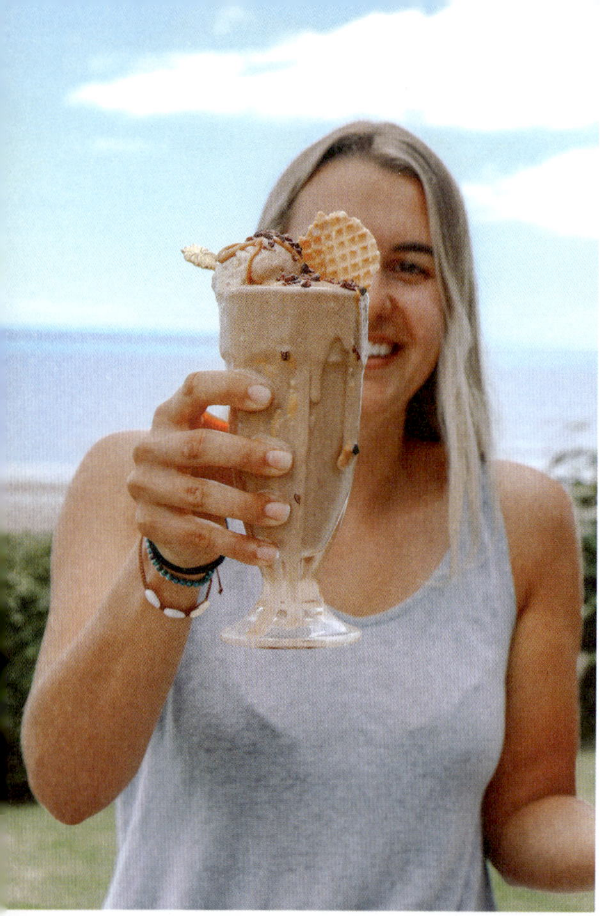

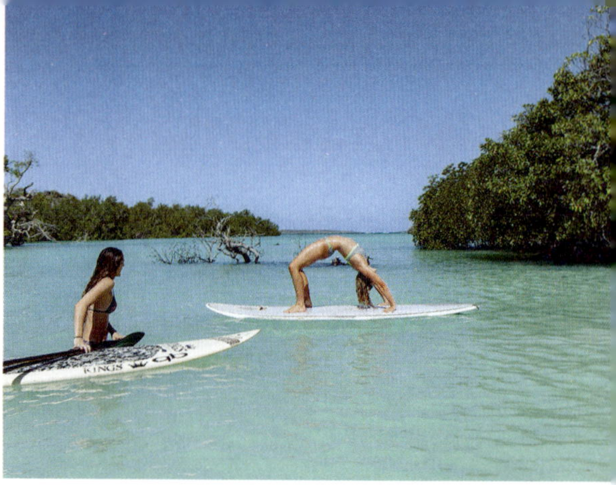

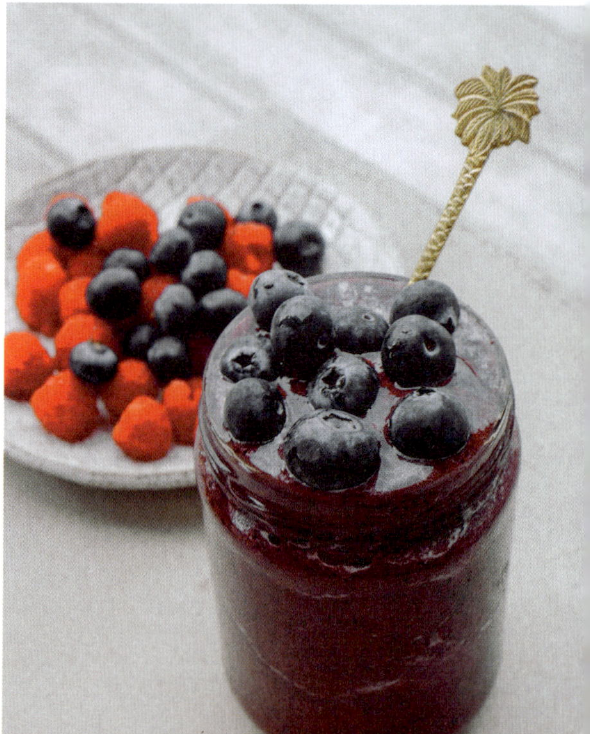

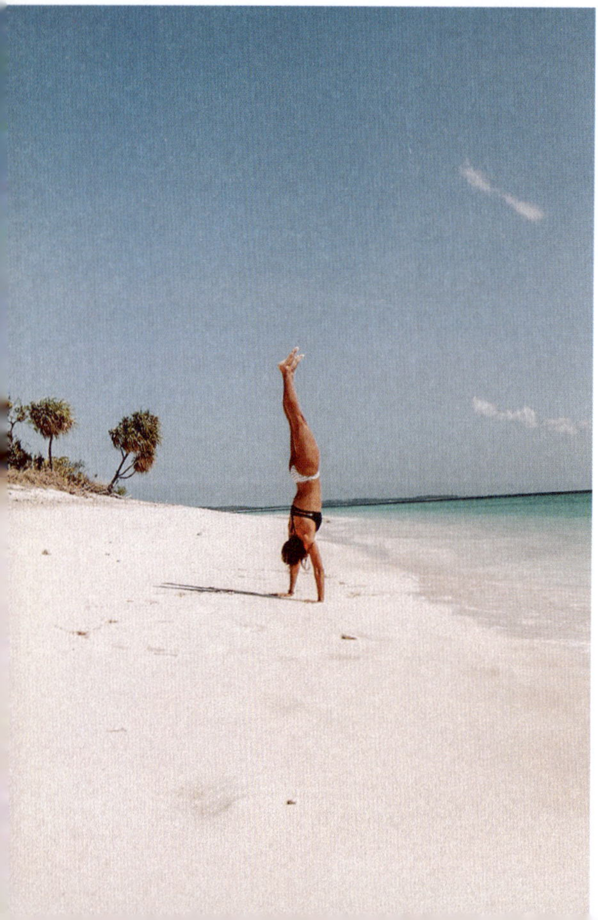

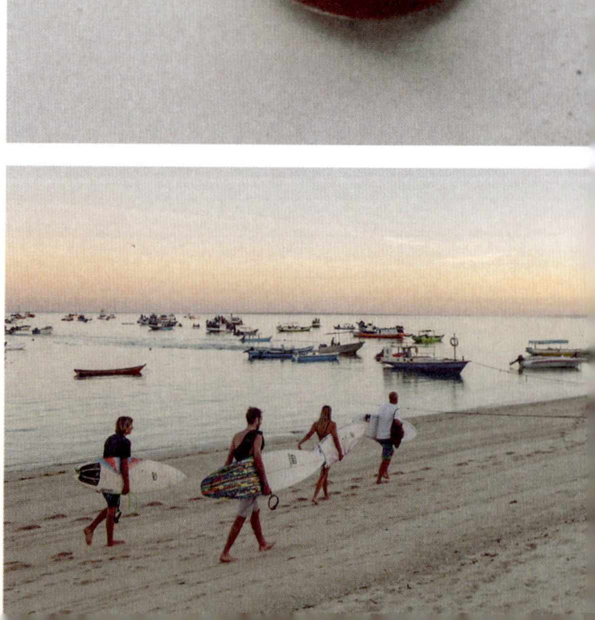

Peanut Butter Freak Shake

Serves 1 • 5 minutes • GF

I could happily live off a steady diet of peanut butter. This shake has a moreish creamy texture that melts in your mouth.

2 frozen bananas
2 Tbsp peanut butter
1 Tbsp cacao powder
¼ cup soy milk

Topping
1 scoop Coconut Salted Caramel Ice Cream (see p. 203)
Extra peanut butter, wafer biscuits and cacao nibs

Combine all ingredients in a blender and process until smooth. You may have to scrape down the sides a few times. Top with ice cream, extra peanut butter, wafer biscuits and cacao nibs.

Blueberry Muffin Smoothie

Serves 2 • 5 minutes • GF

Another glass of cold, creamy deliciousness, I sometimes make this for an on-the-go breakfast when I don't have much time.

2 cups frozen blueberries
¼ cup gluten-free rolled oats
1 Tbsp peanut butter
1½ cups plant milk
1 Tbsp vanilla protein powder, optional

Add all ingredients to a blender and blend until smooth.

• • • • • • •

Hot Tip: Add more or less liquid depending on whether you prefer a thick or thin consistency.

• • • • • • •

Cheers!

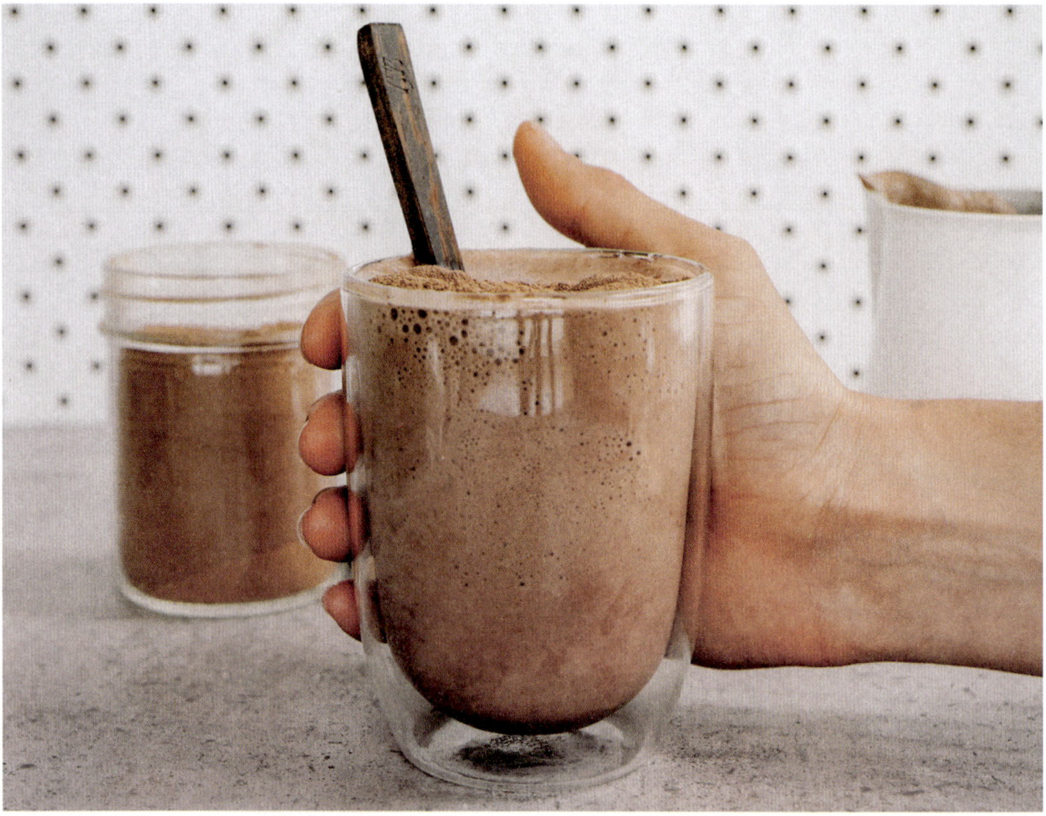

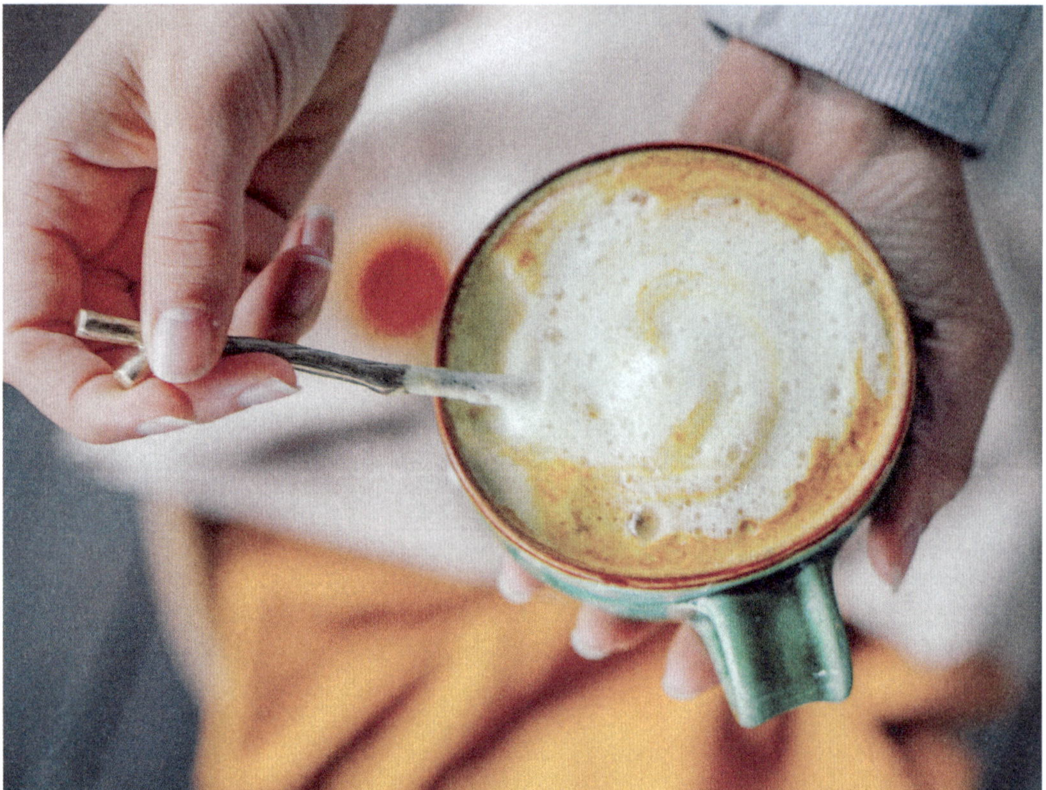

Plant-powered Hot Chocolate

Serves 1 • 5 minutes • GF

This is thick chocolate goodness packed with vitamins and minerals from the dates, cinnamon and Brazil nuts.

1 cup plant milk
1 heaped tsp cacao powder
1 tsp almond butter
½ tsp cinnamon
2 medjool dates, pitted
2 Brazil nuts

Combine all ingredients in a blender or food processor and process to combine.

Heat up the mixture in a pot and top with extra cinnamon.

Golden Hour Latte

Serves 1 • 5 minutes • GF, NF

I've never liked the taste of coffee, so I always order a turmeric latte when I'm out with friends. They are ridiculously easy to make at home.

½ tsp ground turmeric
Pinch of cracked pepper
½ tsp ground cinnamon
¼ tsp ground ginger
¼ tsp ground cardamom
1 tsp honey
1 cup plant milk

Combine turmeric, cracked pepper, cinnamon, ginger, cardamom and honey in a mug. Heat up the milk in a pot. Tip the milk into the mug and mix through.

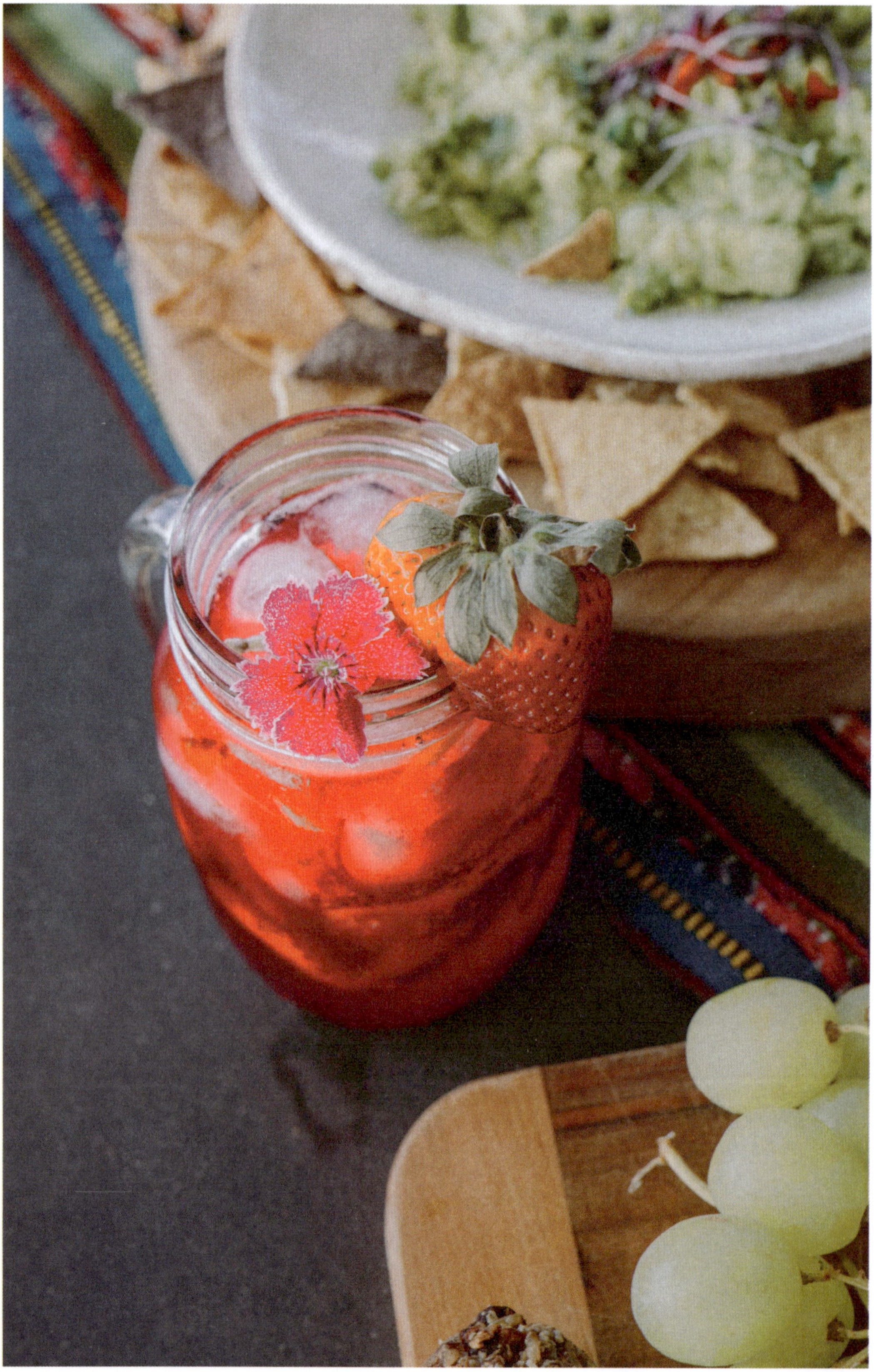

Smashed Strawberry Margarita

Serves 2 • 10 minutes

This is such a tasty summer cocktail. I'm obsessed with the strawberry flavour when paired with the kombucha. Feel free to use any kombucha flavour you like.

6 strawberries, sliced
Juice from 1 lime
Small handful of mint leaves
Large handful of ice
2 cups kombucha
¼ cup tequila, optional

Garnish
Strawberries, sliced
Edible flowers

Divide strawberries, lime juice and mint between two medium-sized glasses. Using the back of a spoon, smash down the strawberries and add ice along with kombucha and mix well. Add tequila for an alcoholic option, if desired.

Garnish with strawberries and edible flowers.

GF NF

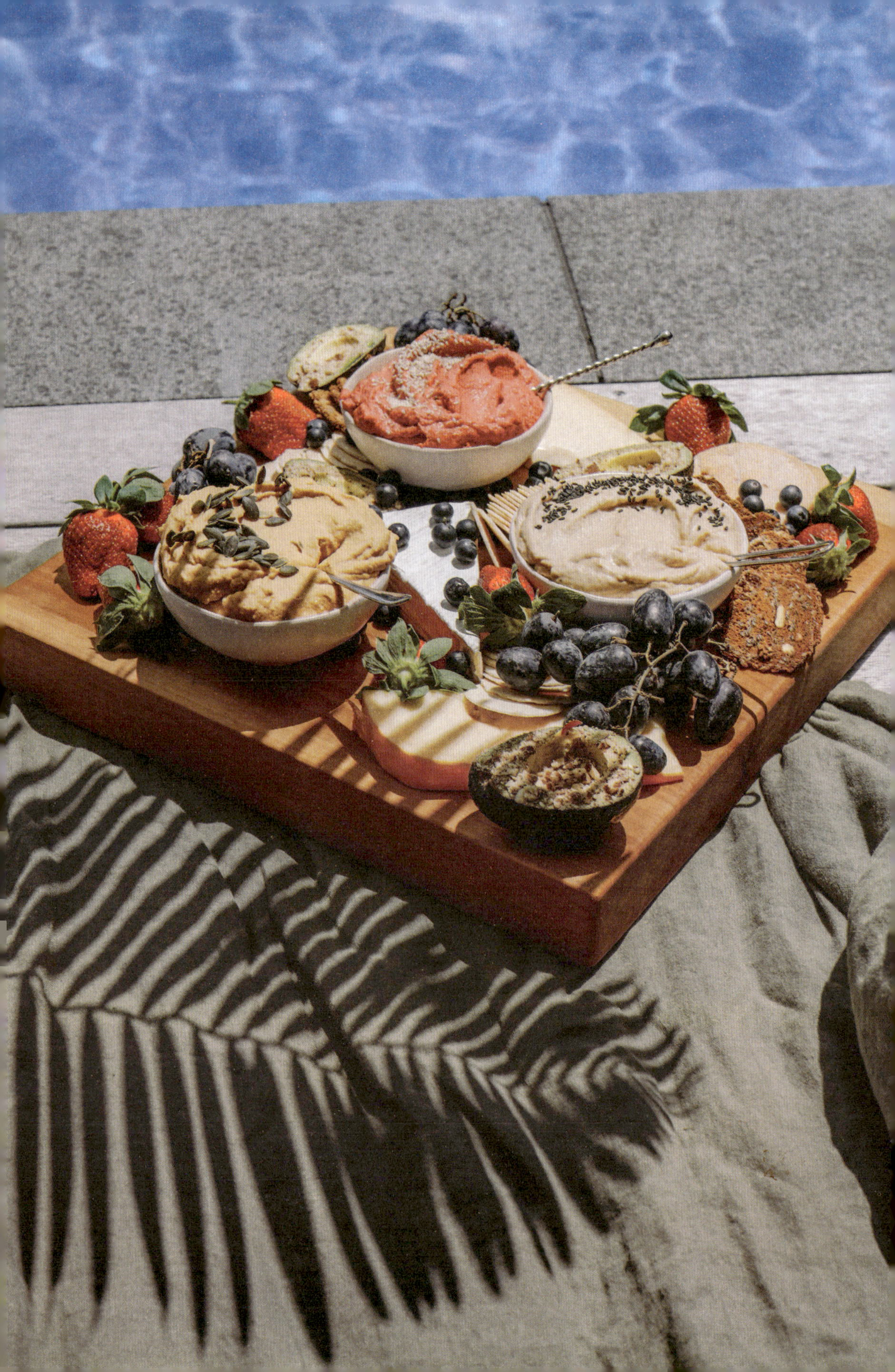

Snack Time

Prepping healthy snacks to nibble on throughout the day has changed the way I eat completely. When it gets to around 3pm and I really want something sweet, having a few bliss balls in the fridge is such a lifesaver. In this chapter I've also included my go-to platter recipes, such as homemade crackers and dips, as well as my favourite sweet snacks, including granola bars and the most delicious lemon and blueberry loaf you'll ever eat!

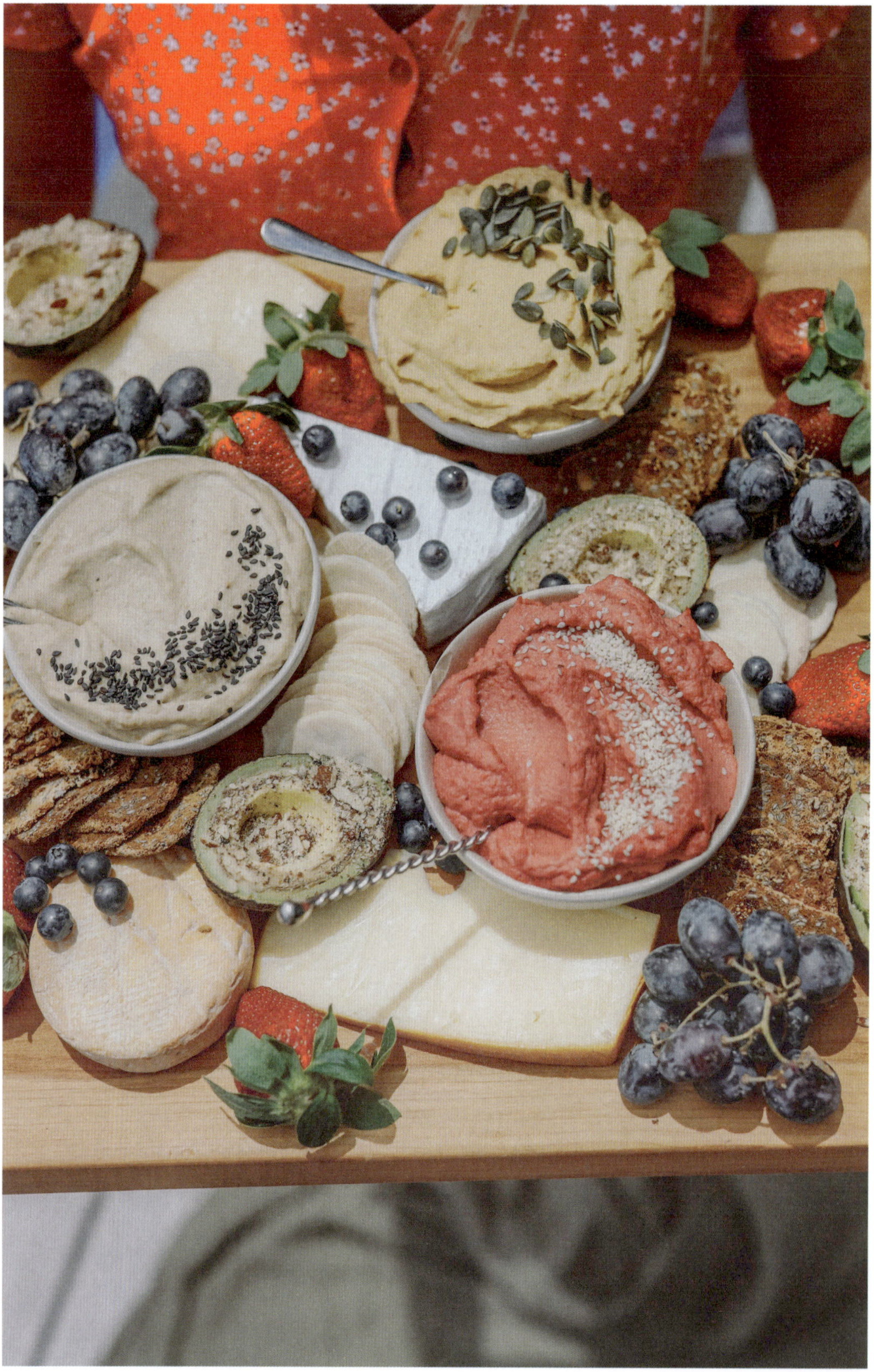

Hummus 3 Ways

Makes 1–2 cups • 20 minutes

I love a good hummus. Perfect for an afternoon snack with some carrots and crackers, but also amazing on sandwiches and wraps.

1. **Creamy Garlic**

400 g can chickpeas, drained and rinsed
3 Tbsp tahini
2 cloves garlic
Juice from ½ lemon
1 tsp maple syrup
½ cup plant milk
Salt and pepper to taste

2. **Beetroot**

400 g can chickpeas, drained and rinsed
1 Tbsp tahini
2 cloves garlic
6 slices canned beetroot
¼ cup plant milk
Salt and pepper to taste

For the Creamy Garlic or Beetroot Hummus, combine all ingredients in a food processor and pulse until smooth. Add more plant milk if needed.

3. **Roast Pumpkin**

200 g pumpkin, peeled, deseeded and roughly chopped
1 Tbsp olive oil
400 g can chickpeas, drained and rinsed
1 Tbsp tahini
2 cloves garlic
Juice from ½ lemon
¼ cup plant milk
Salt and pepper to taste

Preheat oven to 200°C and line a baking tray with baking paper. Add pumpkin to baking tray with olive oil and roast for 25 minutes until soft and golden.

Place all ingredients, including the roast pumpkin, into a food processor and pulse until smooth. Add more plant milk if needed.

GF NF

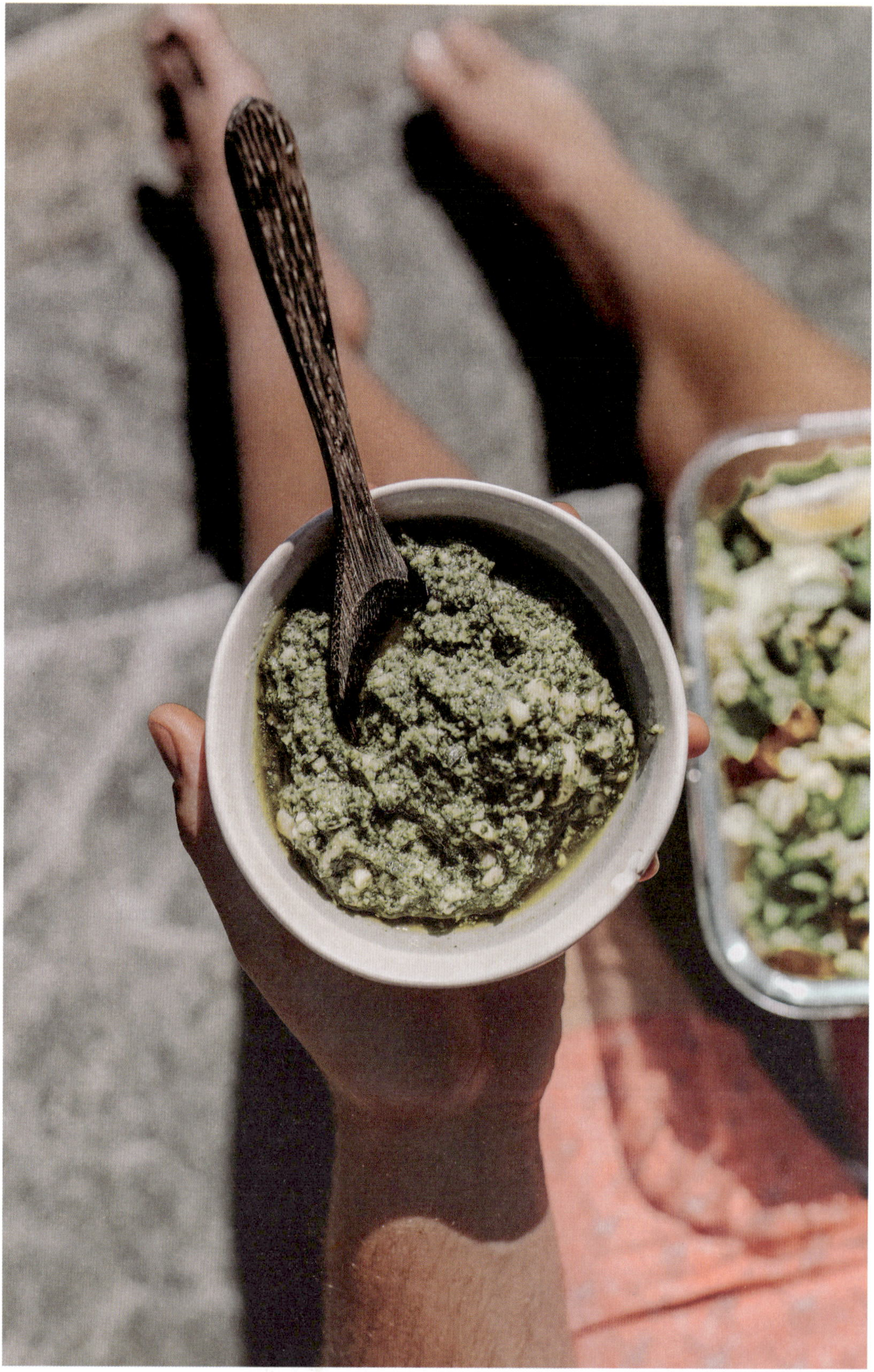

Pumpkin Seed Pesto

Makes 1 cup • 15 minutes

I genuinely think I could eat pesto pasta every day. Making your own pesto is such a good idea as it's full of leafy greens and herbs. The pumpkin seeds give it a really nice texture and taste. This is great to keep in the fridge as it can be used for a bunch of sandwiches, salads and wraps.

2 cups fresh basil
½ cup pumpkin seeds
2 Tbsp nutritional yeast
¼ cup olive oil
1 cup spinach
1 clove garlic
Salt and pepper

Blend all ingredients in a high-powered blender until you reach the consistency you like. You may need to add more olive oil if you want a runnier texture.

. . . .

Hot Tip: Feel free to replace pumpkin seeds with pinenuts or walnuts, if you prefer.

. . . .

Easy Guacamole

Serves 6 • 10 minutes

You can never go wrong with homemade guacamole. This is a super simple, heavenly recipe and can be used to complement a variety of meals or just as an afternoon snack with some good-quality corn chips.

3 large ripe avocados
½ red onion, finely chopped
2 small tomatoes, roughly chopped
1 clove garlic, finely chopped
½ tsp ground cumin
1 chilli, deseeded and finely sliced
½ tsp paprika
Handful of fresh coriander, roughly chopped
Juice from 1 lime
Salt and pepper to taste

To Serve
Corn chips, optional

Scoop avocado flesh into a medium-sized bowl and mash roughly (leaving a few chunky pieces).

Add remaining ingredients and mix well to combine.

Serve with corn chips or add as a condiment to meals, such as the Wholesome Black Bean Nachos with Cashew Cheese (see p. 175).

GF NF

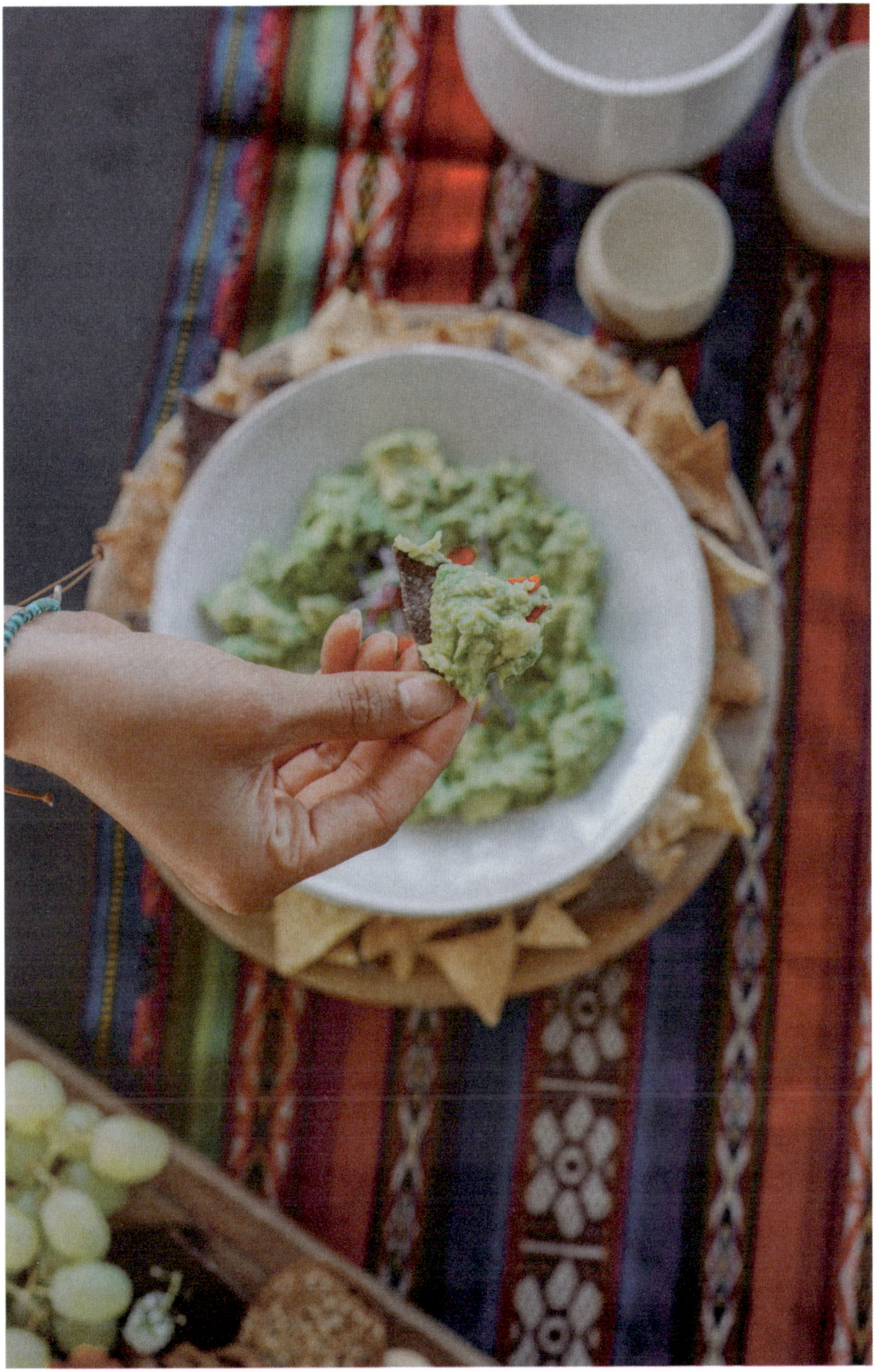

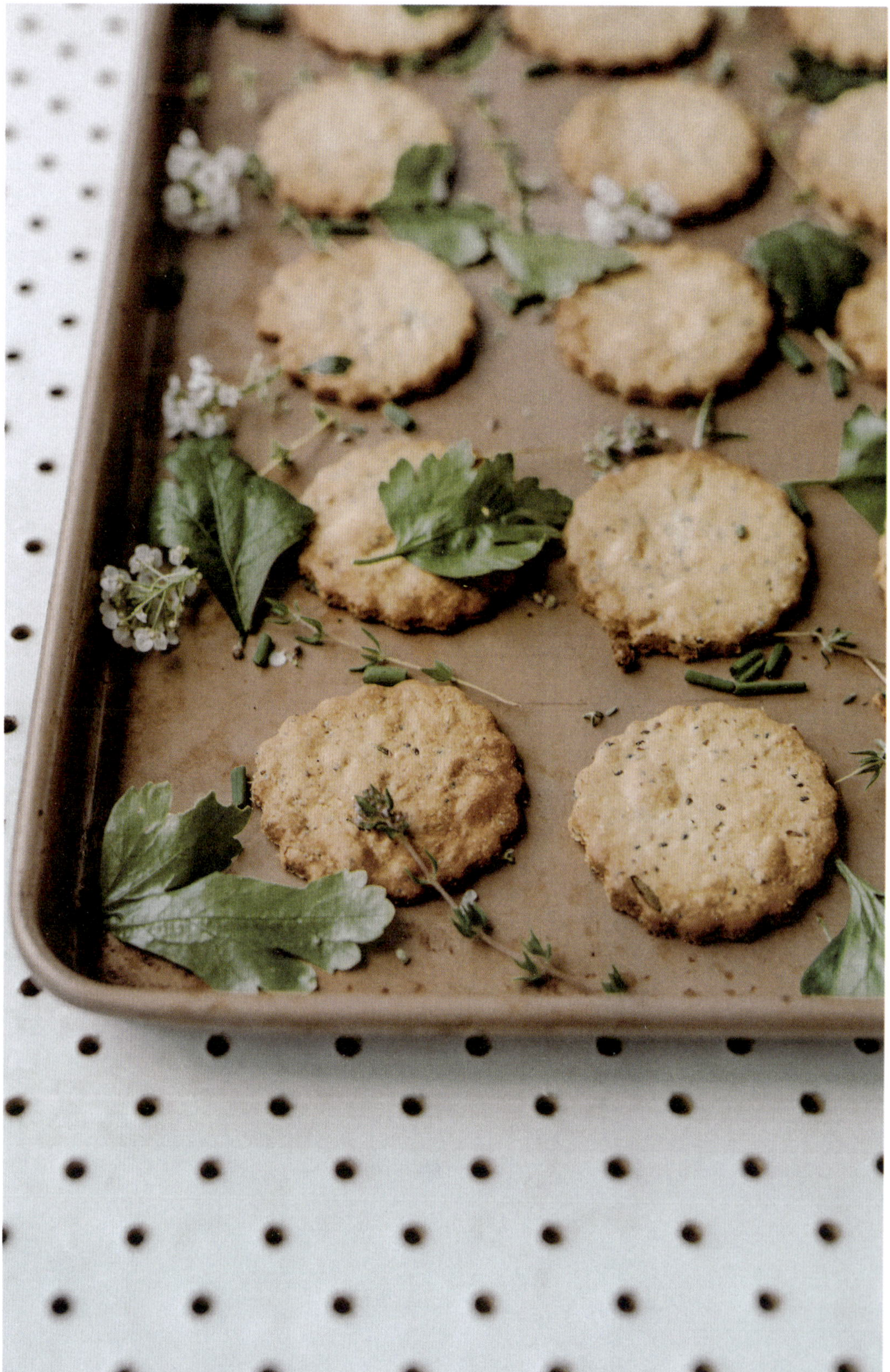

Chickpea Herb Crackers

Makes around 15 crackers • 40 minutes

These are the perfect addition to an afternoon platter or to pair with a tasty dip. The fresh herbs create such an amazing burst of flavour. These are always a big hit and no one can believe I make them from scratch.

2 cups chickpea flour
1 cup almond meal
1 Tbsp chia seeds
1 Tbsp olive oil
1 Tbsp maple syrup
¼ cup finely chopped rosemary
¼ cup finely chopped parsley
¼ cup finely chopped thyme
½ tsp baking powder
¼ tsp salt
¼ cup water

Preheat oven to 180°C and line a baking tray with baking paper.

Add all ingredients to a bowl and mix well. Use your hands to form a dough (if the dough is too dry you may need to add a dash more water).

Between two sheets of baking paper roll out the dough until it's thin and even. Using a sharp knife, cut the dough into small pieces. Alternatively, use a cookie cutter.

Bake in the oven for 25 minutes or until golden.

GF

Bliss Balls

Makes 8–12 • 10 minutes

Bliss balls are the perfect morning snack. All of these recipes take less than 10 minutes to prepare and they taste absolutely delicious. Once you have a good base, you can experiment with different ingredient variations. If you have a nut allergy, pumpkin or sesame seeds make a great alternative.

1. **Fig and Tahini**
8 dried figs
1 cup almonds
2 Tbsp tahini

2. **Chocolate Orange**
1 cup mixed nuts
5 medjool dates, pitted
¼ cup cacao powder
Juice from 1 orange

3. **Banana Bread**
1 cup cashews
2 cups gluten-free rolled oats
3 medjool dates, pitted
1 banana
½ cup chocolate chips or cacao nibs

4. **Blueberry and Coconut**
1 cup gluten-free rolled oats
2 cups frozen blueberries
2 Tbsp peanut butter
1 cup desiccated coconut

Add all ingredients to a food processor and blend. The mixture should be slightly sticky. Using your hands, roll tablespoonfuls of the mixture into snack-sized balls.

Store in the fridge for up to 7 days.

. . . .

Hot Tip: These bliss balls can be frozen if required. Just remove them 5 minutes before eating.

. . . .

GF

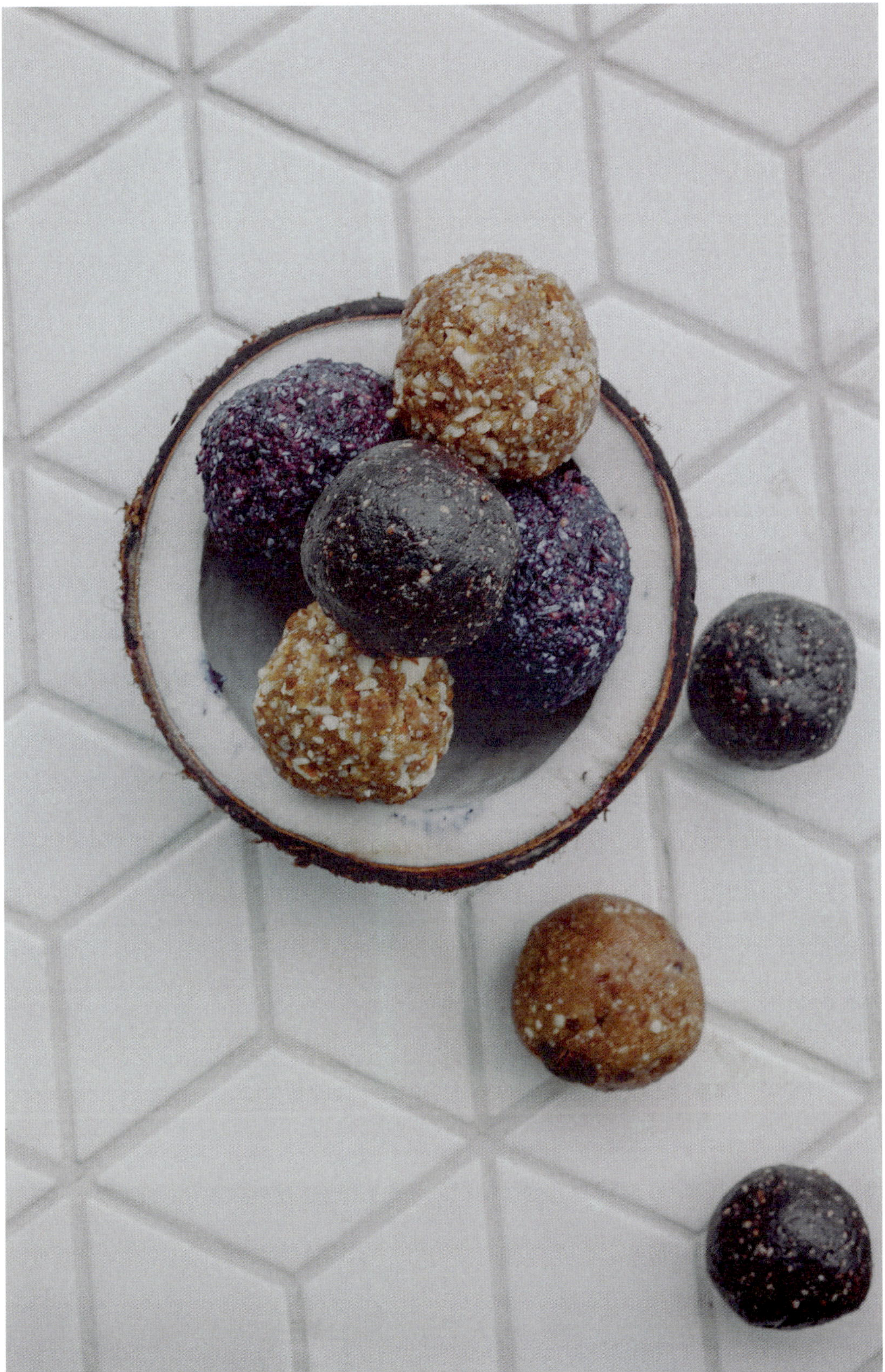

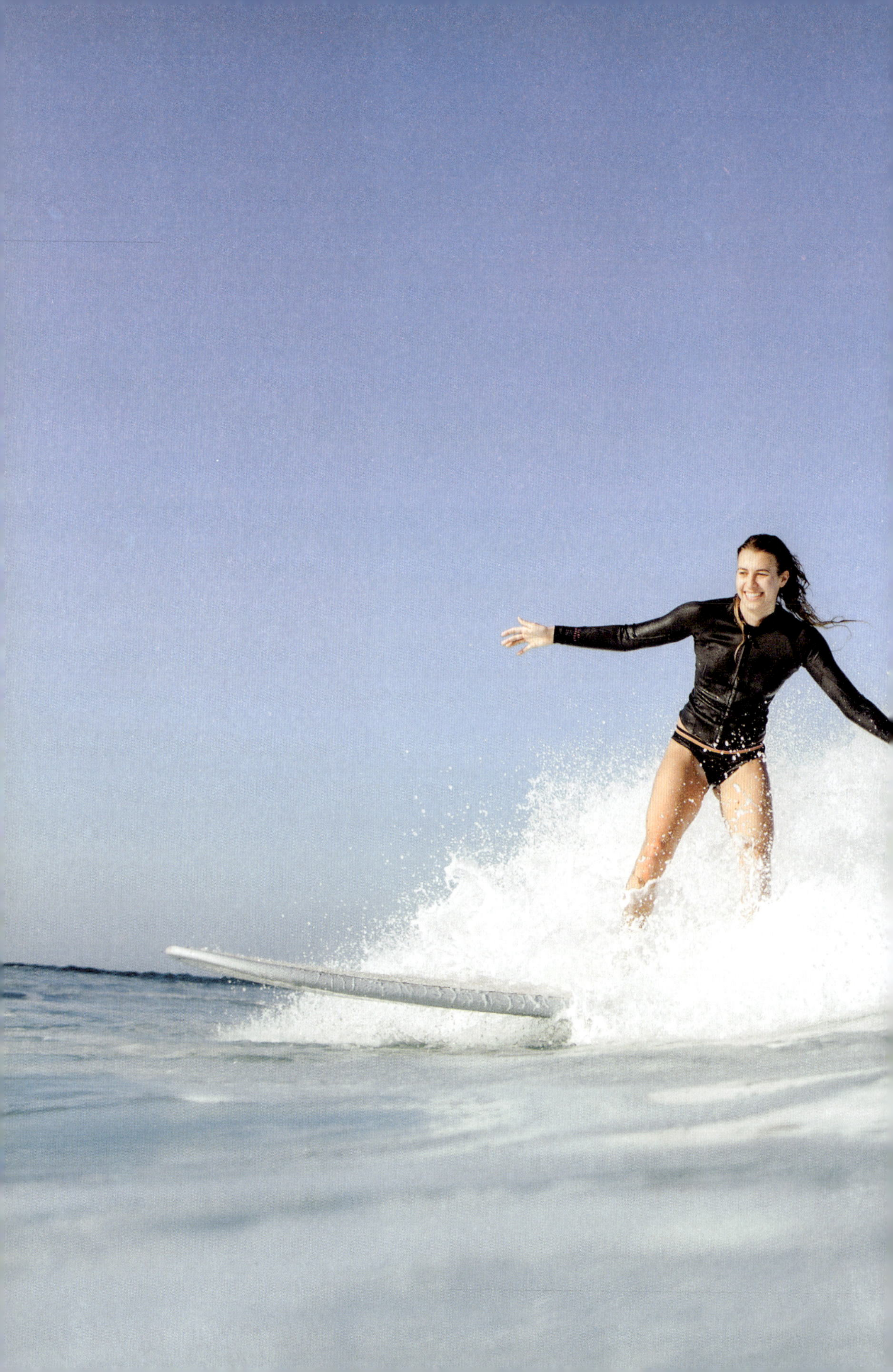

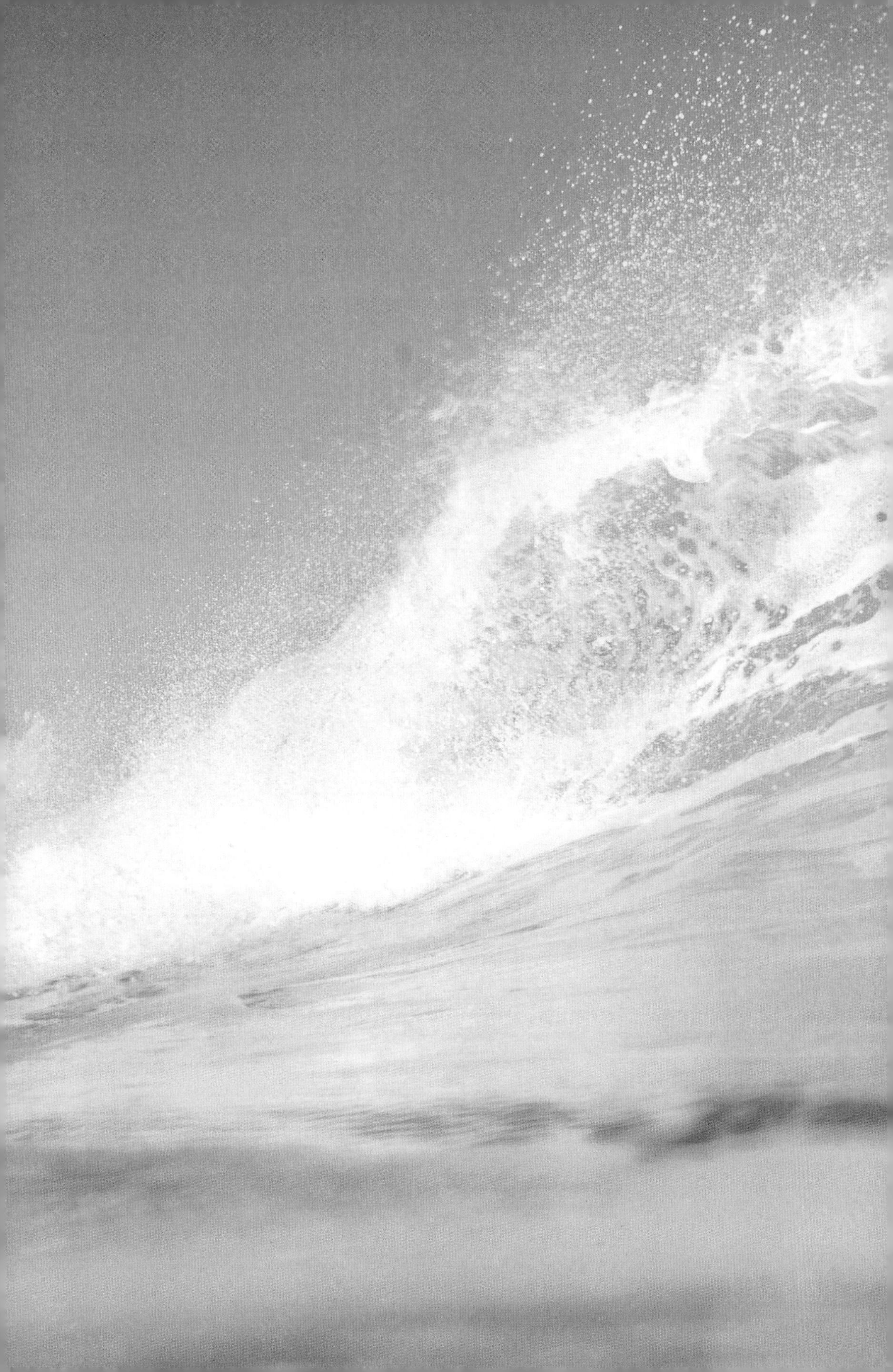

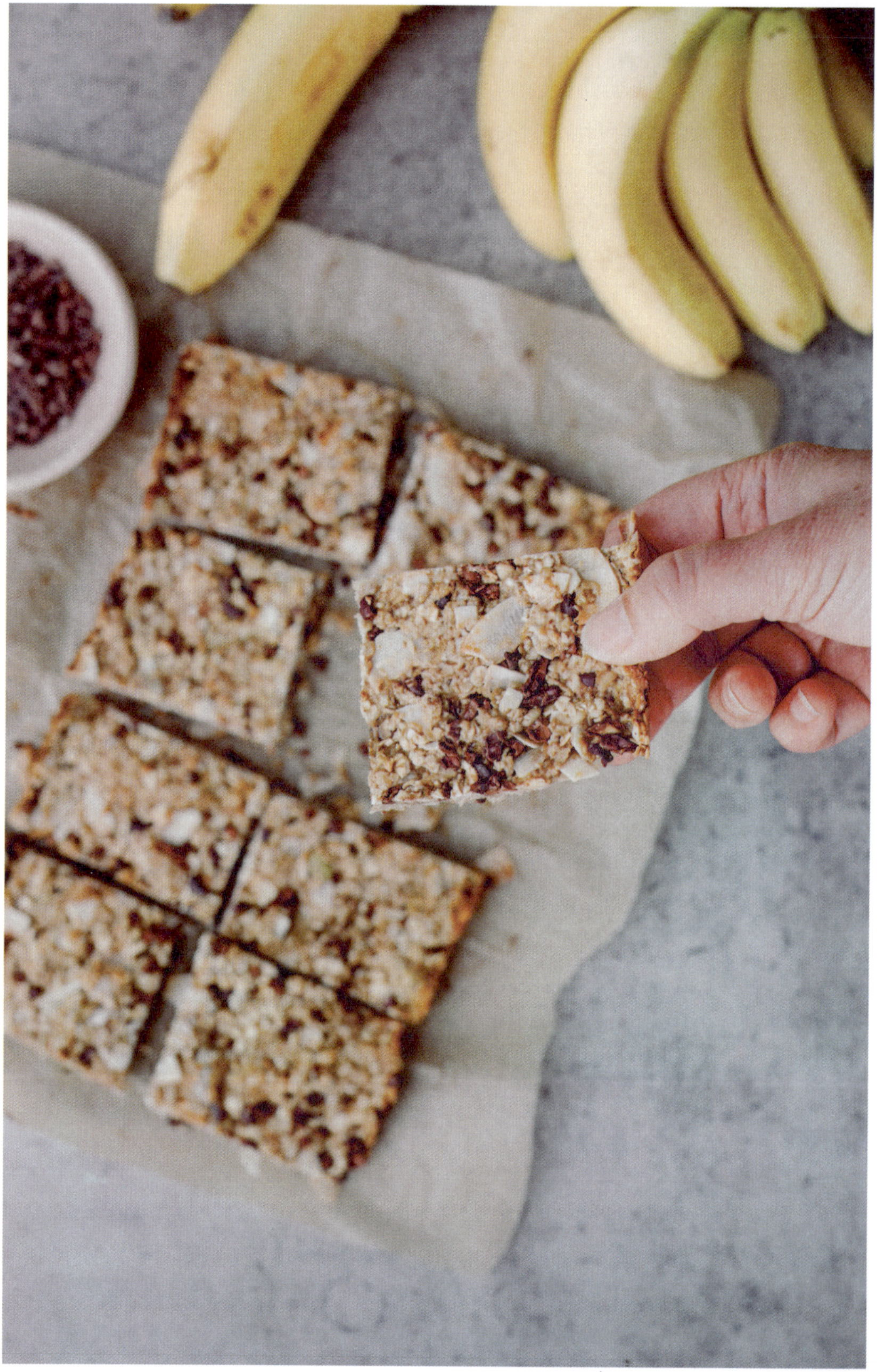

Chunky Monkey Granola Bars

Serves 8 • 30 minutes

These granola bars are naturally sweetened with bananas and a little maple syrup. It's all made in one bowl — couldn't be easier!

2 medium-sized bananas, mashed
2 Tbsp peanut butter
¼ cup maple syrup
1½ cups gluten-free rolled oats
½ cup coconut chips
½ cup cacao nibs or chocolate chips

Preheat oven to 180°C and line a slice tin with baking paper.

Add all ingredients to a bowl and mix until well combined.

Tip mixture into slice tin and press down firmly. Bake for 20 minutes or until golden.

Remove from oven and refrigerate for at least 30 minutes before slicing (this helps bind them together).

. . . .

Hot Tip: Instead of cacao nibs or chocolate chips, you can always add things like berries, raisins and nuts.

. . . .

GF

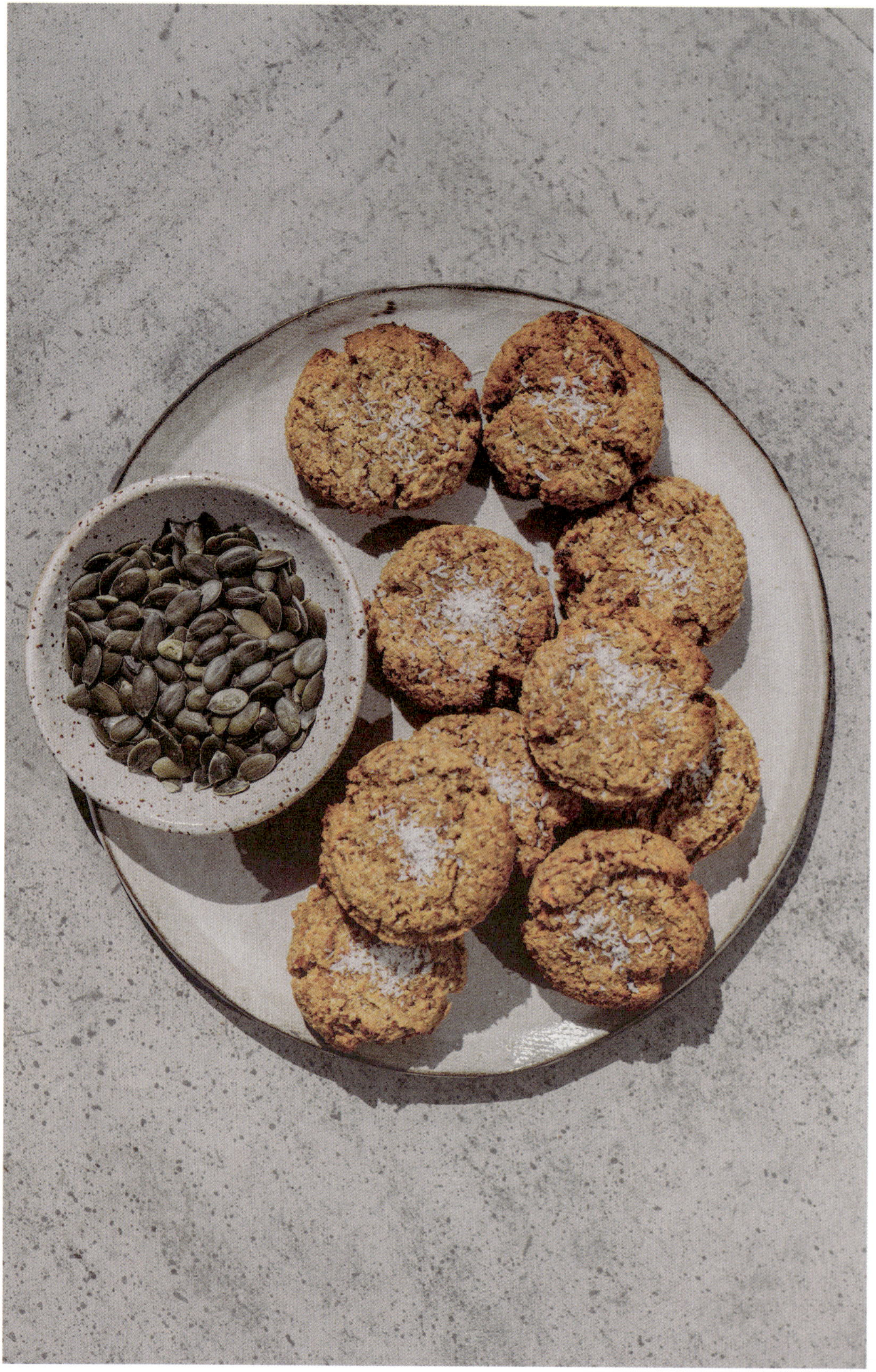

Date and Carrot Cookies

Makes 10 cookies • 30 minutes

These are probably the easiest cookies you'll ever make. You can chuck everything straight into the food processor, creating hardly any dirty dishes. These cookies are sweetened with fresh dates, which makes them super low in sugar, and the cinnamon, ginger and nutmeg will make your house smell delicious!

8 medjool dates, pitted and soaked in hot water for 10 minutes
1½ cups grated carrot
1½ cups almond meal
1 tsp ground cinnamon
1 tsp ground ginger
½ tsp ground nutmeg
⅓ cup desiccated coconut
½ cup tapioca flour
½ tsp baking powder
½ tsp baking soda
¼ tsp salt
Desiccated coconut, to garnish

Preheat oven to 180°C and line a baking tray with baking paper.

Place dates, carrot, almond meal, cinnamon, ginger, nutmeg and coconut into a food processor and blend until the mixture becomes a sticky paste. Add tapioca flour, baking powder, baking soda and salt, and pulse until combined.

Scoop tablespoonfuls of mixture onto the tray and press down lightly with a fork. Bake in the oven for around 20 minutes until golden but soft in the middle. Once cooled, garnish with desiccated coconut.

GF

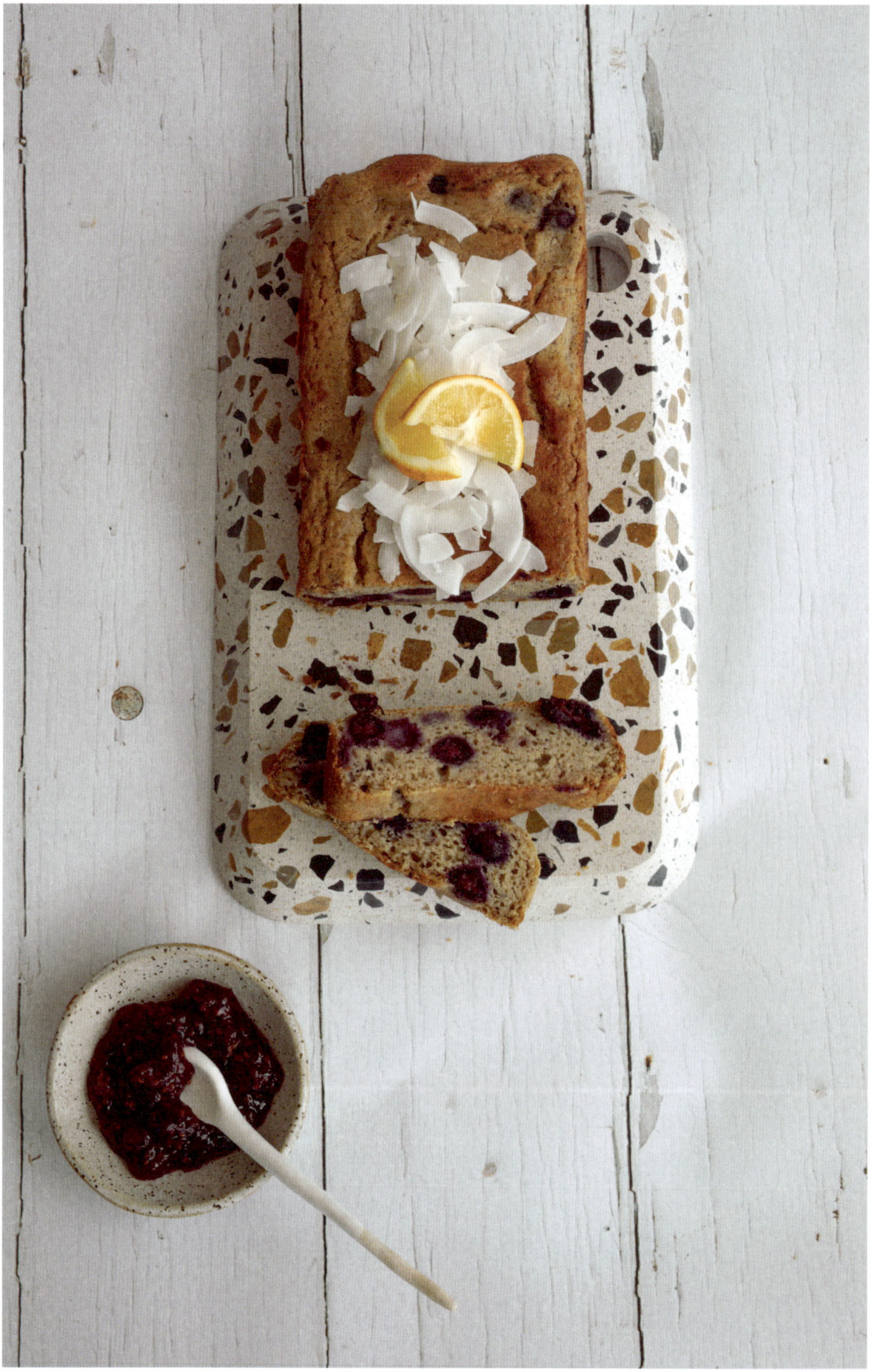

Lemon Blueberry Loaf

Serves 6 • 75 minutes

This loaf is decadently moist with the fresh combination of blueberries and lemon. Not only is this recipe bursting with tangy lemon but the buckwheat adds a slight nutty flavour. Use any flour you have handy.

1 cup plant milk
2 Tbsp flaxmeal
¼ cup maple syrup
¼ cup vegetable oil
1 tsp vanilla
Zest and juice from 1 lemon
1 cup buckwheat flour
2 tsp baking powder
Pinch of salt
1 cup blueberries

Preheat oven to 180°C and line a 10 x 20 cm loaf tin with baking paper.

Place plant milk, flaxmeal, maple syrup, oil, vanilla and lemon zest and juice in a medium-sized bowl and mix to combine.

In a separate large bowl, stir together flour, baking powder, salt and blueberries. Add wet ingredients to the dry and fold together — do not overmix.

Transfer to the loaf tin and place in the oven for 45–50 minutes until golden and cooked through.

. . . .

Hot Tip: Adding blueberries to the dry mix stops the entire loaf turning purple.

. . . .

GF NF

Mushroom Arancini Balls with Homemade Parmesan

Makes around 10 balls • 45 minutes

I've tried a few arancini recipes before and they were really difficult to make — so I decided to create a super easy version that was packed with flavour.

1 cup brown rice
200 g button mushrooms
2 cloves garlic, crushed
1 cup Sunflower Parmesan (see p. 211)

Preheat oven to 180°C and line a baking tray with baking paper.

Rinse rice then add to a pot with 2 cups water. Bring to the boil, stirring regularly, then turn heat down to low and cover. Leave pot covered over heat for 6 minutes without disturbing. Remove from heat and set aside for 5 minutes. Lift lid and fluff up rice with a fork.

Finely dice mushrooms with a knife or in a food processor then add to a pan over a medium heat along with the garlic and cook for about 5 minutes.

Add cooked rice and Sunflower Parmesan to pan and stir well to combine. Remove from heat.

Using your hands, roll tablespoonfuls of mixture into golf-ball-sized balls. Place them on the tray and bake in the oven for 30 minutes or until golden.

GF NF

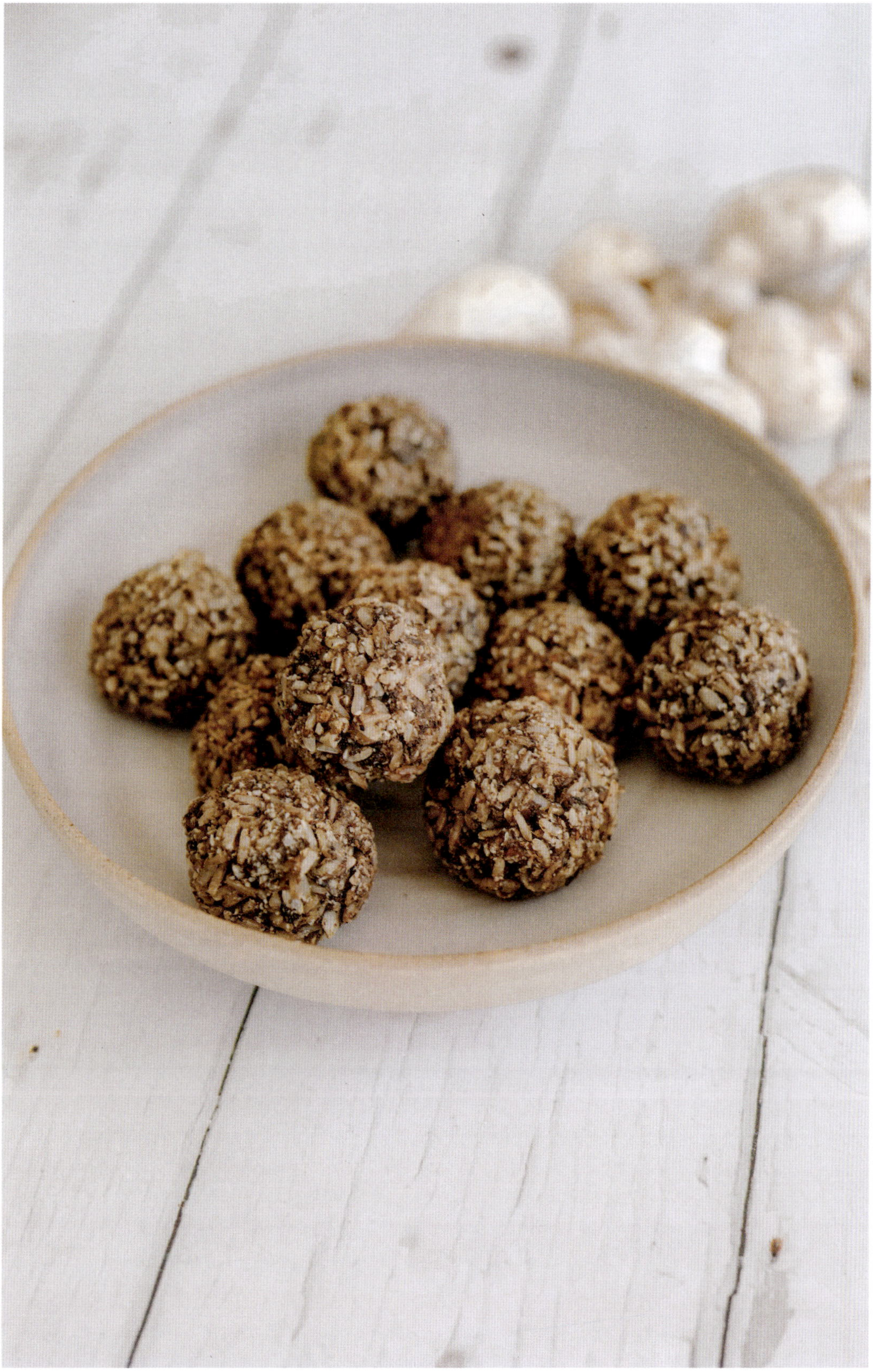

Beetroot Falafels

Serves 4 • 35 minutes

Making homemade falafels is way easier than you think. I make them at least once a week for lunch with a simple side salad and dressing. I wanted to create a unique flavour, and the beetroot creates the perfect texture, colour and taste.

2 medium-sized beetroot, quartered
1 small onion
2 cloves garlic
1 large handful of fresh parsley
1 large handful of fresh coriander
400 g can chickpeas, drained
1 tsp smoked paprika
1 tsp ground cumin
1 tsp ground coriander
¼ cup chickpea flour
1 tsp baking soda

Preheat oven to 180°C and line a baking tray with baking paper. Place beetroot on baking tray and cook for around 20 minutes until soft.

Pulse onion, garlic, parsley and coriander in a food processor until finely chopped but still a bit chunky. Tip mixture into a bowl and rinse out food processor.

Place chickpeas and cooked beetroot in food processor and pulse until a chunky paste is formed. Add beetroot mixture to chopped herbs. Add remaining ingredients and mix until combined.

Use a large tablespoon to shape mixture into balls and place on baking tray. Bake in oven for around 25 minutes.

. . . .

Hot Tip: Serve with Creamy Garlic Hummus (see p. 81).

. . . .

GF NF

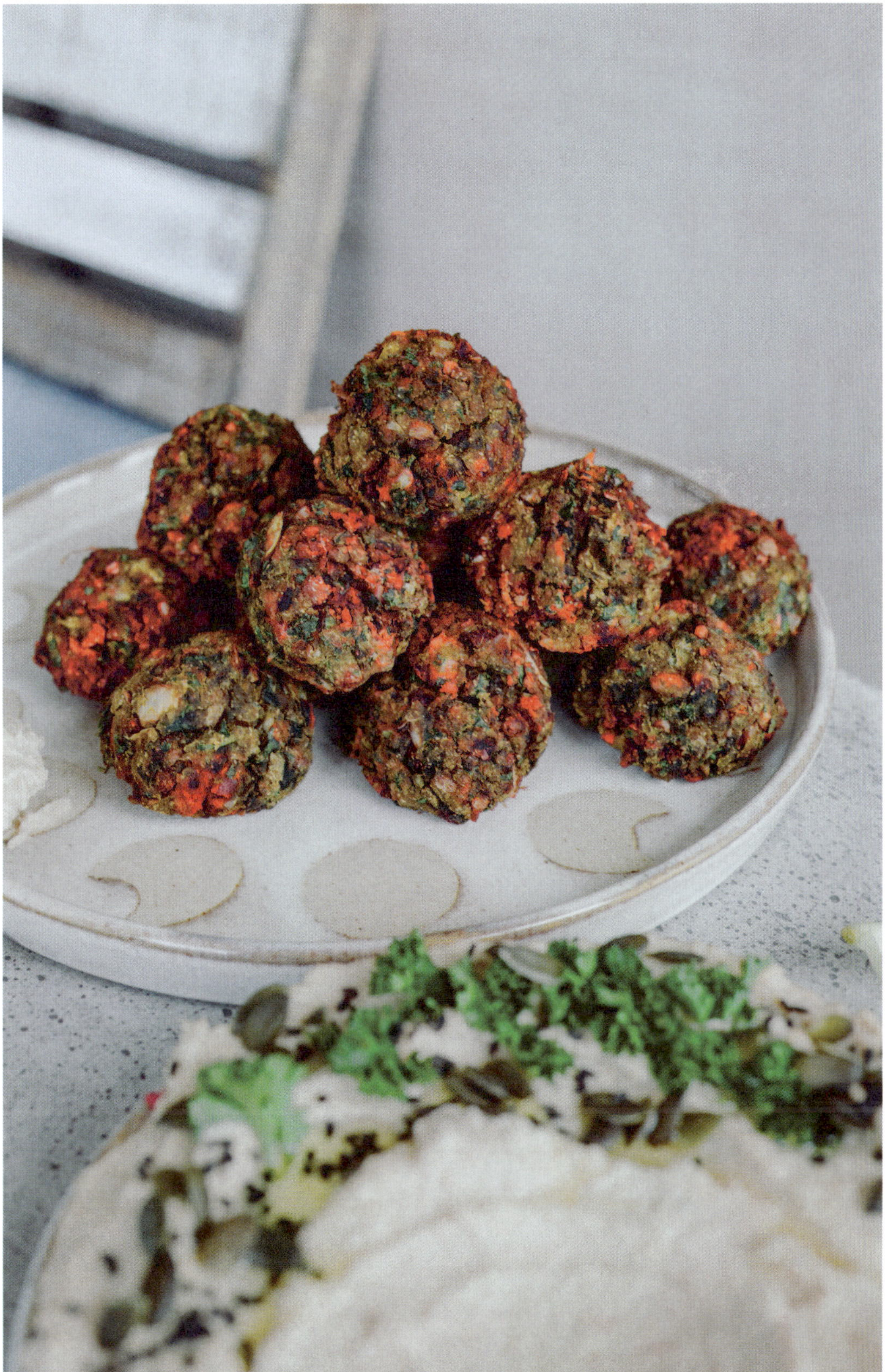

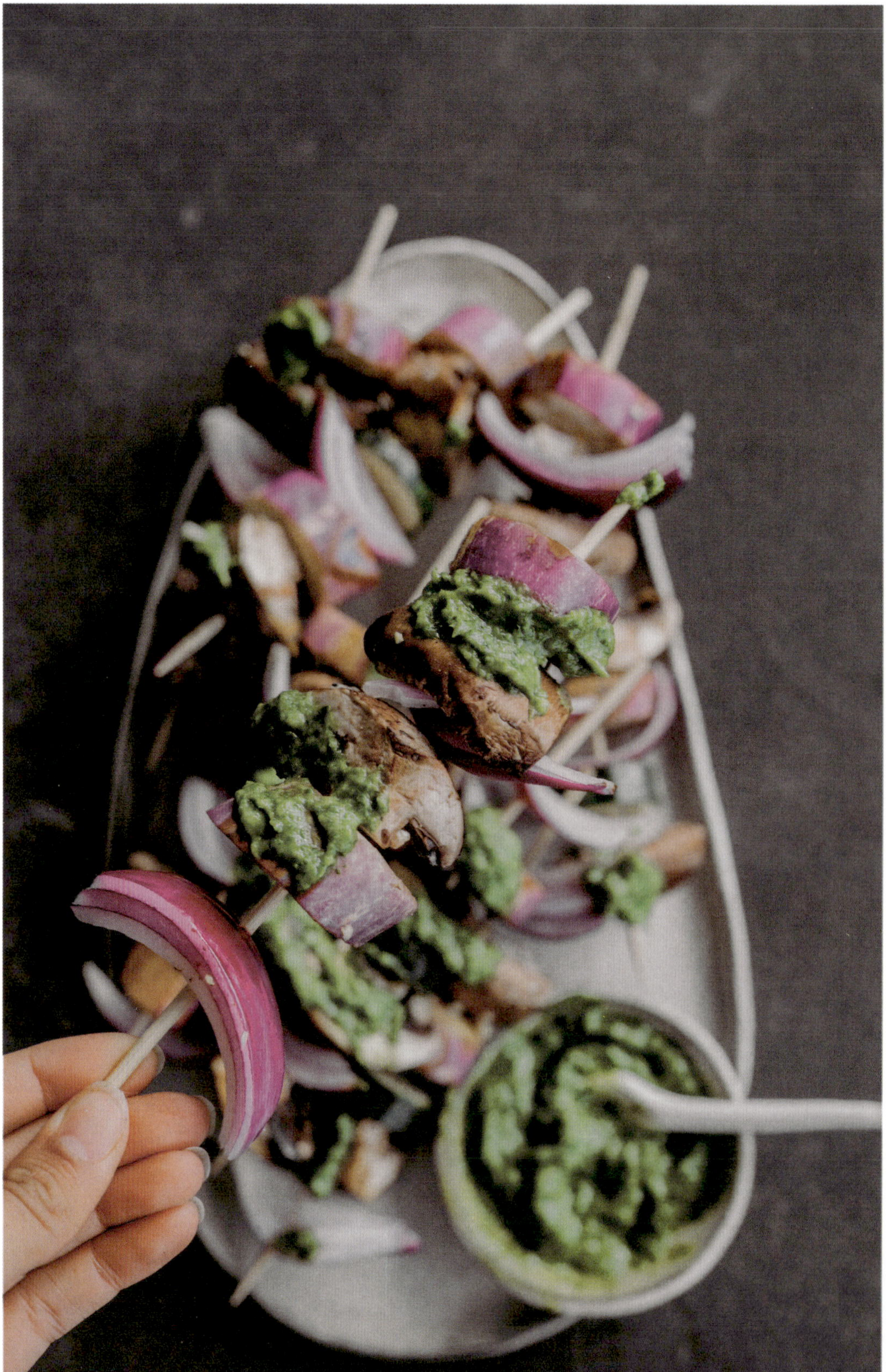

Veggie Skewers with Chimichurri Sauce

Serves 6 • 45 minutes

An excellent and easy-to-prepare plant-based dish for a family barbecue. I can't believe I never liked eggplant as a kid as it's probably one of my favourite vegetables now, especially paired with chimichurri sauce.

2 eggplants, cut into cubes
1 zucchini, thickly sliced
250 g mushrooms, halved
1 red onion, sliced into wedges
3 cloves garlic, crushed
2 Tbsp olive oil
Salt and pepper

Chimichurri Sauce
3 cloves garlic
1 chilli, deseeded
1 cup fresh coriander
1 cup fresh parsley
½ avocado
Juice from 1 lime
1 Tbsp maple syrup

Add eggplants, zucchini, mushrooms and red onion to a bowl along with garlic, olive oil, salt and pepper. Toss everything together and prepare your skewers.

Thread vegetables in layers onto skewers until full. Just be sure to leave enough room at each end for flipping and to prevent the vegetables from falling off.

Place skewers on a preheated barbecue or hot pan and cook for 5–8 minutes each side until golden and soft.

To make Chimichurri Sauce: Add all ingredients to a food processor and pulse until combined.

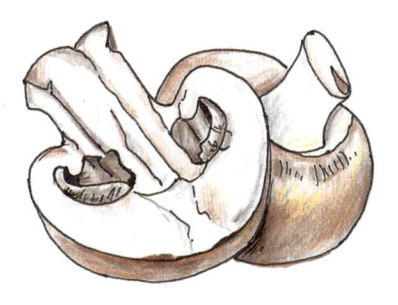

GF NF

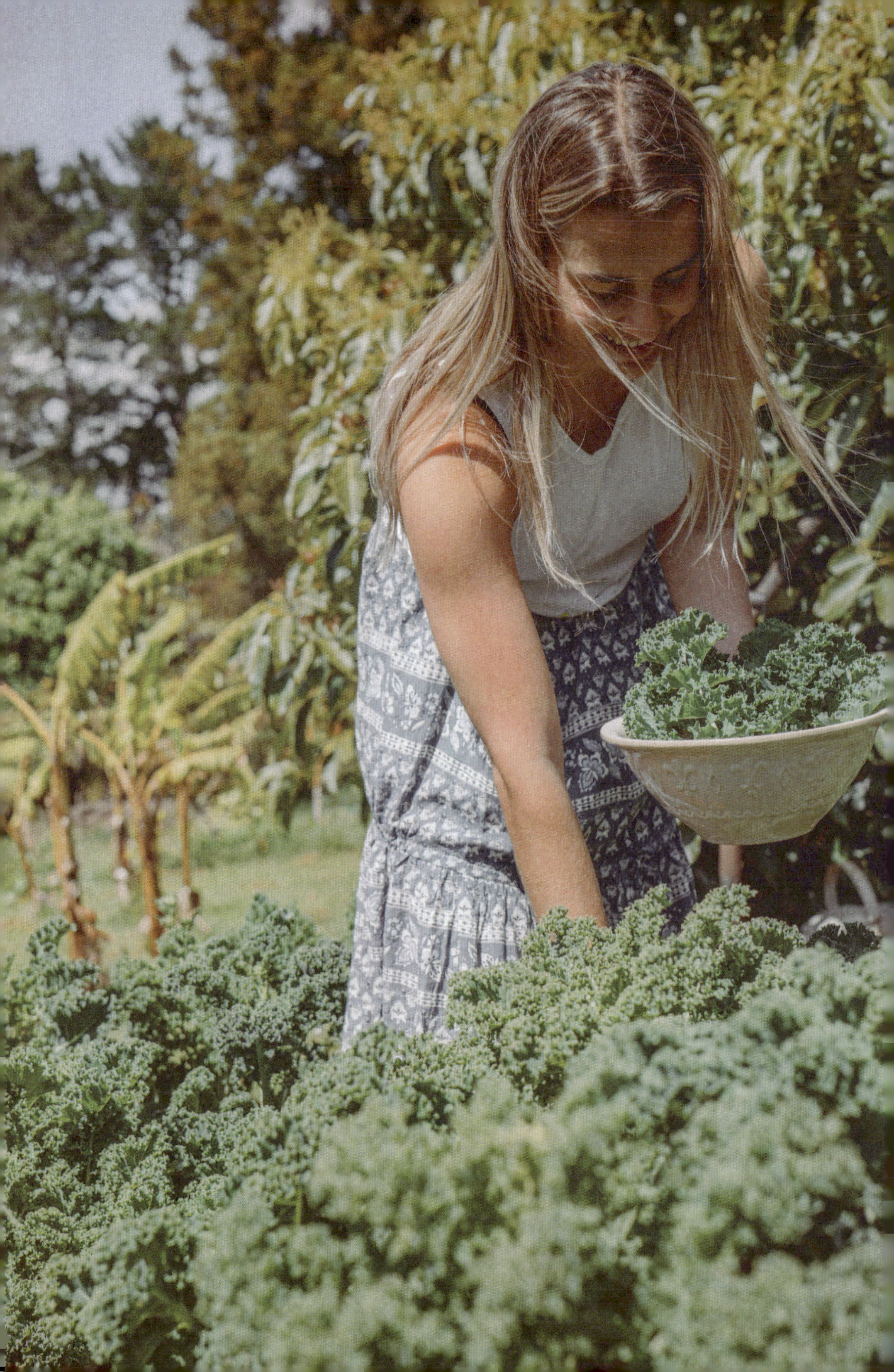

Sun-kissed Salads

I know salads aren't everyone's cup of tea, but they play such an important role in my life and I wanted to share some of that goodness with you. There are so many ways to make salads something you crave rather than dread eating. I love to experiment with a bunch of colours, textures and flavours. A good salad dressing can often lift a salad to another dimension, too. Like most kids I was never fussed on salad until my mum started salad-eating competitions between me and my brothers. That meant (me being the most competitive person in the world) that suddenly salads were a big part of my life. A couple of my favourites include the Rainbow Papaya Salad (see p. 111) and the Curried Potato Salad with Cashew Dressing (see p. 121).

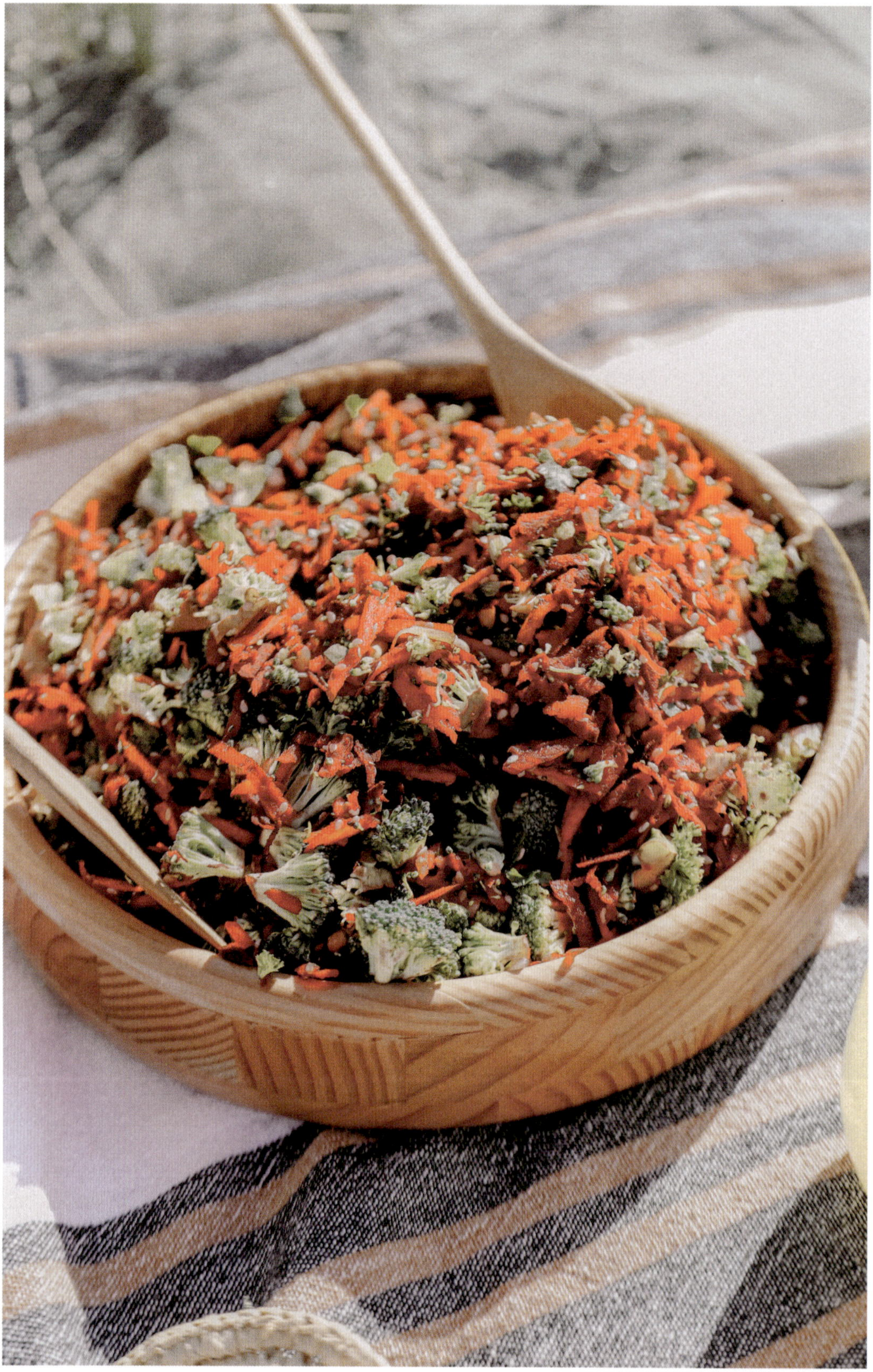

Broccoli Slaw

Serves 4 • 30 minutes

I never thought I liked coleslaws because I'd only ever had the soggy ones from the supermarket. Mum started making this a few years ago and now I'm hooked.

1 large carrot, grated
1 apple, grated
1 large beetroot, grated
1 head broccoli, roughly chopped
Handful of parsley, finely chopped
¼ cup sunflower seeds
¼ cup sesame seeds
1 Tbsp Cashew Aioli (see p. 214)
1 tsp wholegrain mustard
Juice from ½ lemon

Add all ingredients to a bowl and mix well to combine.

Hot Tip: Swap broccoli for cabbage to make it a classic coleslaw.

GF

Simple Kale and Avocado Salad

Serves 4 • 15 minutes

This is one of my signature side salads. I know lots of people aren't massive kale fans, but I promise that by massaging the kale with the creamy dressing, it creates a whole new flavour and way softer texture.

6 cups chopped kale
3 spring onions, finely chopped
2 avocados, sliced

Dressing
2 Tbsp Cashew Aioli (see p. 214)
1 Tbsp nutritional yeast
1 tsp wholegrain mustard
1 clove garlic, crushed
Juice from ½ lemon
1 tsp maple syrup

To make the dressing: add all the ingredients to a jar or small bowl and mix or shake well.

Combine kale and spring onion in a bowl.

Tip dressing onto kale and massage it through (this helps soften the kale). Arrange sliced avocado in a pattern on top.

. . . .

Hot Tip: Pomegranate seeds or fresh mango both add a wonderful sweetness to this salad.

. . . .

GF

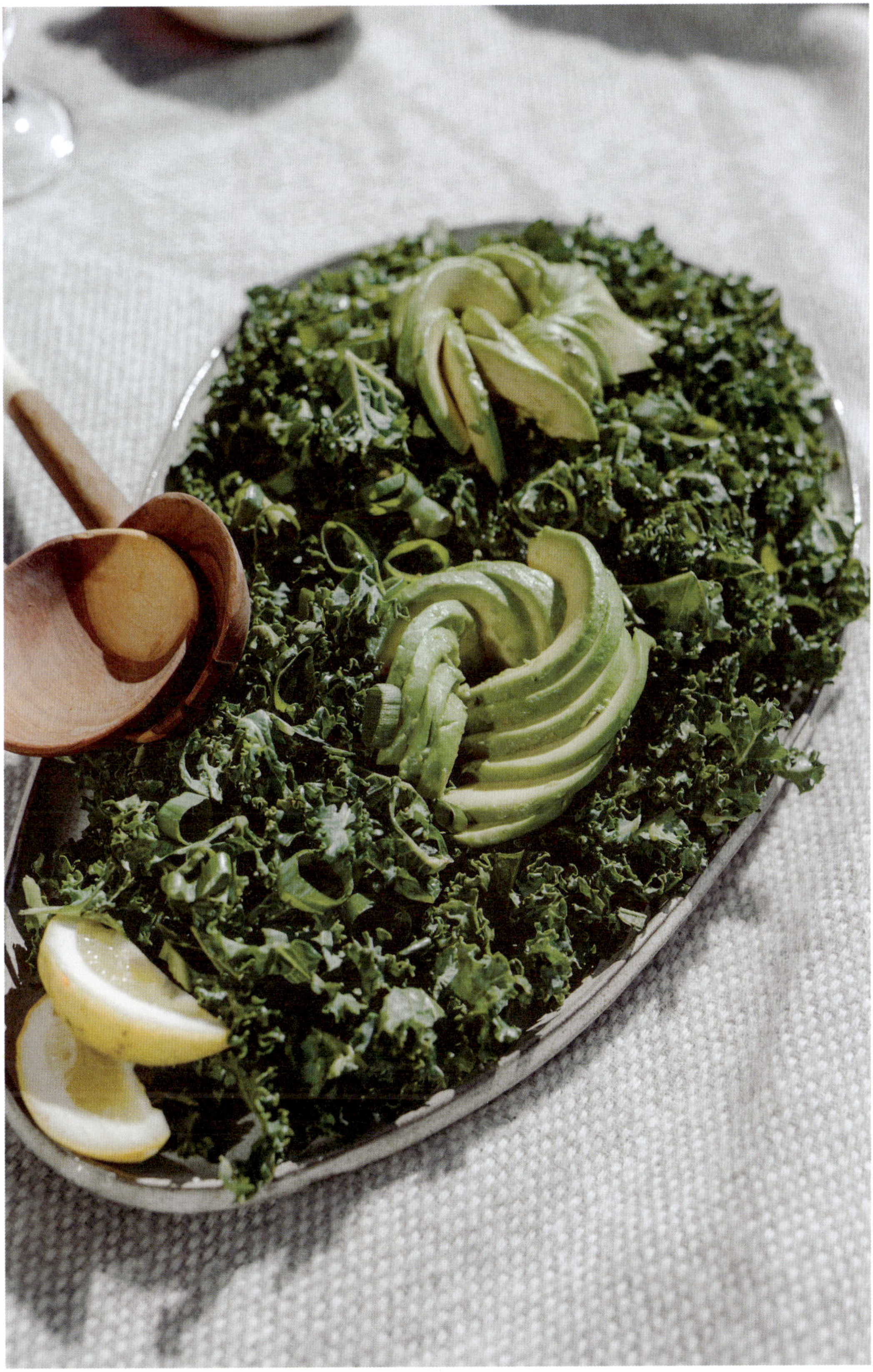

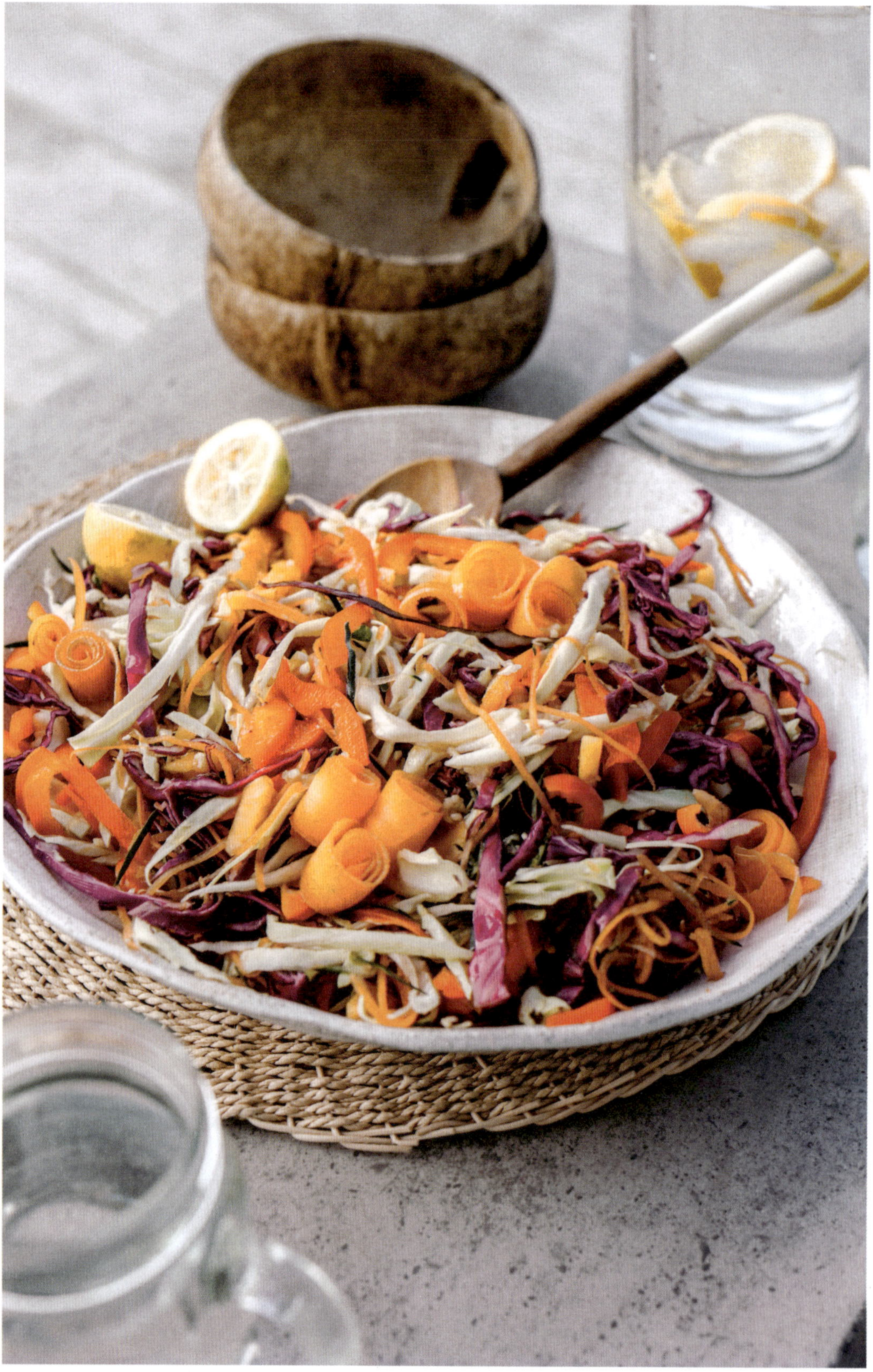

Rainbow Papaya Salad

Serves 4 • 30 minutes

Papaya Salad is one of my all-time favourite Thai dishes. It's so refreshing and packed with colours and flavours. Green papayas can be hard to source here in NZ, so just use whatever papaya you can find. A ripe orange papaya will be sweeter and a green one will be more sour.

¼ purple cabbage, thinly shredded
¼ green cabbage, thinly shredded
1 red capsicum, deseeded and thinly sliced
2 large carrots, julienned
1 cucumber, julienned
1 hard papaya, peeled, deseeded and thinly sliced
¼ cup Vietnamese mint, chopped
1 spring onion, chopped
2 Tbsp sesame seeds
¼ cup Ginger Sesame Dressing (see p. 210)

Combine cabbage, capsicum, carrots, cucumber, papaya, mint, spring onion and sesame seeds in a large bowl.

Add dressing and toss to combine.

GF NF

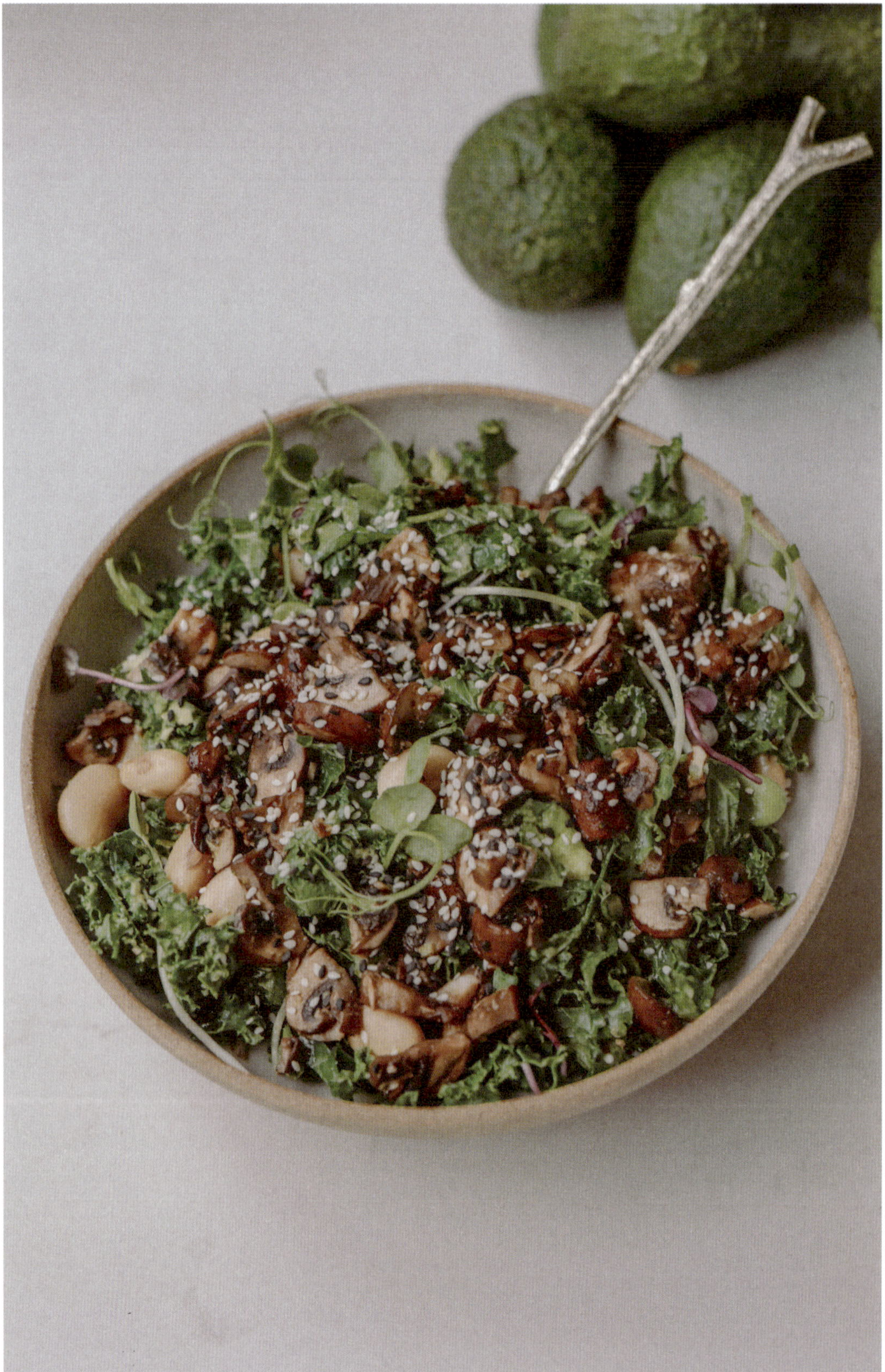

Miso Mushrooms with Kale and Butterbeans

Serves 2 • 20 minutes

I love adding miso to mushrooms — I think it creates such an exquisite flavour combination. Especially when combined with the butterbeans and tahini dressing.

200 g button mushrooms, sliced
1 tsp miso paste
1 Tbsp olive oil
1 tsp soy sauce or tamari
6 stalks kale, finely chopped
ACV Tahini Dressing (see p. 210)
400 g can butterbeans, drained and rinsed
1 cup microgreens
2 Tbsp sesame seeds

Heat a pan over high heat. Add mushrooms, miso paste, olive oil and soy sauce or tamari. Cook mushrooms for 10 minutes until soft.

In a medium-sized bowl, toss kale with Tahini Dressing and massage through (this will soften the kale).

Add butterbeans, microgreens, miso mushrooms and top with sesame seeds.

. . . .

Hot Tip: Chickpeas are a great alternative to butterbeans.

. . . .

GF NF

Tofu Poke Bowl

Serves 2 • 40 minutes

Sushi is a must-have every week for me, and I came up with this one-bowl dish as a way of integrating a few of my favourite sushi ingredients without all the fiddliness. The best part is you can really add anything you want to this bowl of tasty goodness.

1 cup quinoa or brown rice
300 g firm-style tofu
1 Tbsp soy sauce or tamari
1–2 tsp grated ginger
½ medium-sized cucumber, sliced
1 carrot, julienned
1 avocado, sliced
2 sheets nori, shredded
Ginger Sesame Dressing
   (see p. 210)
Microgreens, to garnish
Fresh coriander, to garnish

Preheat oven to 200°C and cook brown rice or quinoa according to instructions (see p.98).

Cut tofu into cubes and coat with soy sauce (or tamari) and ginger then place in oven for around 20–25 minutes or until golden. Flip the tofu halfway through the cooking time so it cooks evenly.

Once tofu and rice are cooked, remove tofu from the oven and place the rice or quinoa in a bowl along with the tofu, cucumber, carrot, avocado and shredded nori. Top with the Ginger Sesame Dressing. Garnish with microgreens and fresh coriander.

. . . .

Hot Tip: You can get super creative with this recipe. Add any veggies you love or have on hand.

. . . .

GF NF

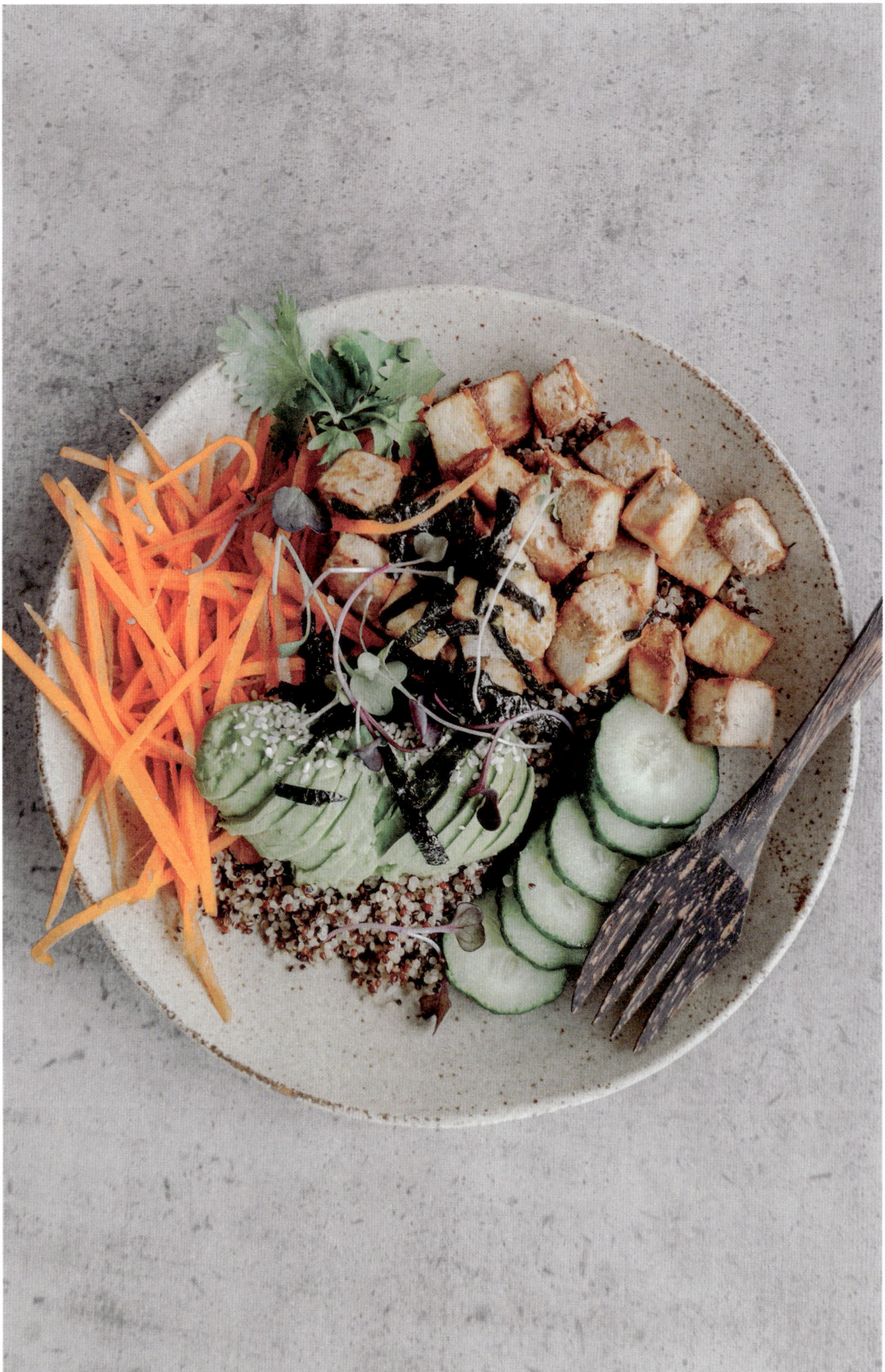

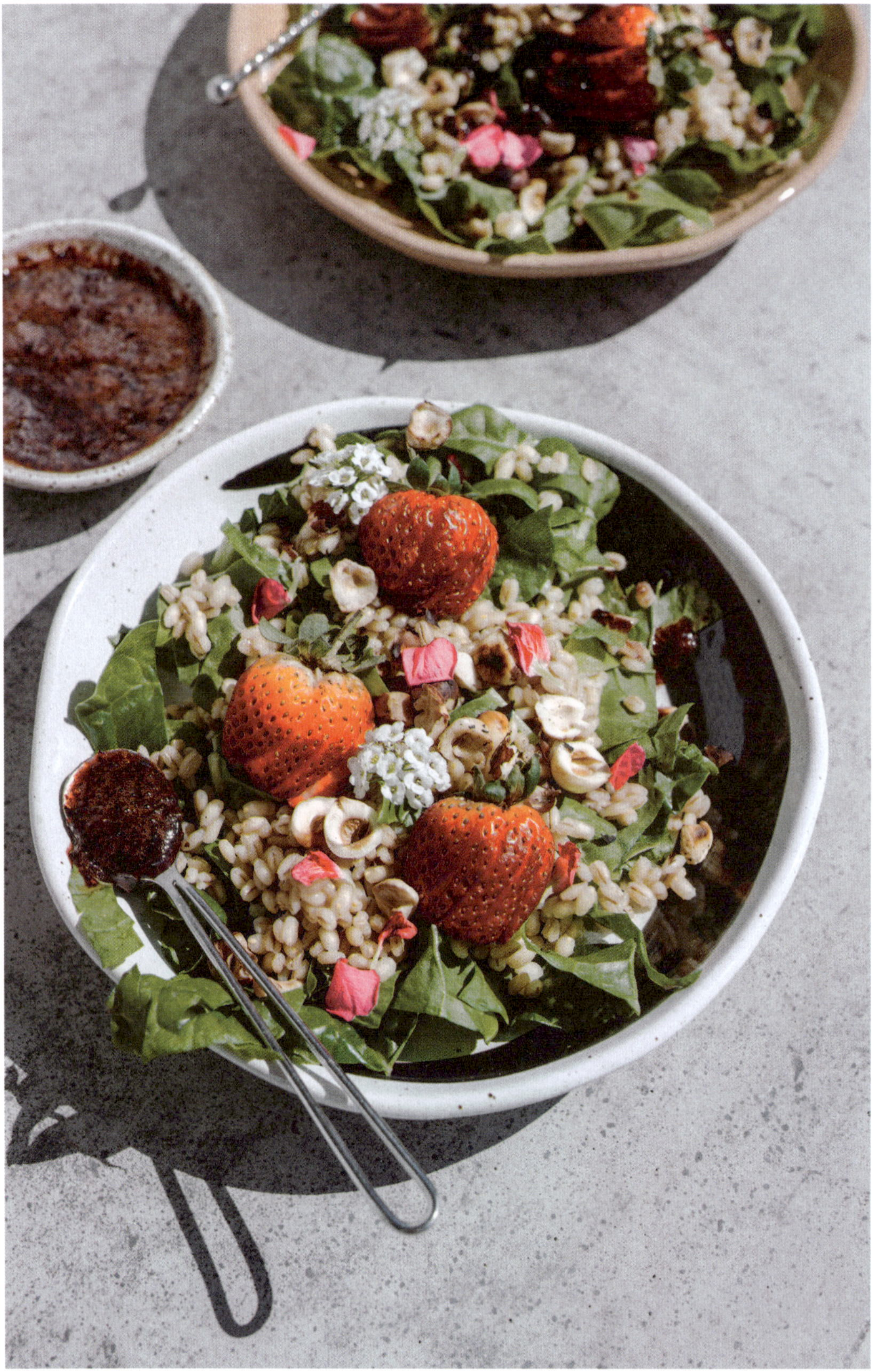

Strawberry and Hazelnut Salad

Serves 2 • 20 minutes

Made with fresh berries and crunchy hazelnuts, this summer salad is perfect for a hot day. Barley is a wholegrain cereal that contains a lot of fibre and B vitamins. It does contain gluten, however, so use brown rice if you're after a gluten-free option.

1 cup pearl barley (or brown rice for gluten-free)
2 cups (80 g) spinach
Handful of strawberries, sliced

Blueberry Vinaigrette
150 g blueberries
½ cup hazelnuts
1 Tbsp balsamic vinegar

Topping
Extra hazelnuts, toasted and chopped

Begin by cooking pearl barley in a pot with 1 cup of water over a medium heat. Boil until all of the water has been absorbed (around 20 minutes). Set aside to cool.

While the barley is cooking, roughly chop spinach and add it to a salad bowl. Toast hazelnuts in a pan for 5 minutes, tossing until golden.

Place blueberries, hazelnuts and balsamic vinegar in a blender and blend until smooth.

Add cooled barley to the salad bowl. Top with the strawberries and extra hazelnuts and drizzle with vinaigrette.

GFO

Roast Cauliflower, Chickpeas and Mango

Serves 4 • 30 minutes

Cauliflower is such an underrated vegetable, and I just love incorporating it into my recipes. This dish is super flavoursome and ideal as a side dish or as a simple lunch.

1 medium-sized cauliflower, chopped
400 g can chickpeas, drained
1 tsp ground turmeric
1 tsp garam masala
1 tsp ground coriander
1 Tbsp olive oil
2 cups baby spinach
1 spring onion, finely chopped
1 large handful of fresh coriander, roughly chopped
1 mango, peeled and sliced
¼ cup sunflower seeds
¼ cup pumpkin seeds
⅓ cup Curried Yoghurt Dressing (see p. 210)

Preheat oven to 200°C. Combine cauliflower, chickpeas, ground turmeric, garam masala, ground coriander and olive oil in a bowl and toss to coat. Pour onto a baking tray and roast in the oven for around 20 minutes, or until golden.

While cauliflower is cooking, add baby spinach, spring onion, fresh coriander and mango to a large bowl.

Toast sunflower and pumpkin seeds in a hot pan until starting to brown, then add to bowl. Once cauliflower is cooked, add to salad and mix through along with Curried Yoghurt Dressing.

GF NF

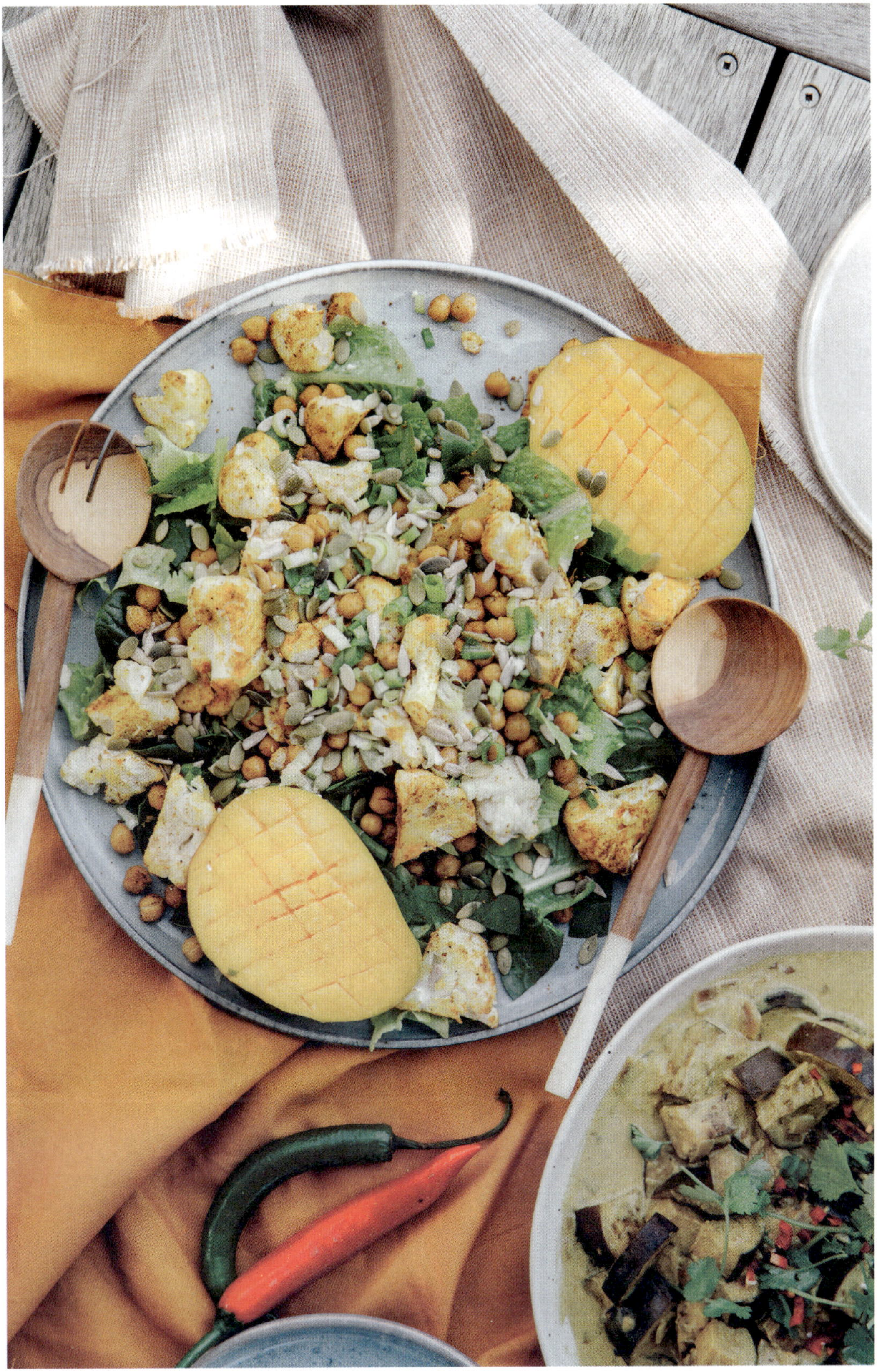

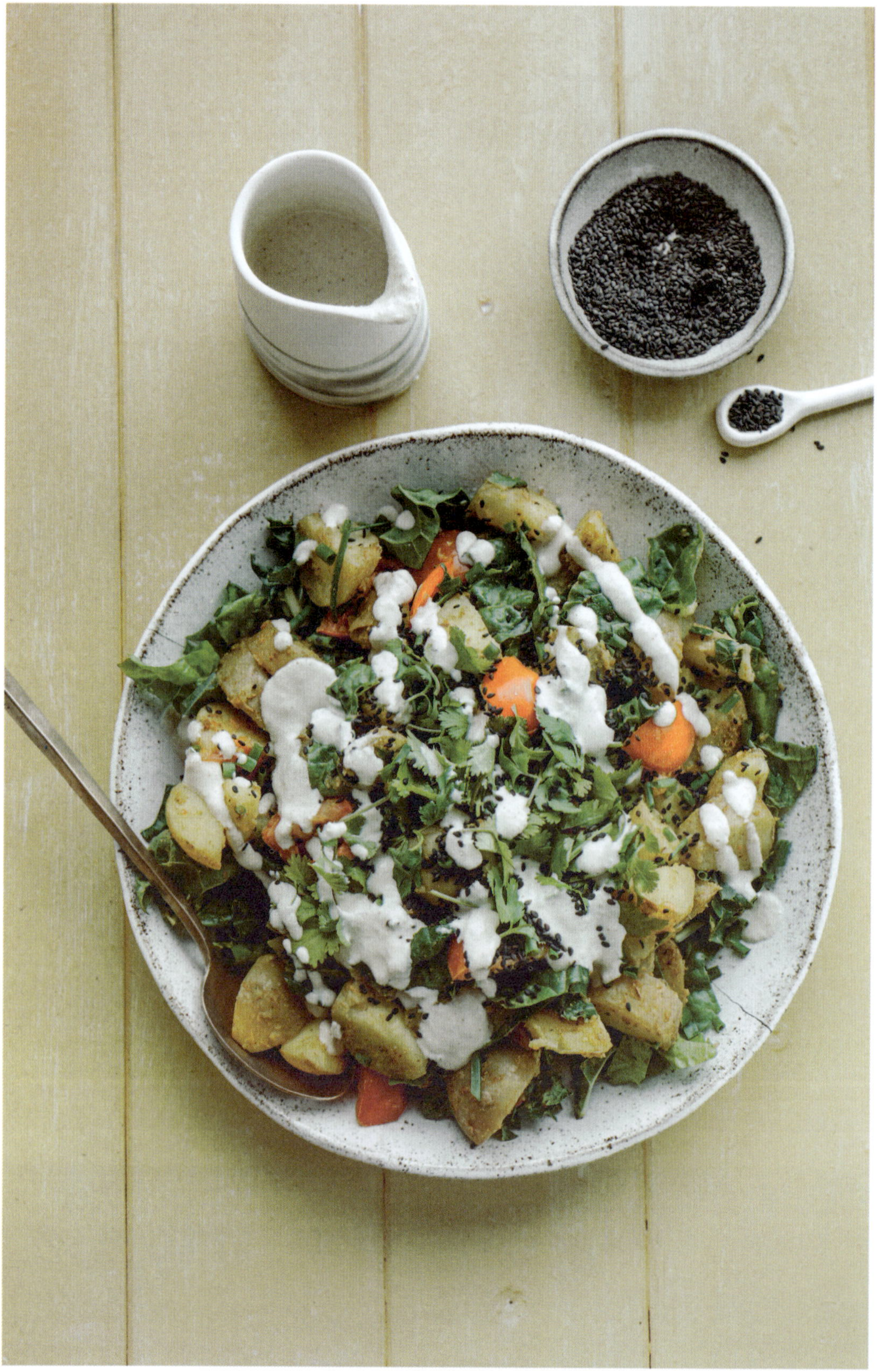

Curried Potato Salad with Cashew Dressing

Serves 6 • 30 minutes

This sensational salad was inspired by the Indian dish Bombay Potatoes. It's made with my Homemade Curry Powder (see p. 211), juicy tomatoes and a little cumin. Paired with a creamy cashew and lemon dressing, I promise, if you weren't a salad lover before, you will be after trying this!

1 kg potatoes, peeled and cut into cubes
1 Tbsp olive oil
1 Tbsp Homemade Curry Powder (see p. 211)
1 tsp ground cumin
1 tsp wholegrain mustard
140 g cherry tomatoes, sliced
3 cups spinach
¼ cup fresh coriander, chopped
¼ cup chives, finely chopped
2 Tbsp black sesame seeds

Cashew Dressing

½ cup raw cashews
½ cup water
Juice from ½ lemon
1 tsp wholegrain mustard
1 clove garlic

Add potatoes to a large pot and cover with water. Bring to the boil and leave to simmer for 10–15 minutes until tender. Drain and set aside.

To a large frying pan over medium heat, add olive oil, curry powder and cumin, and sauté for 1 minute until fragrant. Add potatoes and toss to coat in the spices. Add mustard, tomatoes and spinach and stir to combine.

Transfer potato salad to a large bowl and top with fresh coriander, chives and black sesame seeds.

To make the dressing, blend all ingredients together until smooth then pour over the top of the salad and toss to coat.

GF

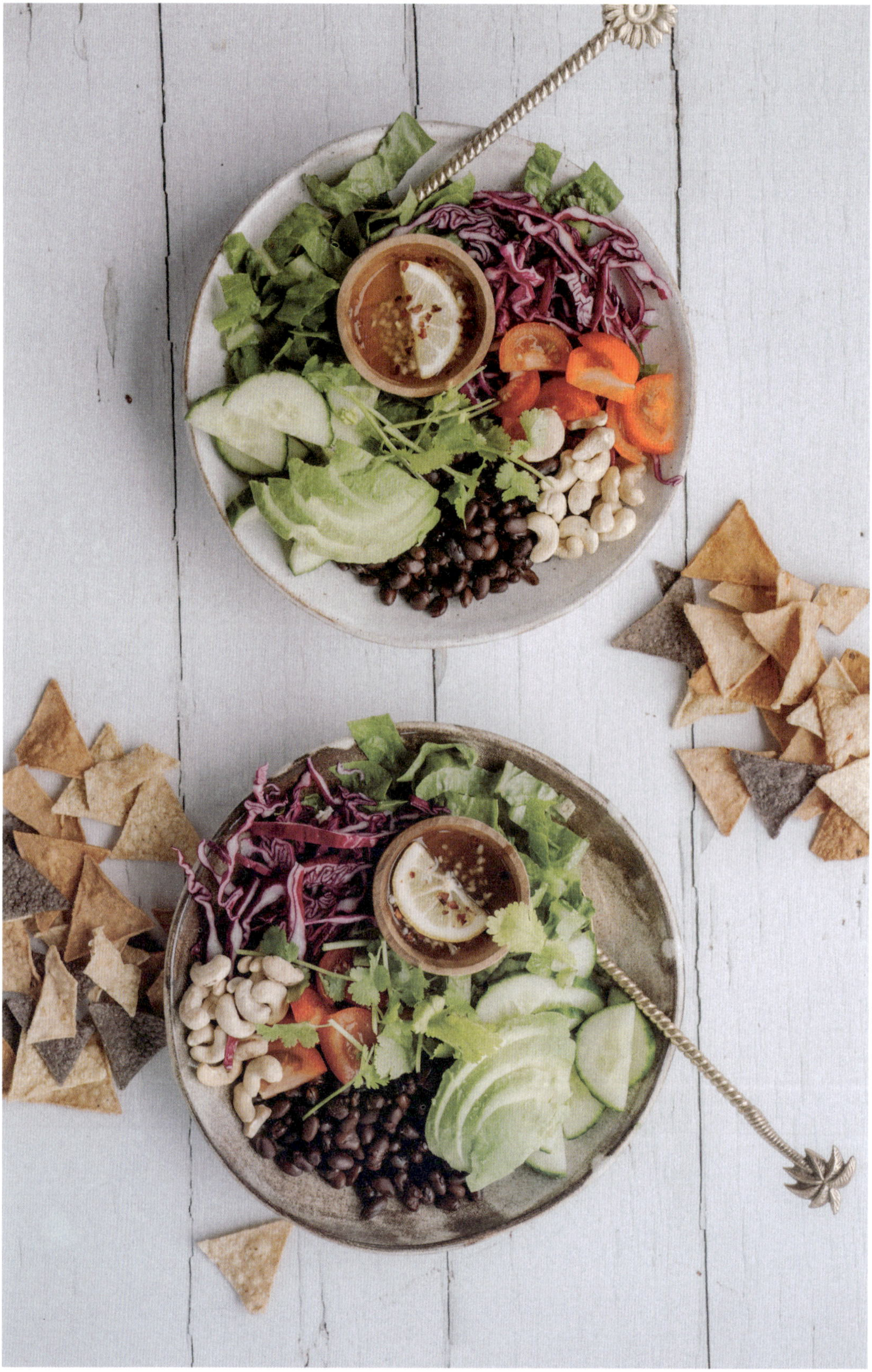

Burrito Bowls

Serves 2 • 25 minutes

When I'm short on time I make a one-bowl meal using whatever vegetables I have in the fridge. This is my favourite bowl variation as I totally love Mexican food. I usually pair this dish with the Sweet and Tangy Dressing on page 210.

400 g can black beans, drained
½ cup brown rice
2 cups roughly chopped cos lettuce
¼ cup thinly sliced purple cabbage
2 tomatoes, sliced
1 avocado, sliced
1 cup sliced cucumber
½ cup cashews
Handful of fresh coriander
Sweet and Tangy Dressing
   (see p. 210)

Rinse rice then add to a pot with 1 cup water. Bring to the boil, stirring regularly, then turn heat down to low and cover. Leave pot covered over heat and set aside for 5 minutes. Lift lid and fluff up rice with a fork.

Divide all ingredients between two bowls and top with Sweet and Tangy Dressing.

• • • • • • •

Hot Tip: For a lighter lunchtime version, try leaving out the brown rice.

• • • • • • •

GF

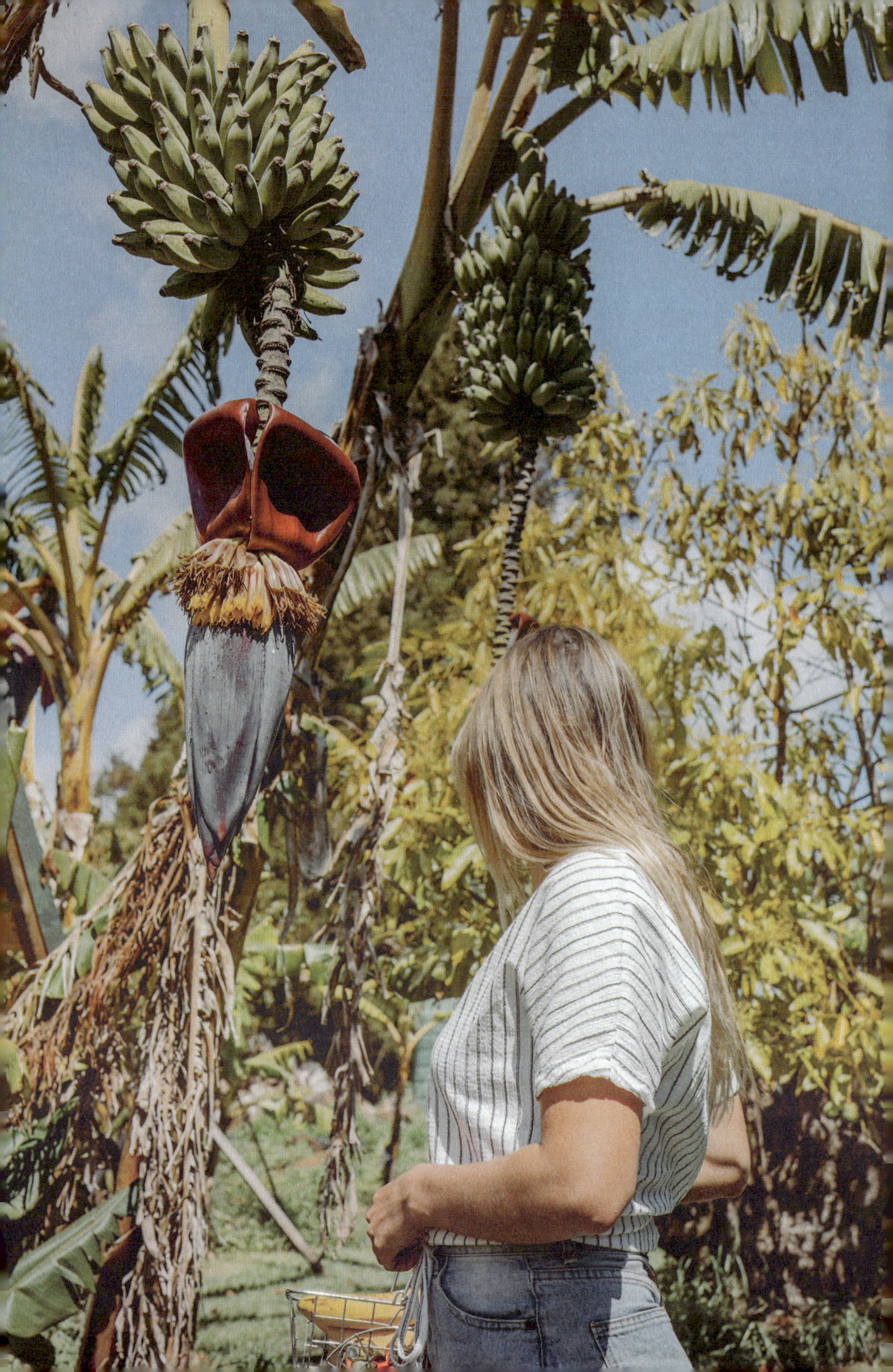

4 for $5

LOCAL CAPSICUMS
SPRAY FREE GREENS & BEETROOT
LOCAL MUSHROOMS

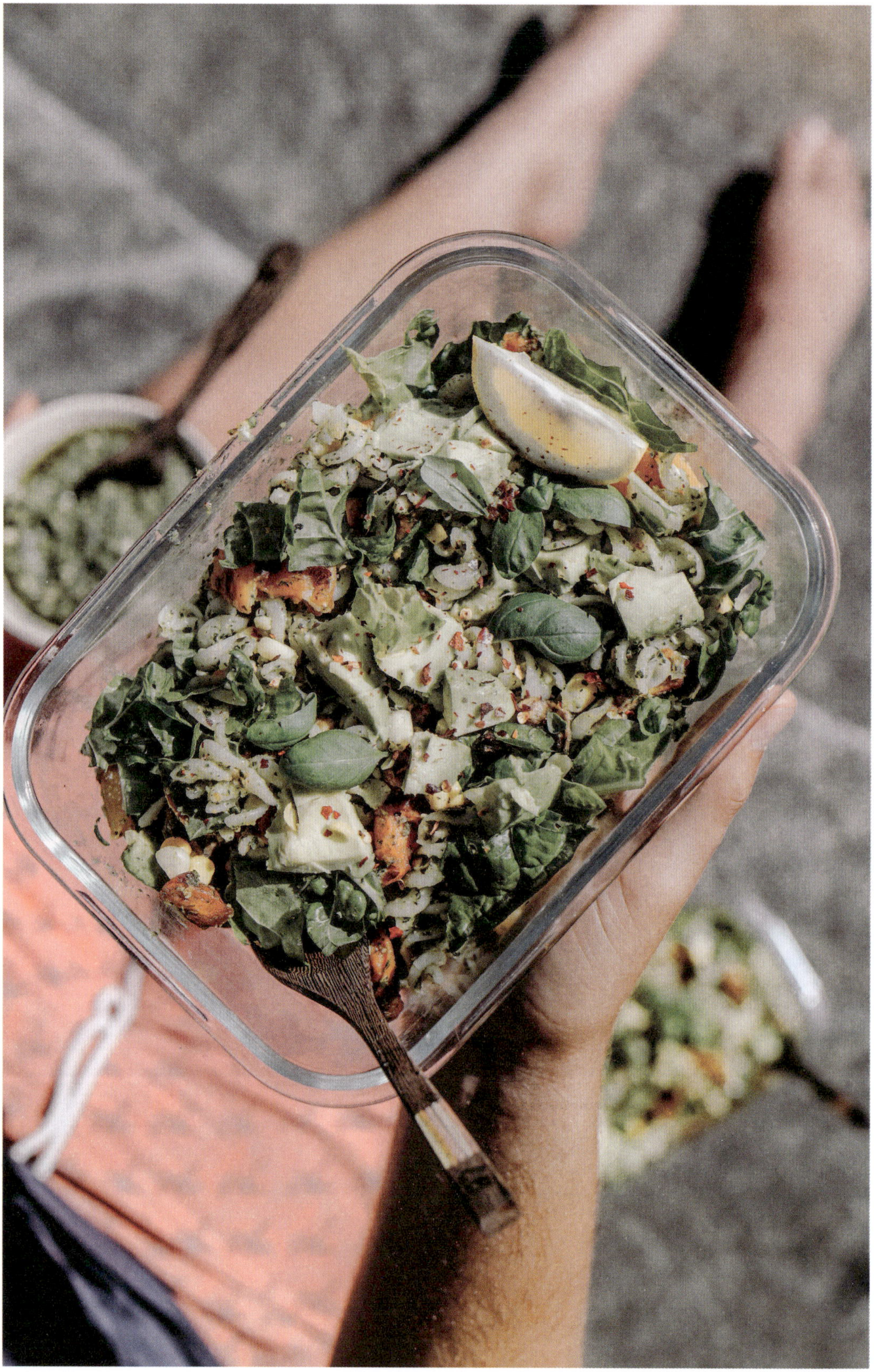

Andrew's 'World-Famous' Pesto Pasta

Serves 4 • 30 minutes

After months of him nagging me, I finally agreed to include a recipe from my partner in this book. I knew straight away he was going to choose this dish (mainly because it's the only thing he makes), but without praising him too much, it's seriously delicious.

1 large kumara (sweet potato), peeled and chopped into cubes
2 Tbsp olive oil
250 g pasta (we use gluten-free quinoa pasta)
100 g white button mushrooms, sliced
10 cherry tomatoes, halved
1 cup fresh, frozen or canned corn kernels
Large handful of spinach, roughly chopped
½ cup Pumpkin Seed Pesto (see p. 83)
Salt and pepper to taste
Handful of fresh basil
1 avocado, sliced
1 Tbsp Sunflower Parmesan to serve (see p. 211)

Preheat oven to 200°C and line a baking tray with baking paper. Place kumara on a tray with 1 Tbsp of the olive oil and bake in the oven for 20 minutes or until cooked.

Cook pasta in a large pot of salted boiling water, until just cooked. Drain, rinse and set aside.

In a large frying pan or wok, sauté mushrooms, tomatoes and corn with remaining olive oil over medium heat for 5 minutes. Add cooked kumara and pasta to pan along with spinach and pesto. Toss through until everything is coated in the pesto. Season with salt and pepper, and top with fresh basil, avocado and Sunflower Parmesan.

GFO NF

Soba Noodles and Sticky Eggplant

Serves 4 • 20 minutes

This recipe is so simple and bursting with flavour. The mix of fresh ginger and garlic with the vegetables and crunchy cashews goes so well together. The perfect quick lunch on the go.

180 g soba noodles
2 eggplants, diced
4 cloves garlic, crushed
1 Tbsp grated ginger
1 red chilli, deseeded and sliced
2 Tbsp soy sauce or tamari
1 Tbsp maple syrup
Juice from 1 lemon
1 Tbsp olive oil
Small handful of fresh basil, plus extra to serve
3 Tbsp sesame seeds
1 spring onion, sliced

Cook noodles according to packet instructions and set aside.

Add eggplant to a hot frying pan with garlic, ginger, chilli, soy sauce or tamari, maple syrup and lemon juice. Mix well until eggplant is completely covered in sauce. Stir-fry for around 5 minutes until eggplant is tender.

Add noodles to pan along with olive oil and basil. Toss through noodles until combined. Remove from heat and top with sesame seeds, spring onion and basil.

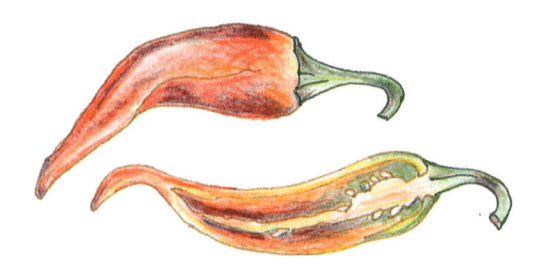

GF NF

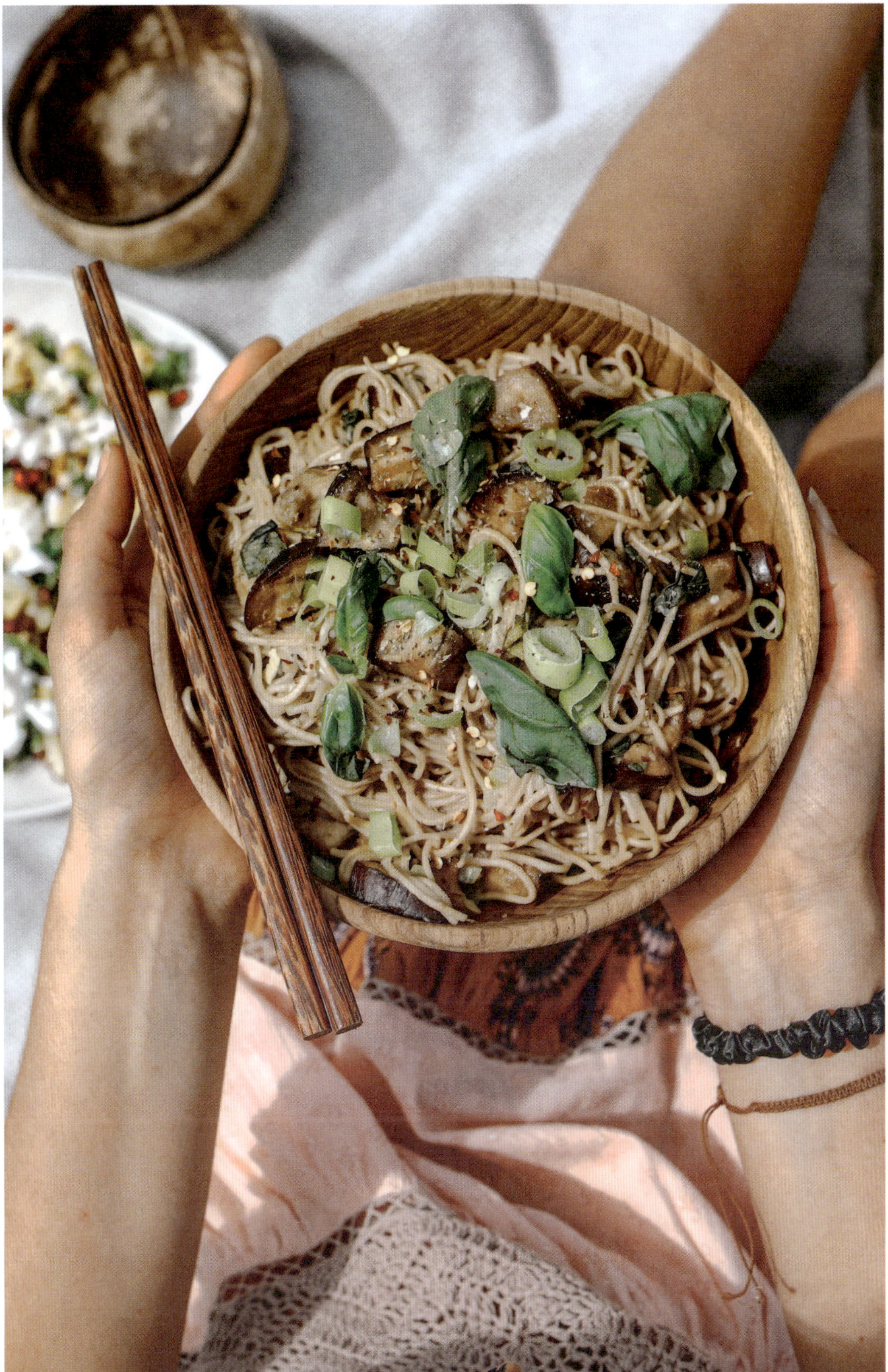

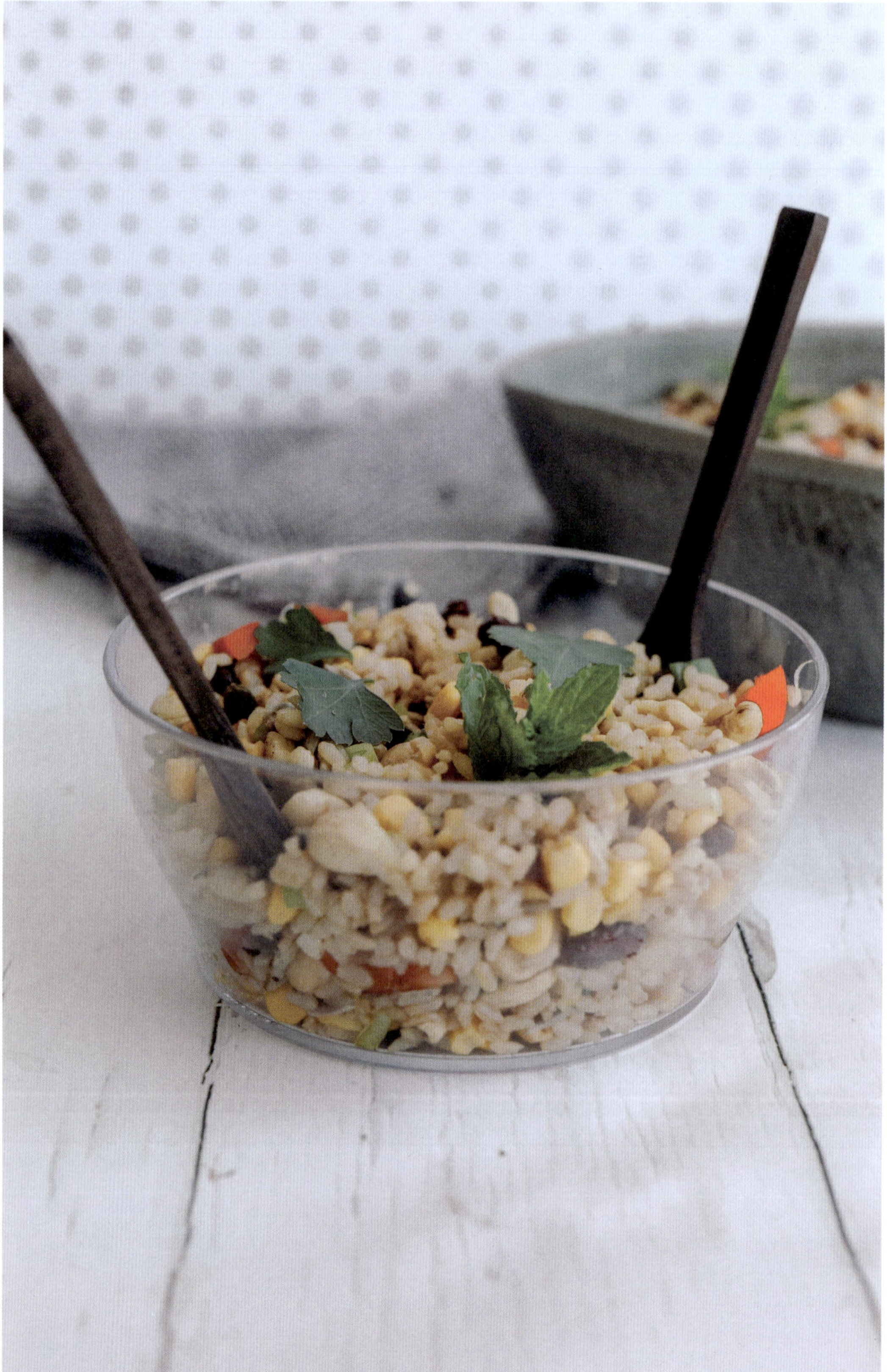

Mum's Brown Rice Salad

Serves 8 • 30 minutes

Mum makes this salad almost every Christmas and it goes down an absolute treat. I always find myself going back for seconds.

2 cups brown rice
3 spring onions, finely chopped
⅓ cup currants or dried cranberries
2 Tbsp sunflower seeds
1 Tbsp pumpkin seeds
1 capsicum, deseeded and diced
120 g pistachios or cashews
1 cup fresh, frozen or canned corn kernels

Dressing
2 Tbsp olive oil
Juice from ½ lemon
2 Tbsp soy sauce or tamari
1 clove garlic, crushed
Salt and pepper to taste

Cook your brown rice by adding it to a medium-sized pot with 4 cups water. Bring to boil, reduce heat, cover and simmer until the water has been absorbed. (This should take around 30 minutes.) Turn off the heat and let the pot sit, covered, for 10 minutes. Remove the lid and fluff up with a fork.

Once the rice has cooled, combine remaining salad ingredients together in a bowl and mix well.

To make the dressing: combine all ingredients in a small bowl and mix well, then add the dressing to the salad and toss.

GF

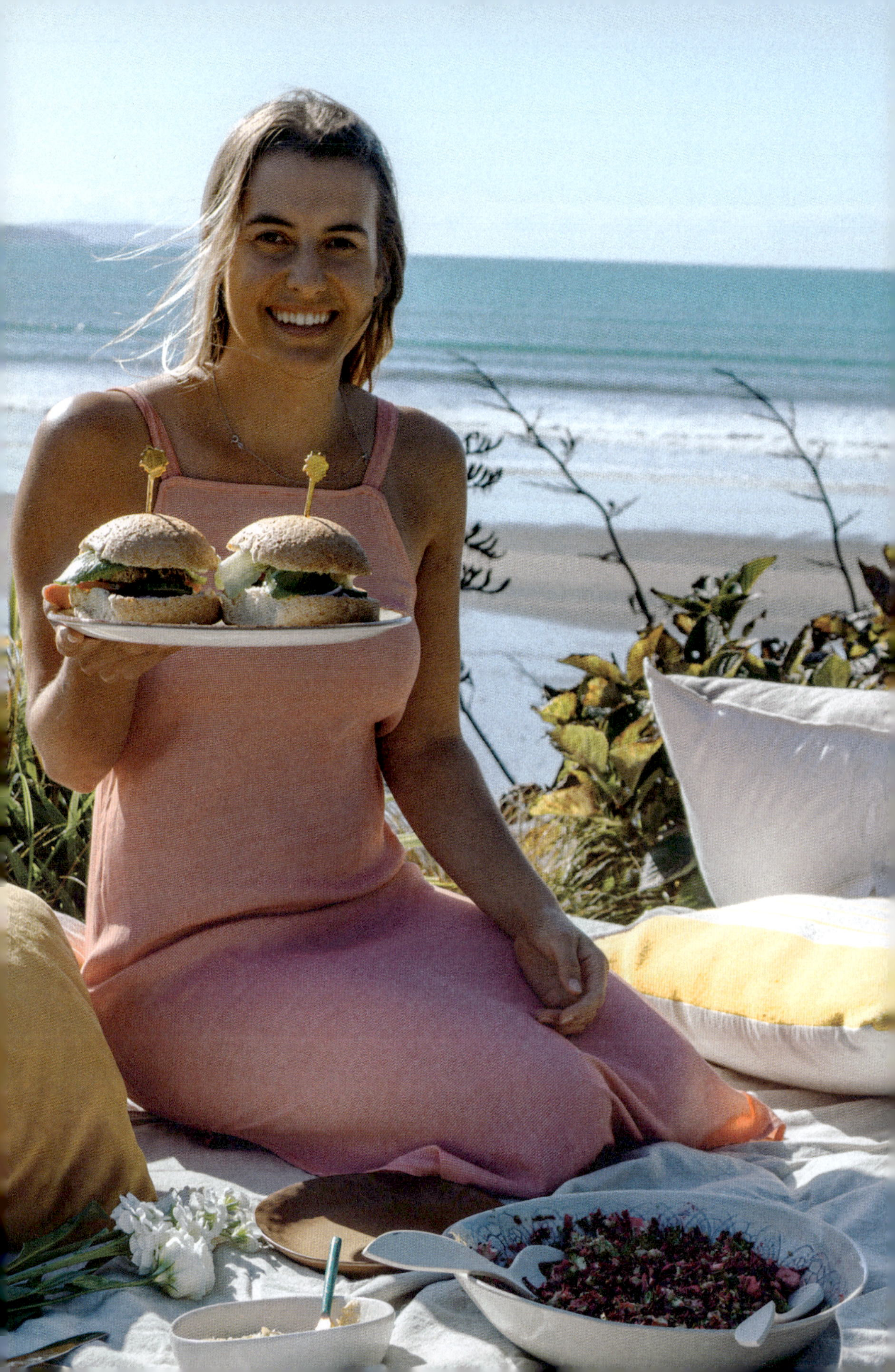

Mouth-watering Mains

In this chapter you'll find a bunch of my favourite family dinners inspired by my travels. From a moreish Sri Lankan Pulled Jackfruit Curry (see p. 149) to a delicious Rainbow Lasagne (see p. 165), this chapter has something for everyone (even the meatlovers). Having a collection of healthy plant-based dinner options is the best way to maintain a balanced lifestyle. Ultimately, there are tons of ways to enjoy a diet filled with more wholefoods, so find what works for you and your family.

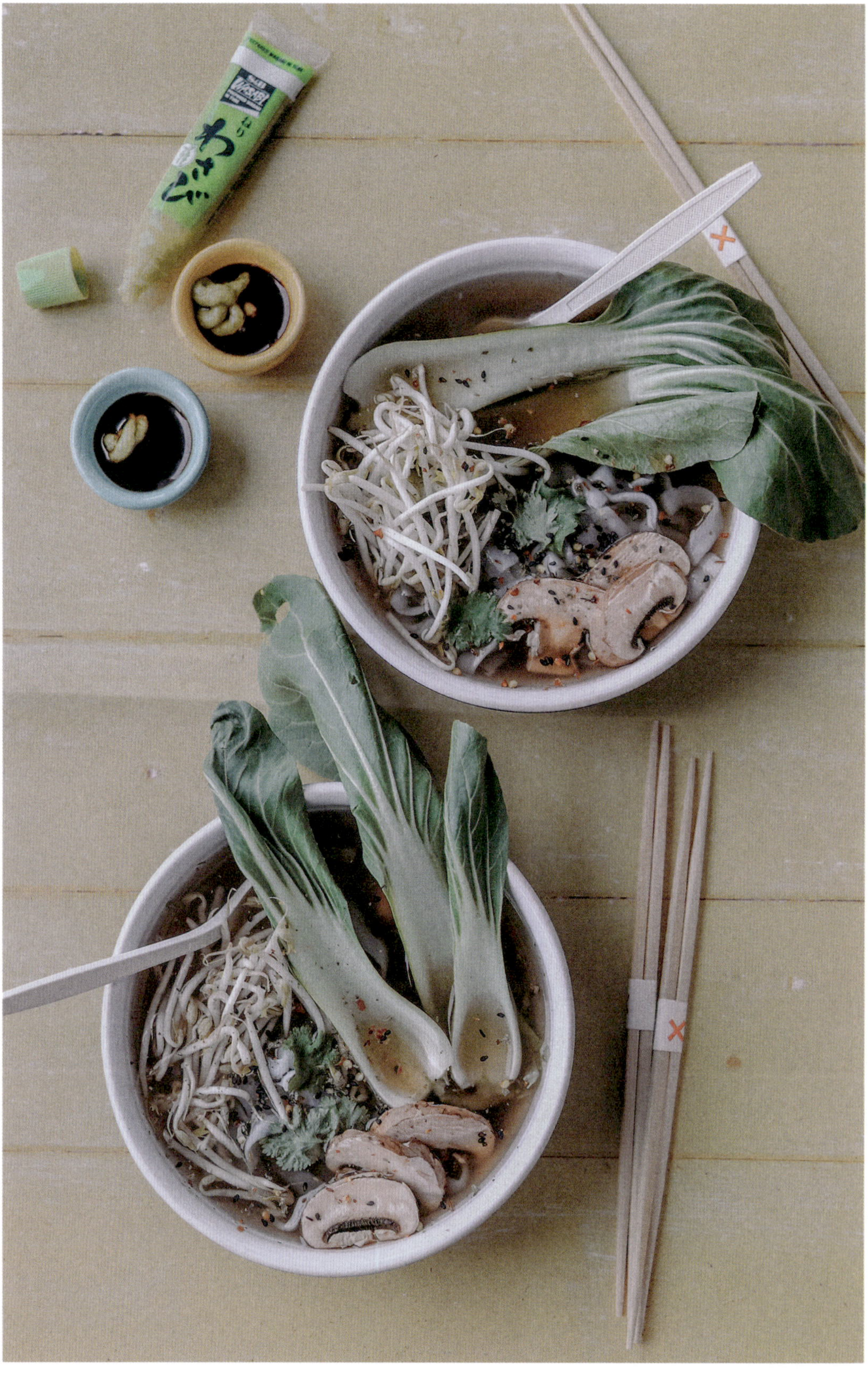
ねり
わさび

Vegetable Pho

Serves 4 • 90 minutes

My all-time favourite Vietnamese dish is pho — I swear, nothing beats noodles with a super flavoursome broth. In Vietnam they eat pho for breakfast — which is actually a pretty awesome way to start the day.

1 leek, thinly sliced
2 carrots, roughly chopped
1 stick celery, roughly chopped
Thumb-sized piece of ginger, grated
1 onion, finely chopped
3 cups roughly chopped button mushrooms
3 cloves garlic, finely chopped
7 cups water
1 Tbsp soy sauce or tamari
Juice from 1 lemon
2 bok choy, washed and leaves separated
1 cup sliced shiitake mushrooms
180 g ramen noodles (or soba noodles if gluten-free)
1 cup mung beans
1 chilli, deseeded and sliced
1 spring onion, finely chopped

Combine leek, carrots, celery, ginger, onion, mushrooms and garlic in a large pot over medium heat with a splash of water to stop the vegetables from sticking.

Once the vegetables start to soften, add water and cover with a lid. Once the stock comes to the boil, add soy sauce or tamari and lemon juice and leave to simmer for at least 1 hour (the longer you let the soup simmer, the more flavour you will create).

Twenty minutes prior to serving, add bok choy, shiitake mushrooms and ramen noodles and leave to cook until noodles are soft.

Serve with mung beans, chilli and spring onion.

GFO NF

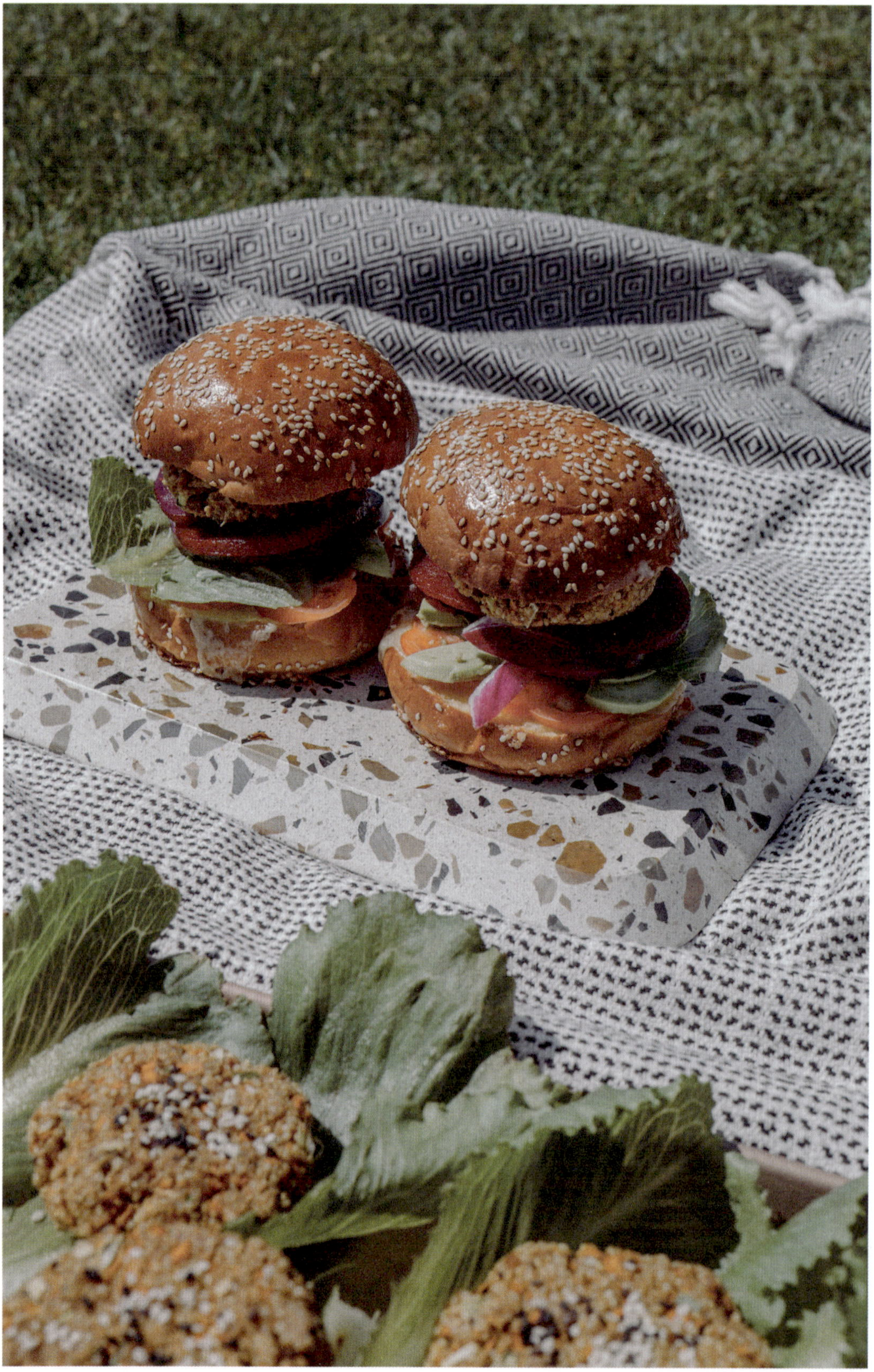

Carrot and Quinoa Burgers

Serves 6 • 60 minutes

Good burgers has always been my guilty pleasure. For me avocado, pickled beetroot, a good aioli and tomato relish are the non-negotiables.

½ cup quinoa

2 large carrots, grated

2 Tbsp flaxmeal

2 tsp ground coriander

2 cm piece ginger, grated

1 tsp ground cumin

2 spring onions, finely chopped

1 Tbsp peanut butter

1 Tbsp sesame seeds

½ cup gluten-free rolled oats

To Serve

Tomato relish and vegan aioli

6 x wholemeal burger buns (GF if desired)

1 red onion, sliced

1 avocado, sliced

2 ripe tomatoes, sliced

1 small cos lettuce, chopped

200 g canned beetroot

Preheat oven to 180°C and line a baking tray with baking paper.

Cook your quinoa according to packet instructions. Add all ingredients to a food processor and pulse until combined (the mixture should be a little chunky).

Shape your mixture into 6 equal-sized patties and place on the baking tray. Cook in the oven for 25 minutes until golden. Alternatively, you can cook them on a barbecue or hot pan with a little bit of oil for around 10 minutes, flipping halfway through.

Add a dollop of tomato relish and aioli to the base of each burger bun. Top with red onion, avocado, tomato, lettuce, beetroot, patties and burger tops.

Serve with a fresh salad or homemade roasties.

GFO

Peanut Butter Noodle Stir-fry

Serves 4 • 20 minutes

This is such an easy dinner option when you don't have much time on your hands. Anything with peanut butter is always an absolute hit in my house, plus it's a great way to make vegetables extra tasty!

1 Tbsp olive oil
1 onion, diced
3 cloves garlic, finely chopped
150 g broccolini
2 carrots, finely sliced
1 capsicum, finely sliced
180 g soba noodles
Satay Sauce (see p. 214)
1 chilli, deseeded and sliced
¼ cup sesame seeds

To a hot pan, add olive oil, onion and garlic, and cook until onion is translucent. Add broccolini, carrot and capsicum and cook until carrot is slightly soft.

Cook noodles according to packet instructions and prepare the Satay Sauce.

Drain noodles and add them to pan, along with the Satay Sauce, making sure everything is coated in sauce.

Top with fresh chilli and sesame seeds.

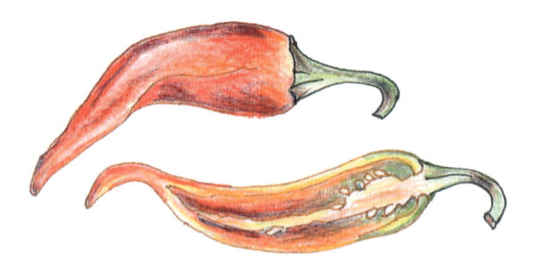

GF

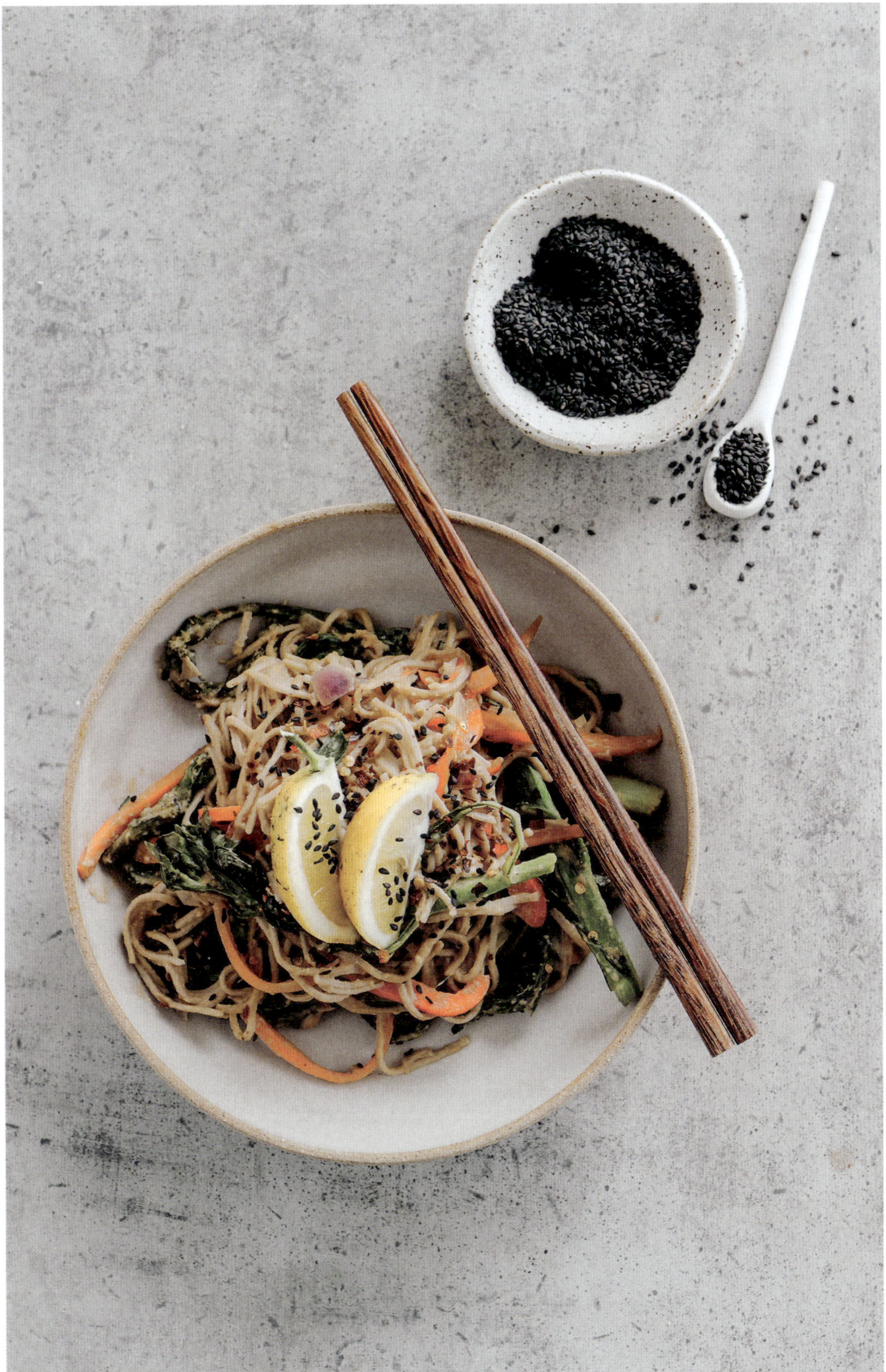

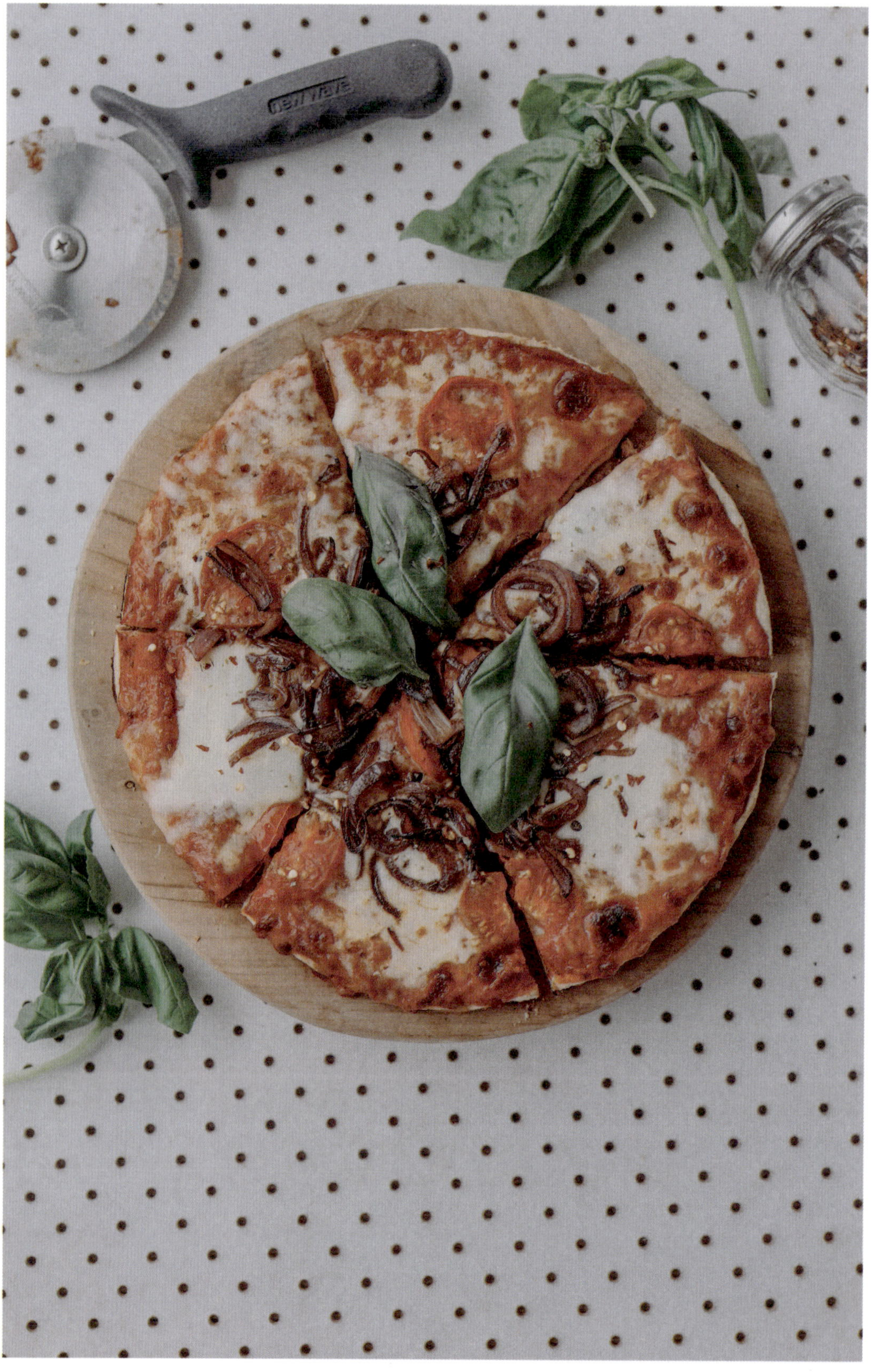
new wave

Herbed Pizza Dough

Serves 6–8 • 3 hours

Homemade pizza dough is a revelation — way tastier, fresher and healthier than store-bought bases. I recommend using a good-quality wholemeal flour. Top with store-bought dairy-free cheese or try my Cashew Cheese (see p. 175) or the cheesy sauce from the Cheesy Potato Gratin (see p. 172).

2 cups warm water
2 tsp active dry yeast
5 cups wholegrain spelt flour
1 Tbsp olive oil
1 Tbsp honey
1 tsp salt
⅓ cup fresh herbs, finely chopped (I like to use rosemary, thyme and parsley)

Combine water and yeast in a bowl and stir. Set aside for 10 minutes or until it turns frothy.

In a separate bowl, place flour, olive oil, honey and salt. Add yeast mixture to bowl and mix with a spoon until combined. Place on a floured bench, along with herbs, and knead until a smooth and elastic ball of dough has formed (should take around 10 minutes).

Place dough in an oiled bowl with a damp tea towel over the top. Leave it in a warm place to rise for two hours.

When dough has doubled in size, punch it down. Place on a floured bench and knead briefly until smooth.

Cut dough into 6–8 equal balls (depending on how large you want your pizzas) and roll into flat rounds.

Preheat oven to 200°C and line a baking tray with baking paper, or use a pizza stone. Top bases with your favourite toppings and cook for about 20 minutes until golden.

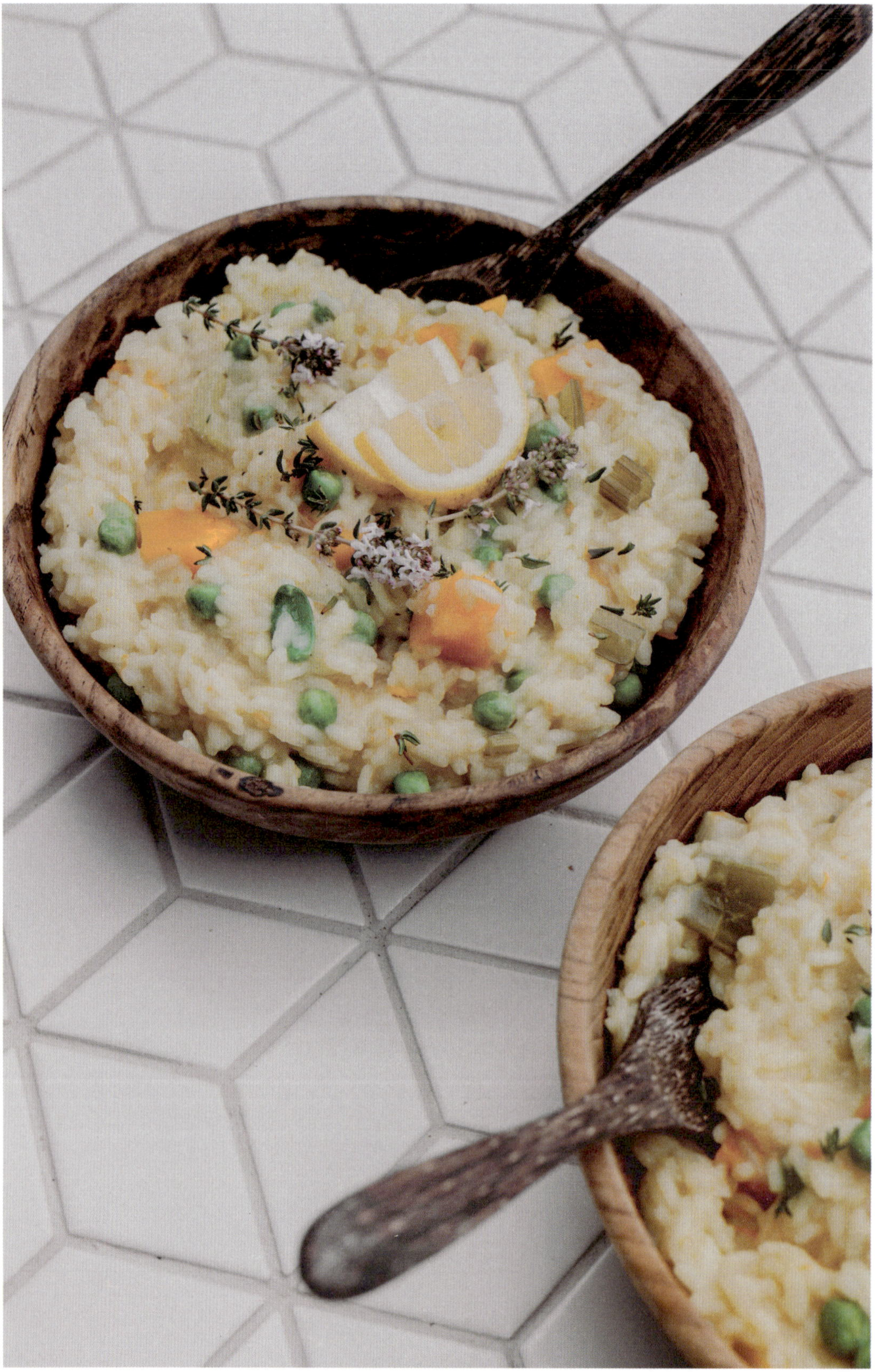

Quick and Easy Butternut Risotto

Serves 6 • 40 minutes

I've been making this butternut risotto for years and it always goes down a treat. It's perfect for when you don't have much in the fridge. You can use any type of rice; however, for brown rice you may need to add more liquid.

1 Tbsp olive oil

1 onion, diced

3 cloves garlic, finely chopped

2 sticks celery, diced

1 medium-sized butternut, peeled, deseeded and diced

500 g arborio or carnaroli rice

6 cups vegetable stock

2 cups plant milk

1 cup frozen peas

1 Tbsp soy sauce or tamari

Juice from 1 lemon

Fresh thyme leaves, plus extra for garnish

Nutritional yeast

Salt and pepper to taste

To a large pot, add olive oil, onion, garlic and celery. Cook over medium heat for 2–3 minutes until onion is translucent. Add butternut and rice and mix through, letting the flavours soak into the rice. Add 1 cup of vegetable stock and stir until liquid is absorbed. Keep adding stock gradually, stirring between cups.

Once stock has been added, cover risotto with a lid for around 10 minutes until stock has been absorbed. Remove the lid and add plant milk, peas, soy sauce or tamari, lemon juice and thyme, and stir until thick and creamy.

Remove from heat and top with more thyme, nutritional yeast, salt and pepper.

Hot Tip: If you don't have any plant milk, water is a great substitute.

GF NF

Pineapple Fried Rice

Serves 6 • 35 minutes

This recipe is packed with vegetables and goes down a treat every time. The sweetness of the pineapple pairs perfectly with the salty ingredients.

2 cups basmati rice
2 Tbsp olive oil
1 onion, diced
2 cloves garlic, finely chopped
1 capsicum, deseeded and diced
1 carrot, diced
2 spring onions, finely chopped, plus extra for garnish
1 chilli, deseeded and thinly sliced
1 Tbsp soy sauce or tamari
1 Tbsp sesame oil
½ cup peas
½ cup corn kernels
1 cup chopped pineapple
Handful of spinach, roughly chopped
½ cup cashews
Chilli flakes to serve, optional

Precook rice (see p. 131) then add to a hot pan with olive oil, onion and garlic. Once onion starts to cook, add capsicum, carrot, spring onions, and chilli.

Once veggies are a little soft, add soy sauce or tamari and sesame oil. Stir through and make sure all vegetables are coated. Add rice along with peas, corn, pineapple, spinach and cashews. Stir together until everything is cooked. Top with extra spring onion and chilli flakes, if desired.

GF

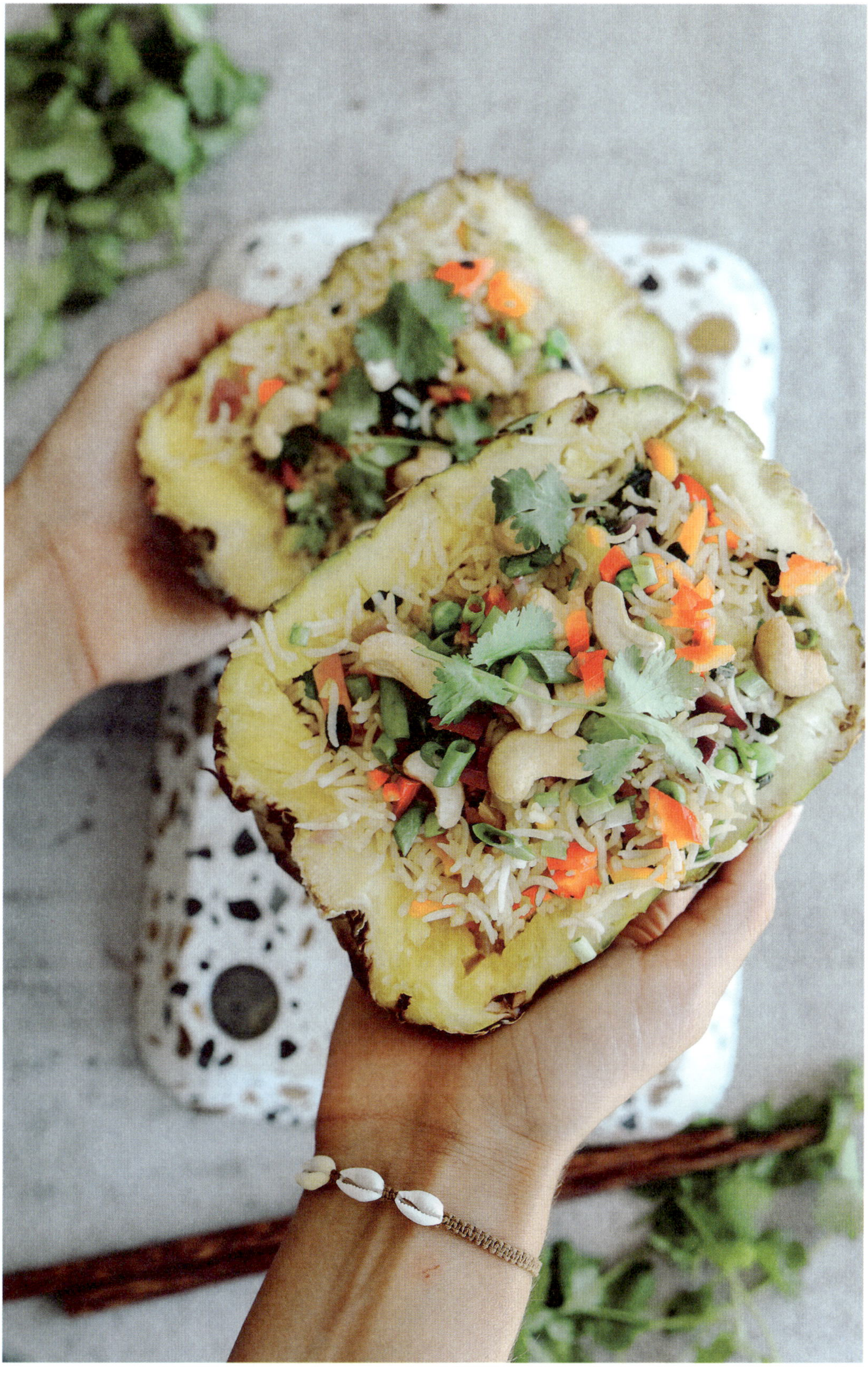

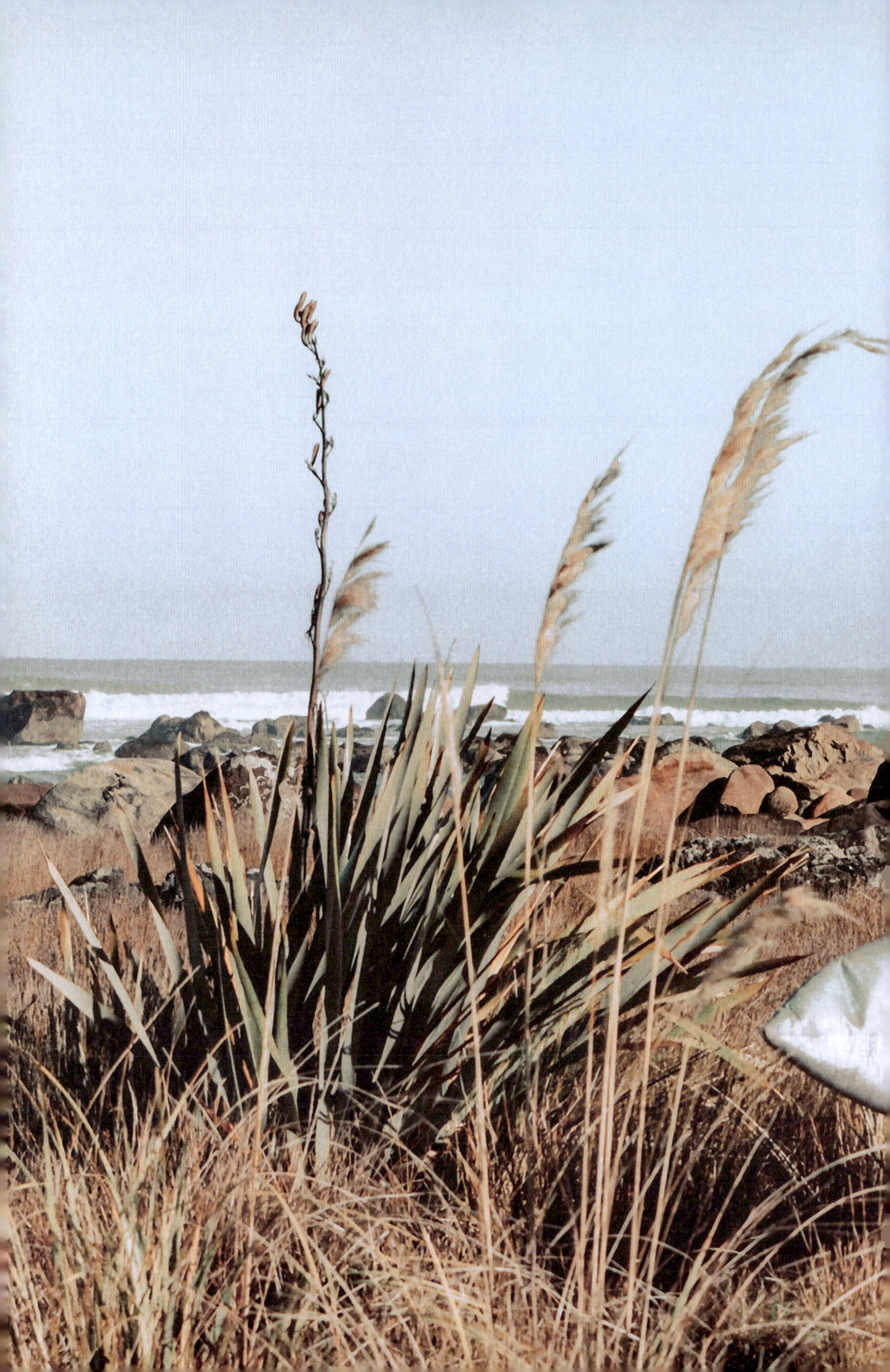

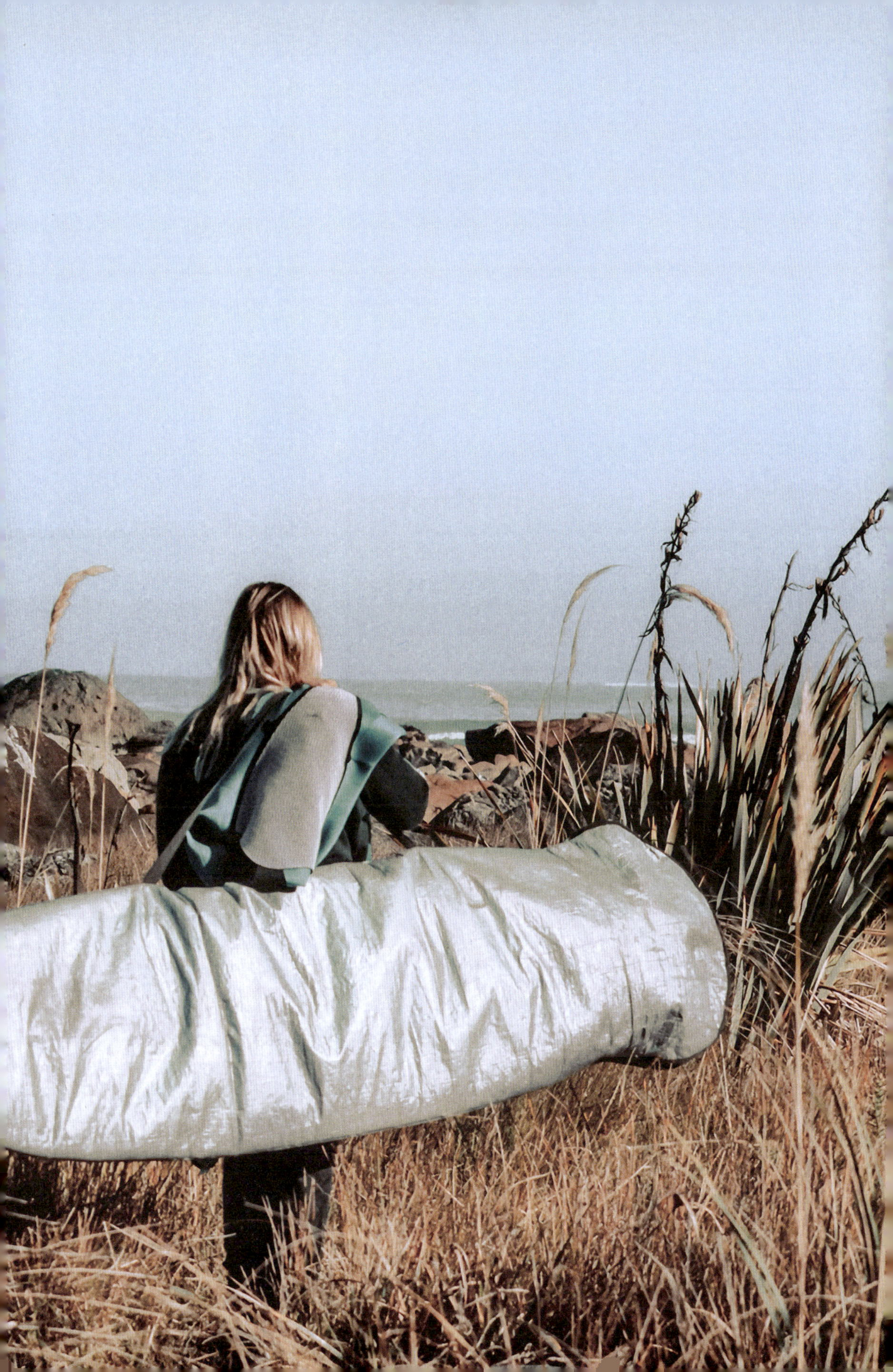

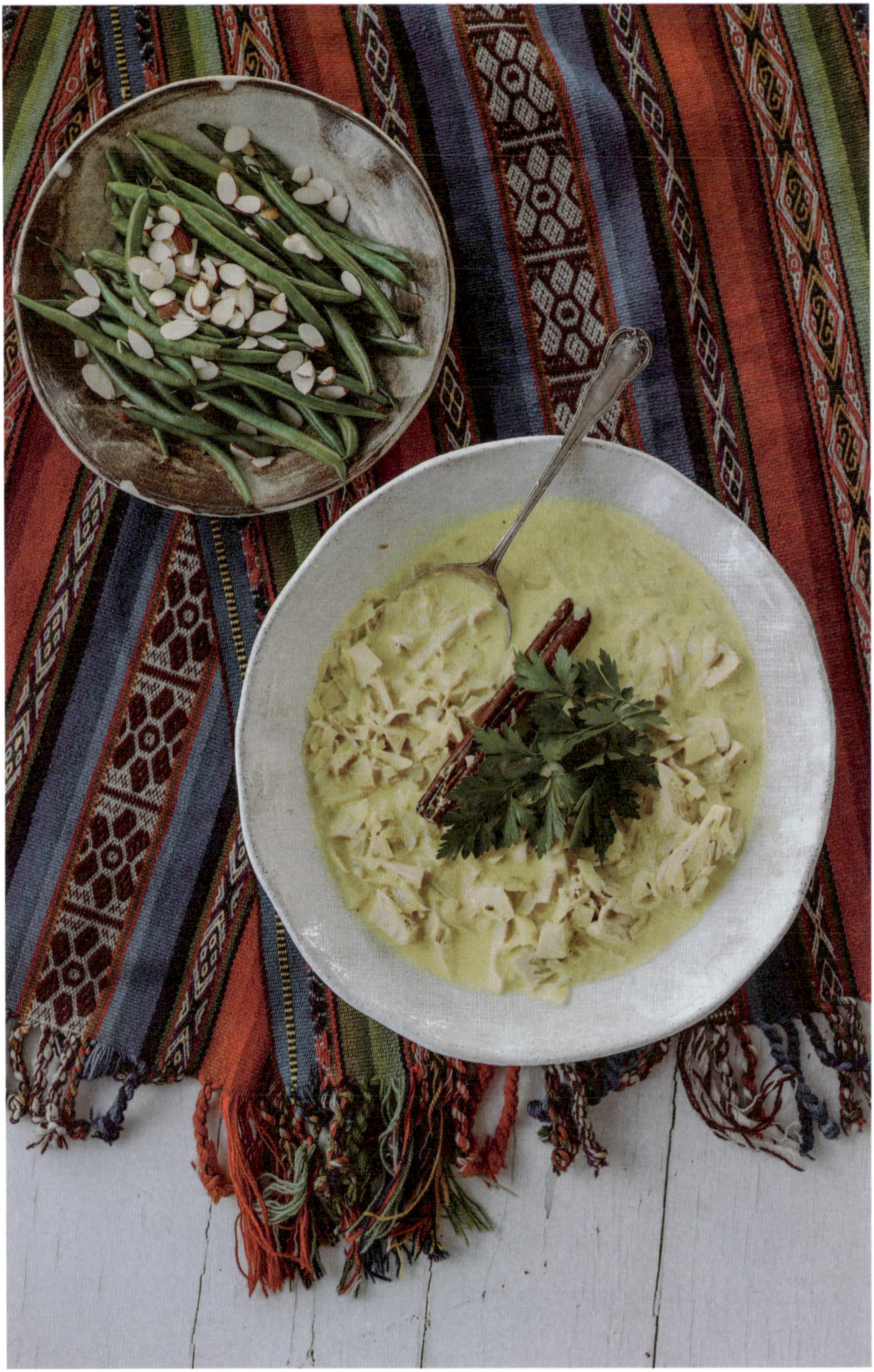

Sri Lankan Pulled Jackfruit Curry

Serves 4 • 60 minutes

I tried jackfruit for the first time when I was in Sri Lanka a few years ago and it got me completely hooked. This is a deliciously unique curry and if you haven't cooked with jackfruit before, this is probably one of the easiest ways to start. The green beans work perfectly to add a little freshness and crunch to the dish.

Jackfruit Curry

- 1 tsp ground coriander
- 1 tsp ground cumin
- 1 tsp Homemade Curry Powder (see p. 211)
- 1 red chilli, halved and deseeded, plus extra to serve
- 1 shallot, finely chopped
- 20 curry leaves
- 1 cinnamon stick
- ½ tsp ground paprika
- ½ tsp ground turmeric
- 400 g can jackfruit
- 400 ml can coconut milk
- 3 Tbsp coconut yoghurt

. . . ingredients continued overleaf

To make the jackfruit curry: Dry roast the coriander, cumin and curry powder in a frying pan and stir until they turn dark brown.

Add chilli, shallot, curry leaves, cinnamon stick, paprika, turmeric and jackfruit to pan, making sure everything is covered in the spices. Add coconut milk and simmer for 15 minutes.

Add coconut yoghurt and continue simmering over a low heat until jackfruit is tender (should take around 20 minutes).

While the jackfruit is softening, cook the brown rice (see p. 131).

. . . recipe continued overleaf

GF

Sweet and Spicy Beans

2 Tbsp sesame oil

2 cm piece fresh ginger, finely chopped

2 cloves garlic, crushed

400 g green beans

1 Tbsp coconut sugar

1 Tbsp lemon juice

½ cup roasted almonds, roughly chopped

To Serve

2 cups brown rice

Large handful of fresh coriander

To make the beans: Heat sesame oil in a wok or large frying pan. Add ginger and garlic and stir-fry for 1–2 minutes. Add beans, coconut sugar and lemon juice and cook for 3–4 minutes, until beans are tender but still slightly crunchy. Add almonds and cook for 1 minute more.

Serve curry and beans with brown rice and fresh coriander.

· · · · · · ·

Hot Tip: Add any vegetables you have on hand. Broccoli or cauliflower work beautifully.

· · · · · · ·

GF

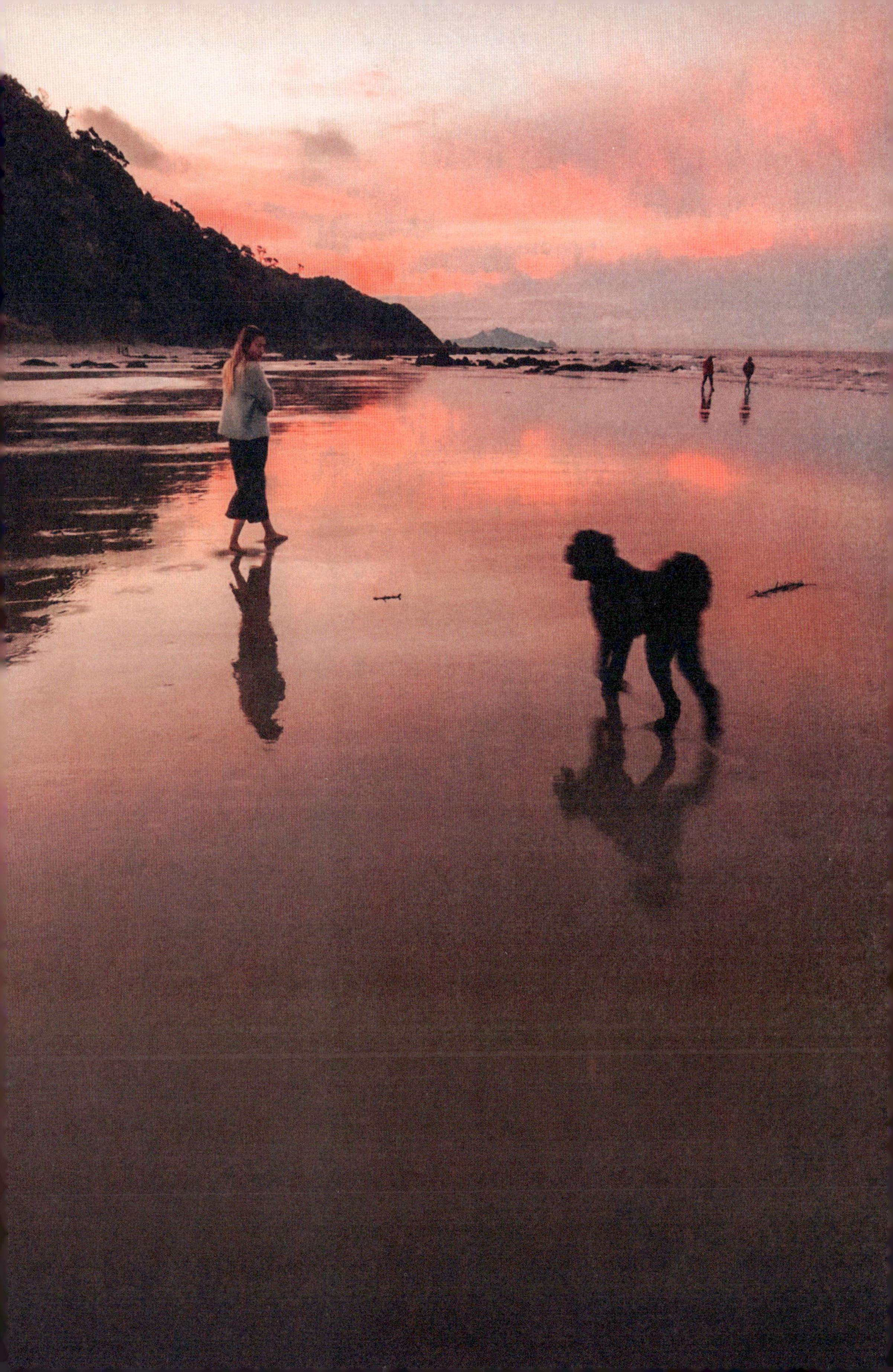

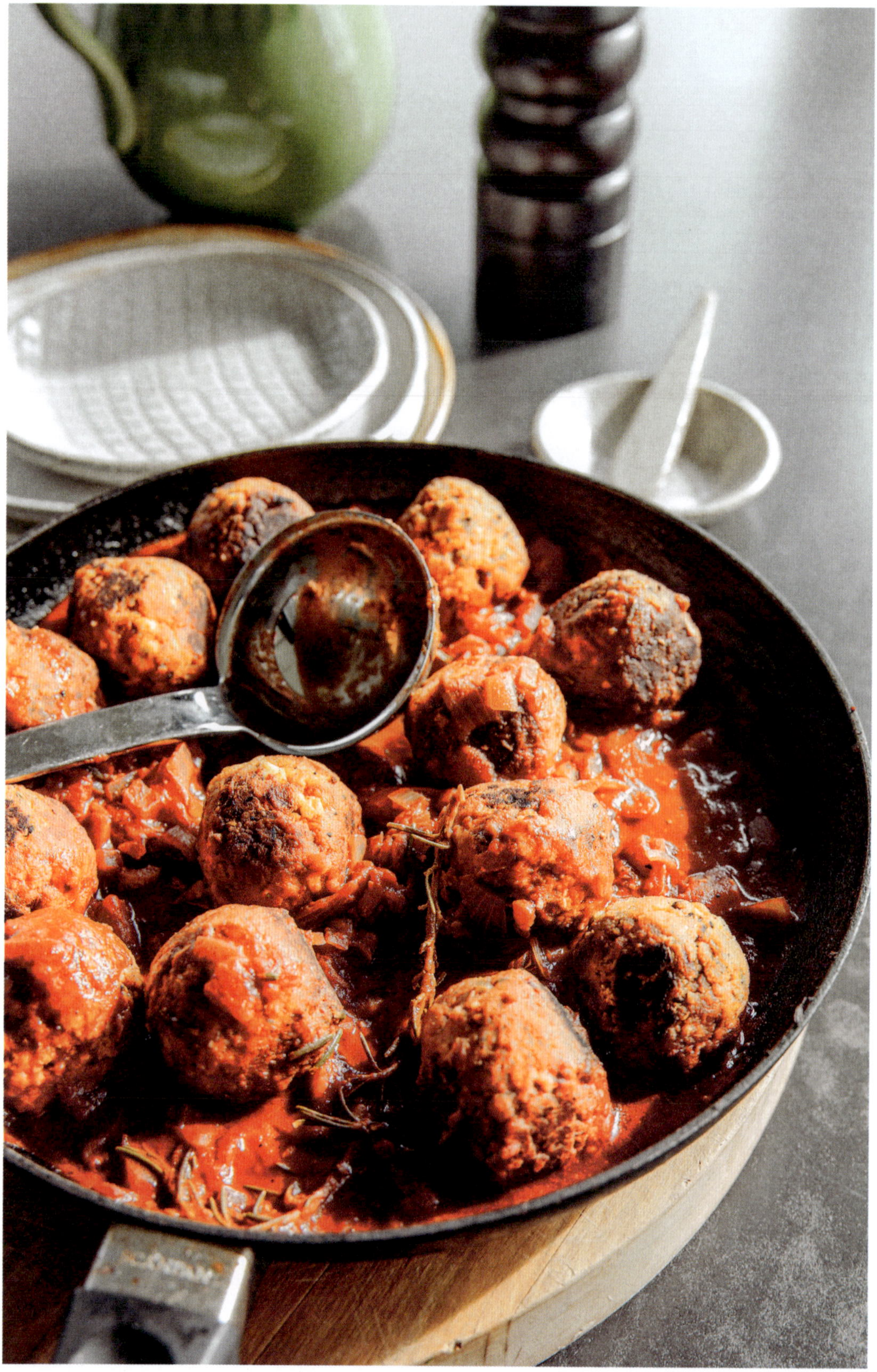

Meatless Meatballs with a Marinara Sauce

Serves 4 • 75 minutes

If you didn't know better, you'd swear that these vegan meatballs were made with meat. You can add any herbs and spices you like to this dish. The marinara sauce really sets it off. I love to serve this dish with spaghetti pasta.

Meatless Meatballs

1 onion, chopped
1 stick celery, chopped
4 cloves garlic
1 Tbsp olive oil
1 Tbsp coriander seeds
1 Tbsp dried sage
1 Tbsp fennel seeds
1 tsp ground paprika
1 tsp ground cumin
1 tsp salt
1 tsp onion power
1 tsp garlic powder
2 Tbsp tomato paste
300 g tofu
1 cup almond meal
1 cup buckwheat flour

. . . ingredients continued overleaf

To make meatless meatballs: In a high-powered blender, blitz onion, celery and garlic. Add to a hot pan along with olive oil, coriander seeds, dried sage, fennel seeds, paprika, cumin, salt, onion powder and garlic powder. Cook for 5 minutes until spices become fragrant.

Add tomato paste then crumble tofu into the pan. Stir through the blitzed ingredients and cook for 5 minutes. Remove from heat and transfer into a large bowl.

Once cool, add almond meal and buckwheat flour to meatball mixture. Knead mixture with your hands until combined. You may need to add more flour to get the right consistency.

. . . recipe continued overleaf

GFO

Marinara Sauce

1 brown onion, chopped
400 g can crushed tomatoes
1 Tbsp miso paste
1 cup vegetable stock
1 cup red wine
1 sprig fresh rosemary

To Serve

Cooked spaghetti pasta (I use gluten-free quinoa pasta)
Roasted Brussels sprouts, optional

To make sauce: Add onion, crushed tomatoes, miso paste, vegetable stock, red wine and rosemary to a hot pan. Simmer for 10 minutes until sauce has reduced then remove from heat and set aside.

Roll meatballs into golf-ball-sized balls and place them back in a hot pan with 2 tablespoons olive oil. Use tongs to move the meatballs around every few minutes until lightly brown all over.

Once meatballs are cooked and crispy on the outside, pour tomato sauce into the pan and sauté for a few minutes until well coated and bubbling.

I like to serve these with spaghetti and roasted Brussels sprouts.

GFO

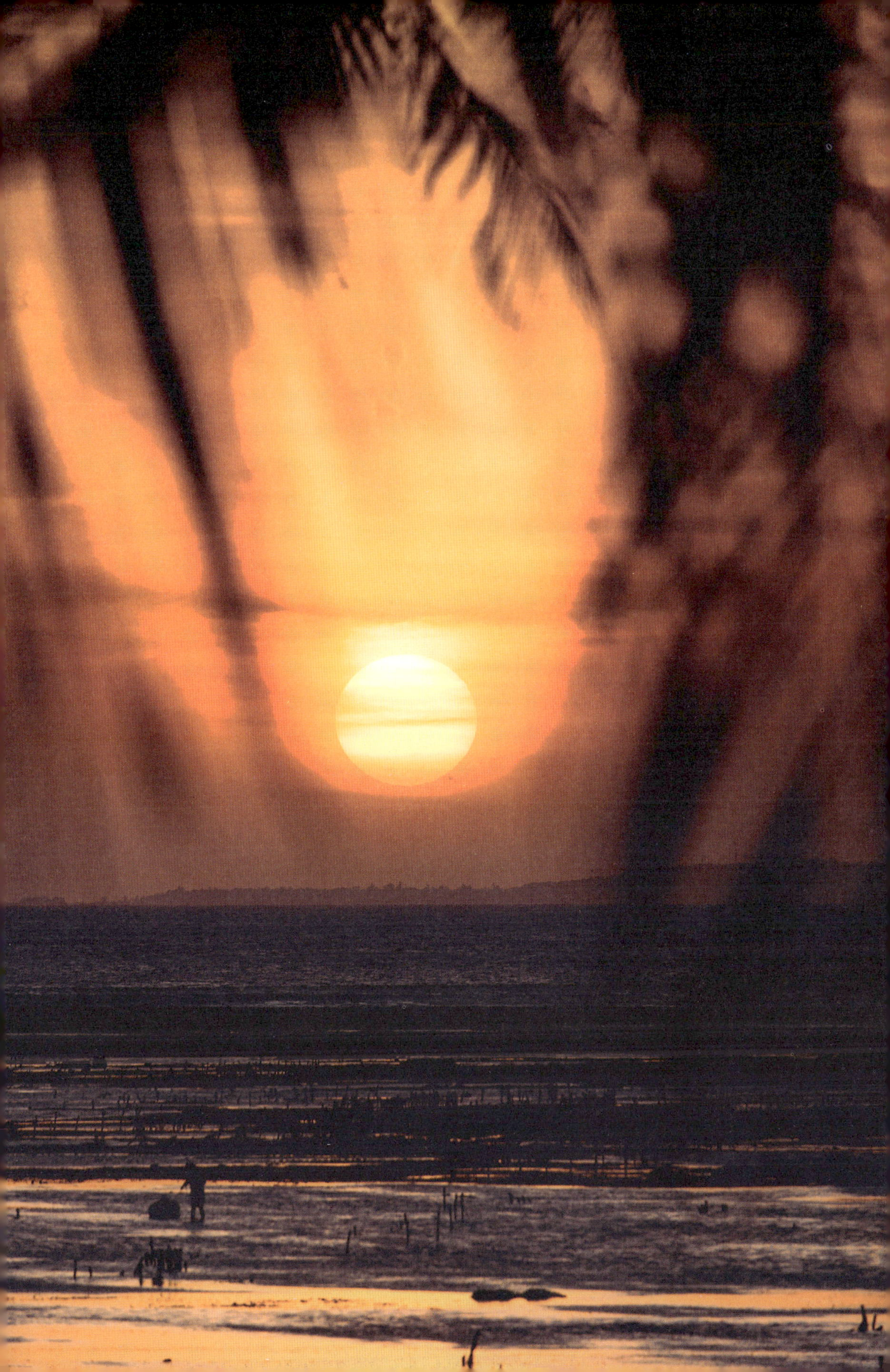

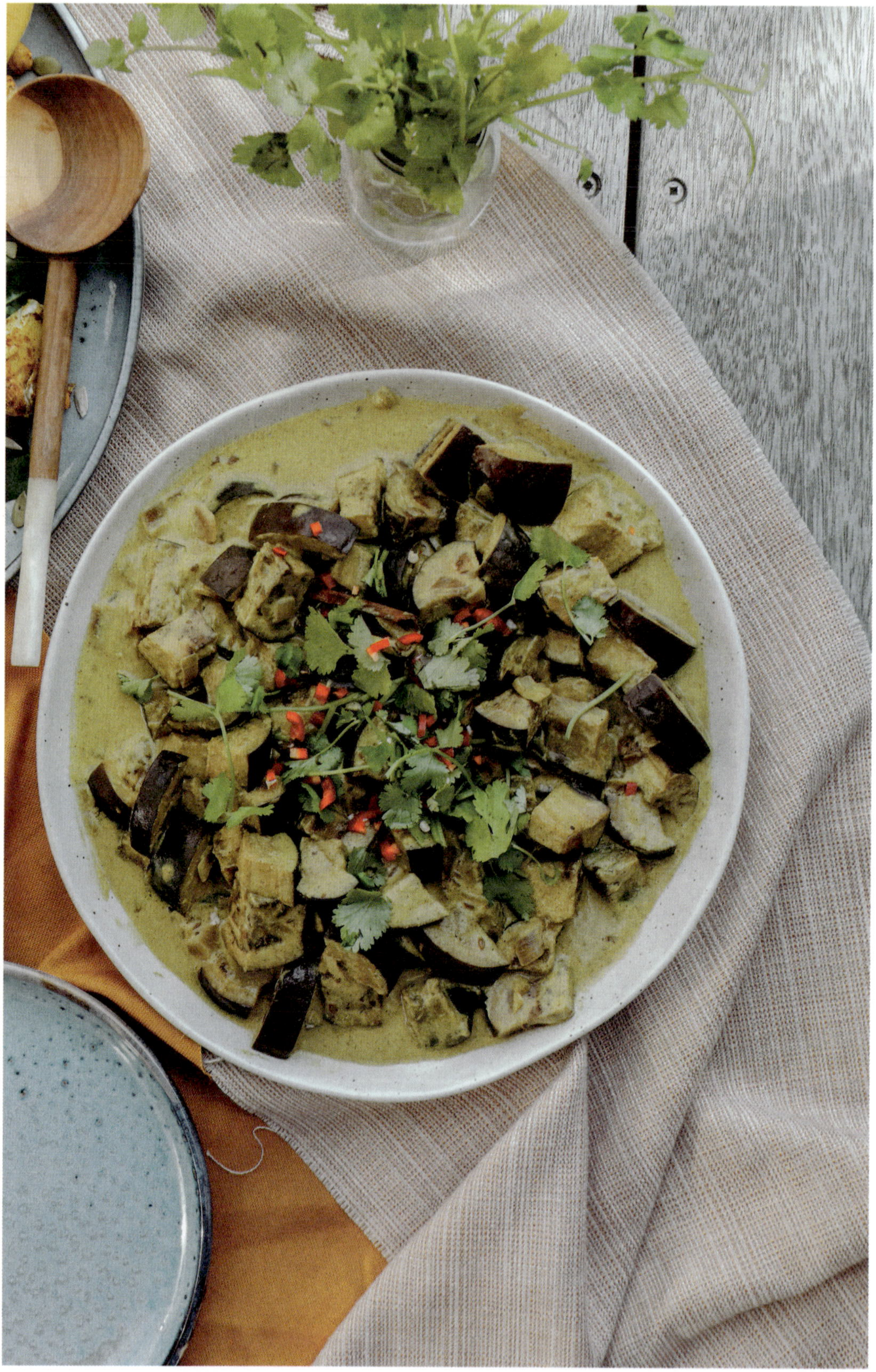

Curried Eggplant

Serves 4 • 30 minutes

I never liked eggplant growing up, but if I'd tried it like this I feel positive I would have quickly changed my mind. This dish makes a stunning addition to a selection of curries and similar condiments, or even just on its own with plain rice.

2 eggplants, cut into cubes
½ tsp ground cinnamon
½ tsp chilli powder
1 tsp ground turmeric
1 Tbsp olive oil
1 onion, finely chopped
2 cloves garlic, thinly sliced
1 tsp fenugreek seeds
1 tsp cumin seeds
1 cinnamon stick
400 ml can coconut milk

To Serve
Fresh coriander
½ chilli, deseeded and finely chopped

Place eggplant in a bowl and toss to coat with cinnamon, chilli powder and turmeric.

To a hot pan over medium heat, add olive oil, onion and garlic, and cook until onion is translucent. Add fenugreek seeds, cumin seeds and cinnamon stick to the pan and cook for another 3 minutes.

Finally, add eggplant and coconut milk, cover and leave to simmer for around 15–20 minutes, stirring occasionally until eggplant is soft.

Transfer to a serving bowl and garnish with fresh oriander and chilli.

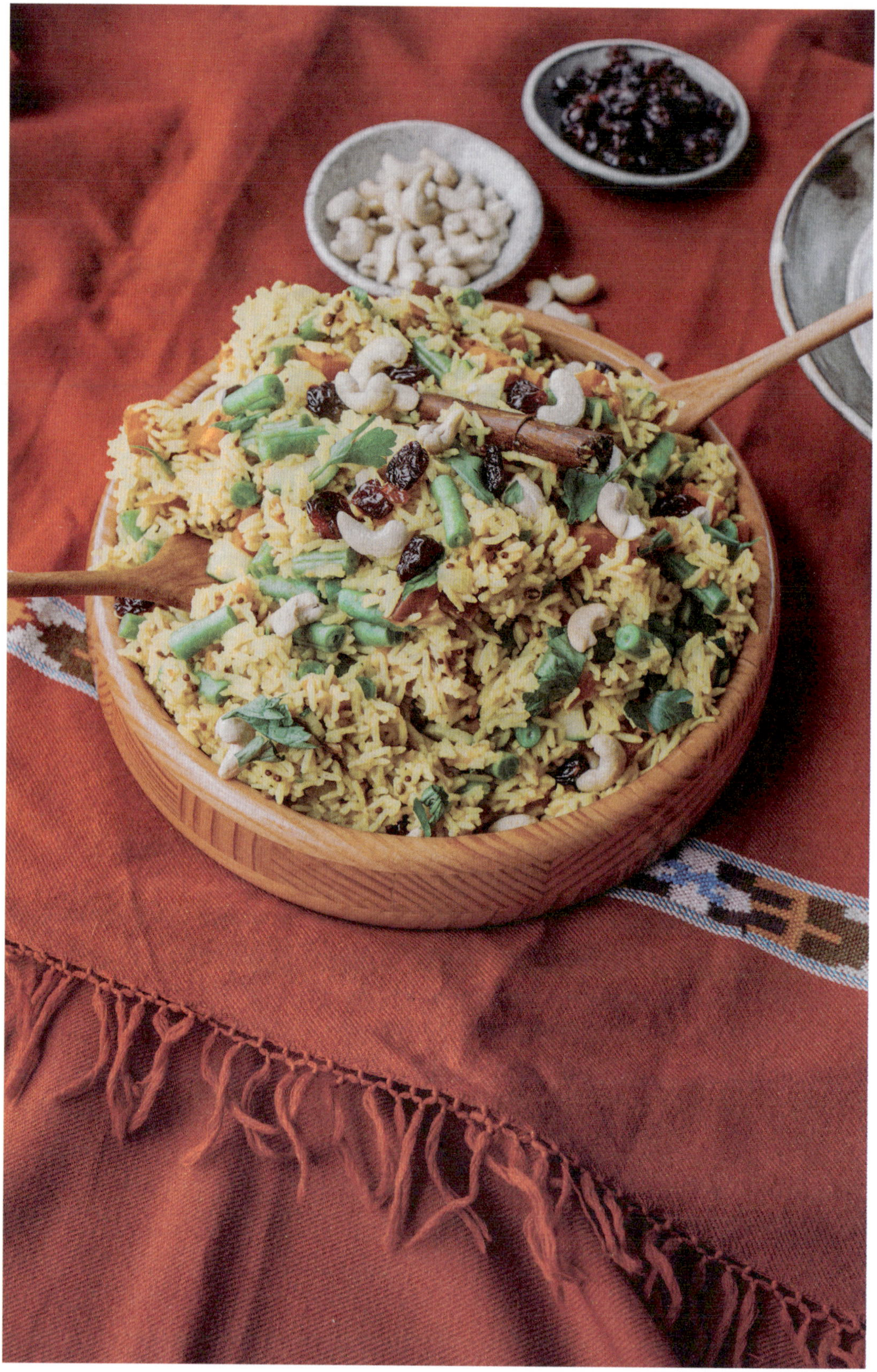

Spiced Cherry Biryani

Serves 5 • 45 minutes

Biryani has been in my life for such a long time and makes for the best family dinners. The dried cherries create the perfect sweetness when paired with the roast cashews.

1 onion, finely diced
1 Tbsp coconut oil
2 cloves garlic, finely chopped
2 Tbsp grated fresh ginger
1 Tbsp mustard seeds
1 cinnamon stick
1 Tbsp coriander seeds
1 tsp ground turmeric
1 carrot, diced
2 small orange kumara, diced
2 cups basmati rice
4 cups vegetable stock
1 zucchini, diced
200 g green beans, chopped
400 g can chickpeas, drained
⅓ cup roast cashews
⅓ cup dried cherries
Large handful of fresh parsley, roughly chopped

In a medium-sized pot, cook onion in coconut oil. Stir until onion is translucent then add garlic, ginger, mustard seeds, cinnamon stick, coriander seeds and turmeric. Cook until fragrant then add carrot and kumara. Stir to combine.

Add rice along with vegetable stock. Cover and leave to simmer for 20 minutes until rice has absorbed almost all the liquid. Finally, add zucchini, beans and chickpeas and stir to combine. Leave to cook until vegetables are soft. Once cooked, top with cashews, cherries and fresh parsley.

• • • • • • •

Hot Tip: If you're using brown rice you will need to add a little extra liquid so it cooks properly.

• • • • • • •

GF

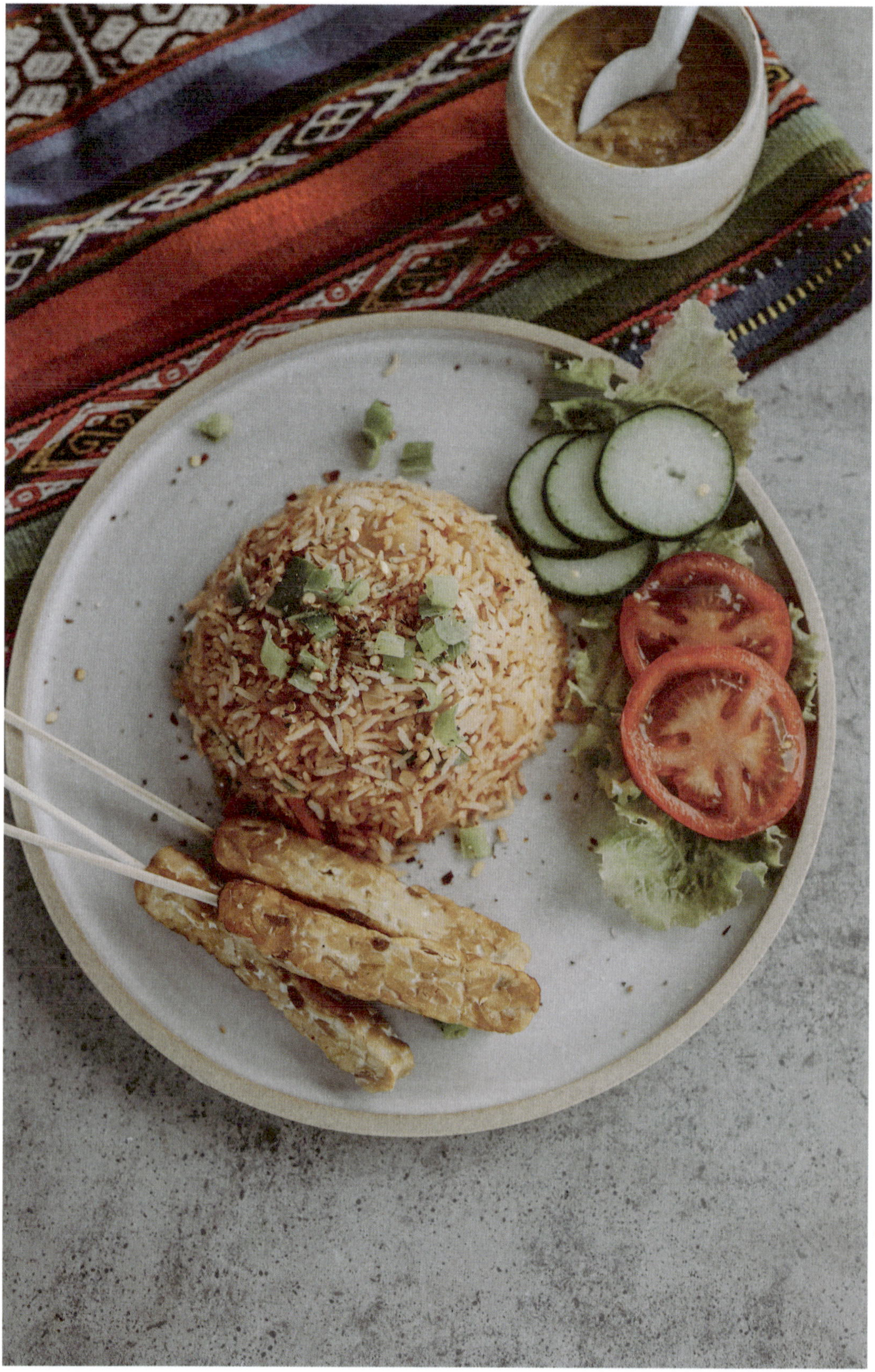

Nasi Goreng

Serves 5 • 40 minutes

When I was 12 I went to a Balinese cooking class while holidaying in Indonesia, which is where I learnt to make this signature dish . . . and I've been adapting it ever since. I like to serve mine with tempeh skewers and my Satay Sauce (see p. 214).

2½ cups white rice
1 Tbsp olive oil
2 shallots, sliced
Thumb-sized piece of ginger, peeled and finely chopped
3 cloves garlic, finely chopped
1 capsicum, deseeded and sliced
1 large carrot, sliced
1 Tbsp tomato paste
1 chilli, deseeded and finely chopped
Juice from 1 lime
2 Tbsp soy sauce or tamari
1 Tbsp sesame oil
5 spring onions, finely chopped

To Serve (Optional)
250 g tempeh, sliced
2 spring onions, roughly chopped
½ cucumber, sliced
1 tomato, sliced
Handful crispy shallots
Satay Sauce (see p. 214)
   (leave out if nut-free)

Precook rice (see p. 131).

To a hot pan, add olive oil, shallots, ginger and garlic, and cook for 5 minutes until fragrant.

Add capsicum and carrot to the pan and cook for another 5 minutes. Tip in cooked rice and add tomato paste, chilli, lime juice, soy sauce or tamari, sesame oil and spring onions. Stir the rice to combine.

If serving with tempeh, add tempeh to a separate hot pan with a bit of oil and soy sauce. Cook for 10 minutes until golden then set aside.

To serve: Scatter spring onions over Nasi Goreng and serve with cucumber, tomato and crispy shallots as well as tempeh topped with Satay Sauce.

. . . .

Hot Tip: Fried rice always tastes better if you cook the rice the day before.

. . . .

GF   NFO

Beetroot Dahl with Coconut Raita

Serves 4 • 45 minutes

When we visited Sri Lanka, the whole family became so obsessed with dhal, my brother refused to eat anything else for breakfast on the whole trip. I wanted to create a unique flavour combination and the earthy sweetness and vibrant colour of beetroot seemed the perfect addition.

1 Tbsp olive oil
3 cloves garlic, finely chopped
1 Tbsp garam masala
1 Tbsp ground cumin
1 large beetroot, peeled and diced
400 g can chopped tomatoes
400 ml can coconut milk
½ cup split red lentils

Raita

1 medium-sized cucumber, diced
1 cup plain coconut yoghurt
½ tsp ground cumin
1 Tbsp chopped fresh mint

To Serve

2 cups basmati or brown rice
¼ cup chopped fresh coriander

Precook rice (see p. 131).

To a large pan or wok over a medium heat, add oil and garlic and stir until fragrant. Add garam masala, ground cumin and beetroot, and stir through until coated in the spices. Add tomatoes, coconut milk and lentils. Cover the pan and leave to simmer for 20 minutes.

To make the raita: Combine all ingredients in a bowl.

Serve with rice and fresh coriander.

GF NF

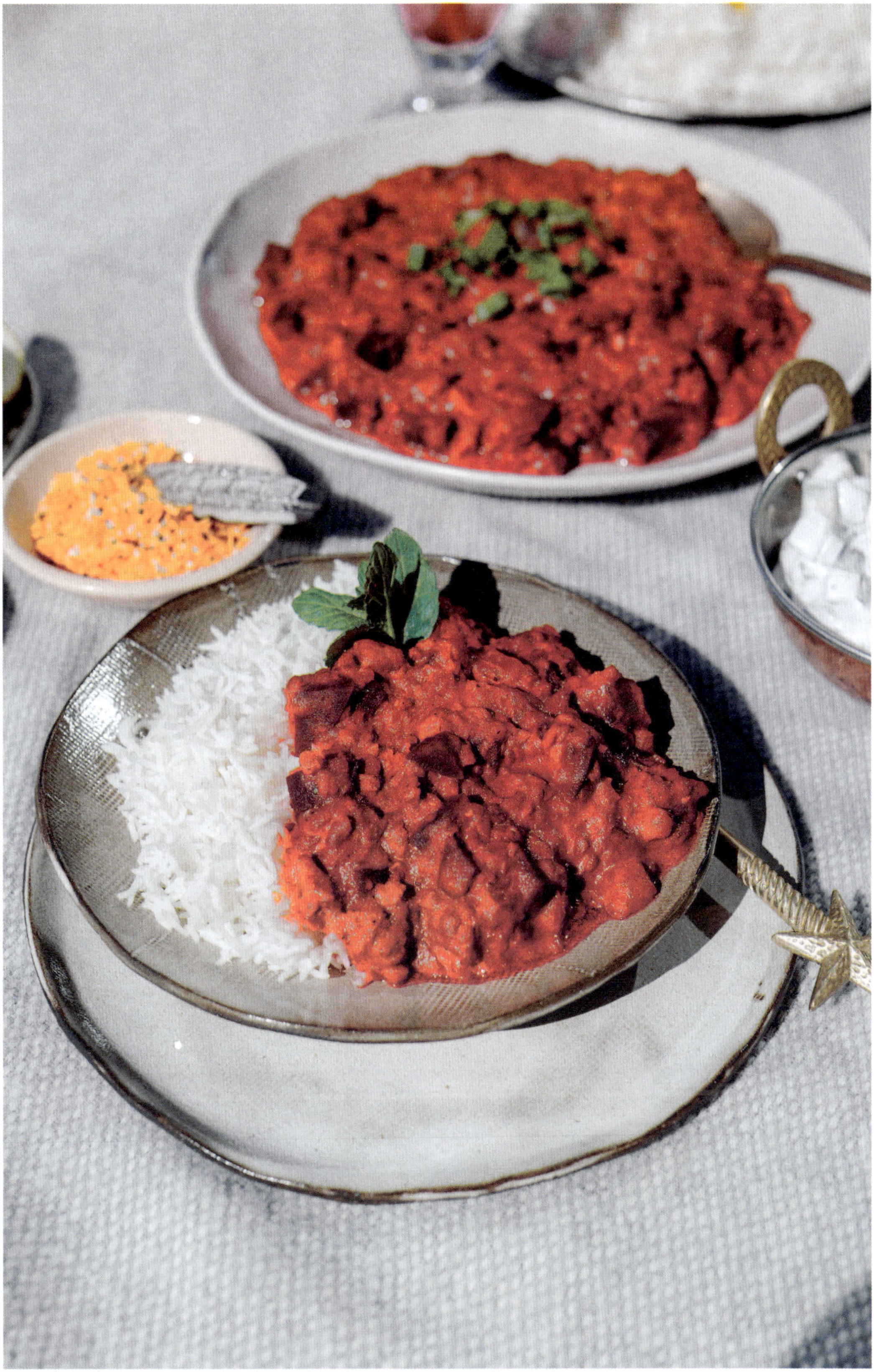

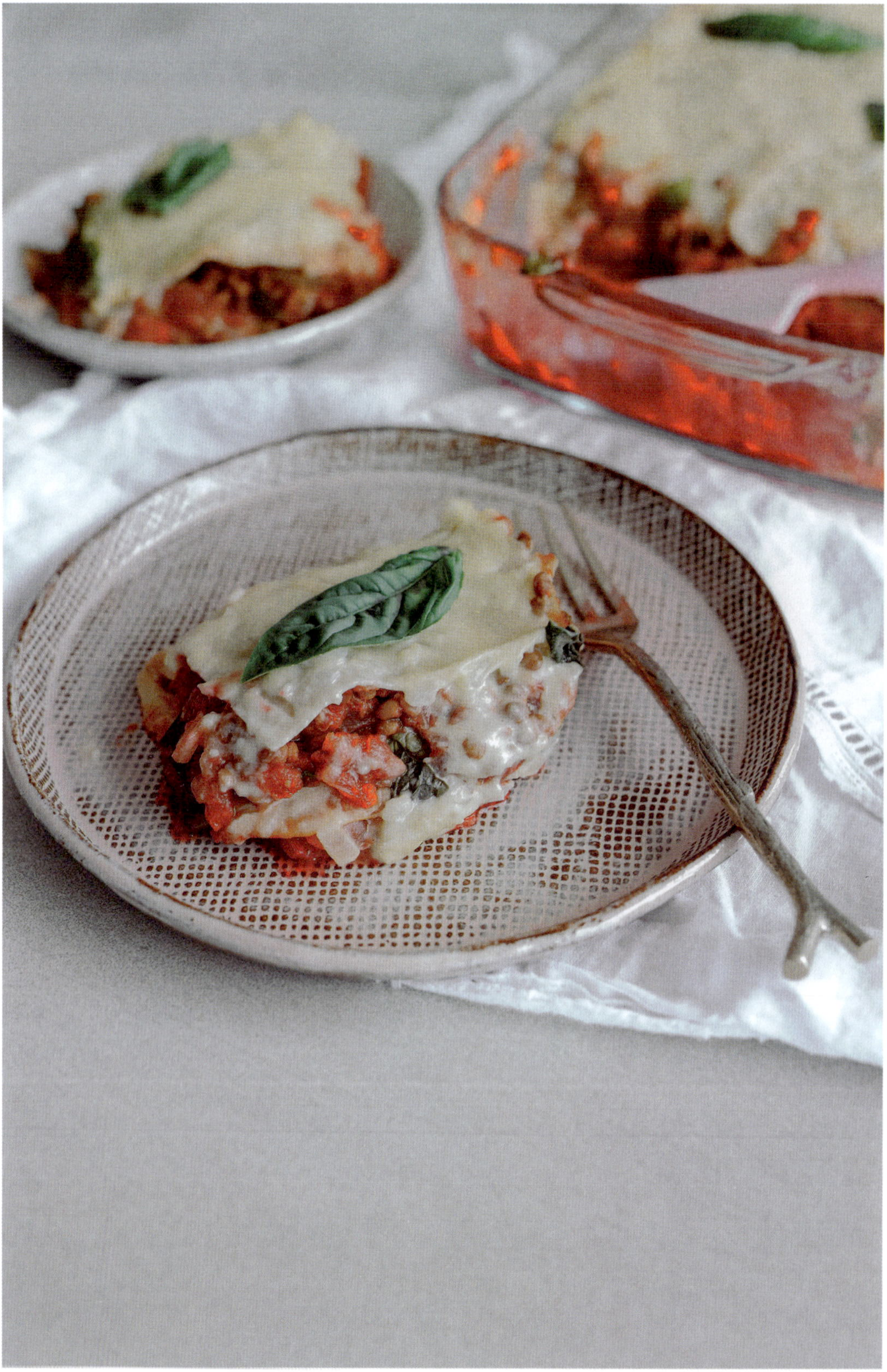

Rainbow Lasagne

Serves 8 • 120 minutes

After trying a lot of lasagnes over the years, I really wanted to make my own plant-based version. My partner's favourite meal of all time is lasagne so I really needed to do it justice. Lentils are packed with iron, magnesium and protein and do an excellent job of creating a 'meaty' tomato sauce.

Béchamel Sauce

1 Tbsp oil

2 cups soy milk

1 onion, diced

2 cloves garlic, finely chopped

1 cup grated vegan cheese

¼ cup white spelt flour (or plain GF)

Lentil Bolognese

1 Tbsp olive oil

1 brown onion, diced

2 x 400 g cans chopped tomatoes

1 tsp ground paprika

1 Tbsp ground coriander

1 Tbsp soy sauce or tamari

1 Tbsp tomato paste

400 g can lentils

. . . ingredients continued overleaf

Preheat oven to 180°C.

To make the béchamel sauce: In a pot, combine oil, milk, onion and garlic. Bring to the boil then simmer and stir through cheese and flour. Once sauce begins to thicken, remove from heat and set aside.

To make lentil bolognese: To a hot pan, add olive oil and onion and sauté until translucent. Add tomatoes, paprika, coriander, soy sauce or tamari, tomato paste and lentils. Cook for 15 minutes then set aside.

. . . recipe continued overleaf

To Assemble

- 500 g gluten-free lasagne sheets
- 1 medium-sized beetroot, thinly sliced
- ¼ butternut pumpkin, thinly sliced
- 3 large handfuls spinach
- 2 cups grated vegan cheese
- Fresh basil, to garnish

To assemble: Line a dish with a layer of lasagne sheets. Top with beetroot then half the lentil bolognese. Add another layer of lasagne sheets followed by butternut, half the béchamel sauce and another layer of lasagne. Add spinach and top with the rest of the lentil bolognese, followed by one final layer of lasagne sheets. Top with remaining béchamel sauce followed by vegan cheese.

Cover lasagne with foil and bake in the oven for 40–50 minutes until cooked through. Remove from oven and leave to sit for 5 minutes before slicing and garnishing with basil.

• • • • • • • •

Hot Tip: If making this recipe nut-free, be sure to check the vegan cheese is nut-free, too.

• • • • • • • •

GFO NFO

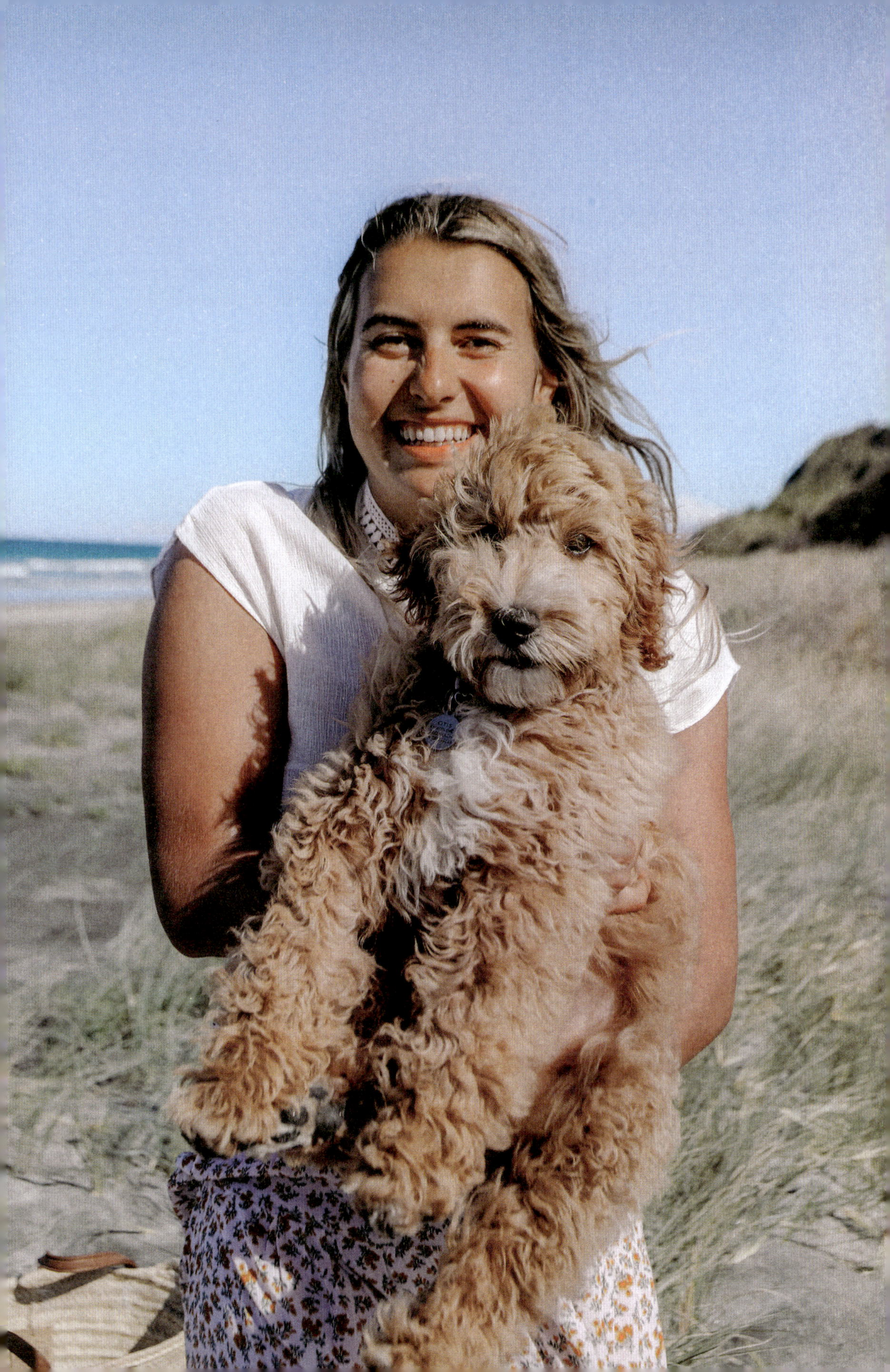

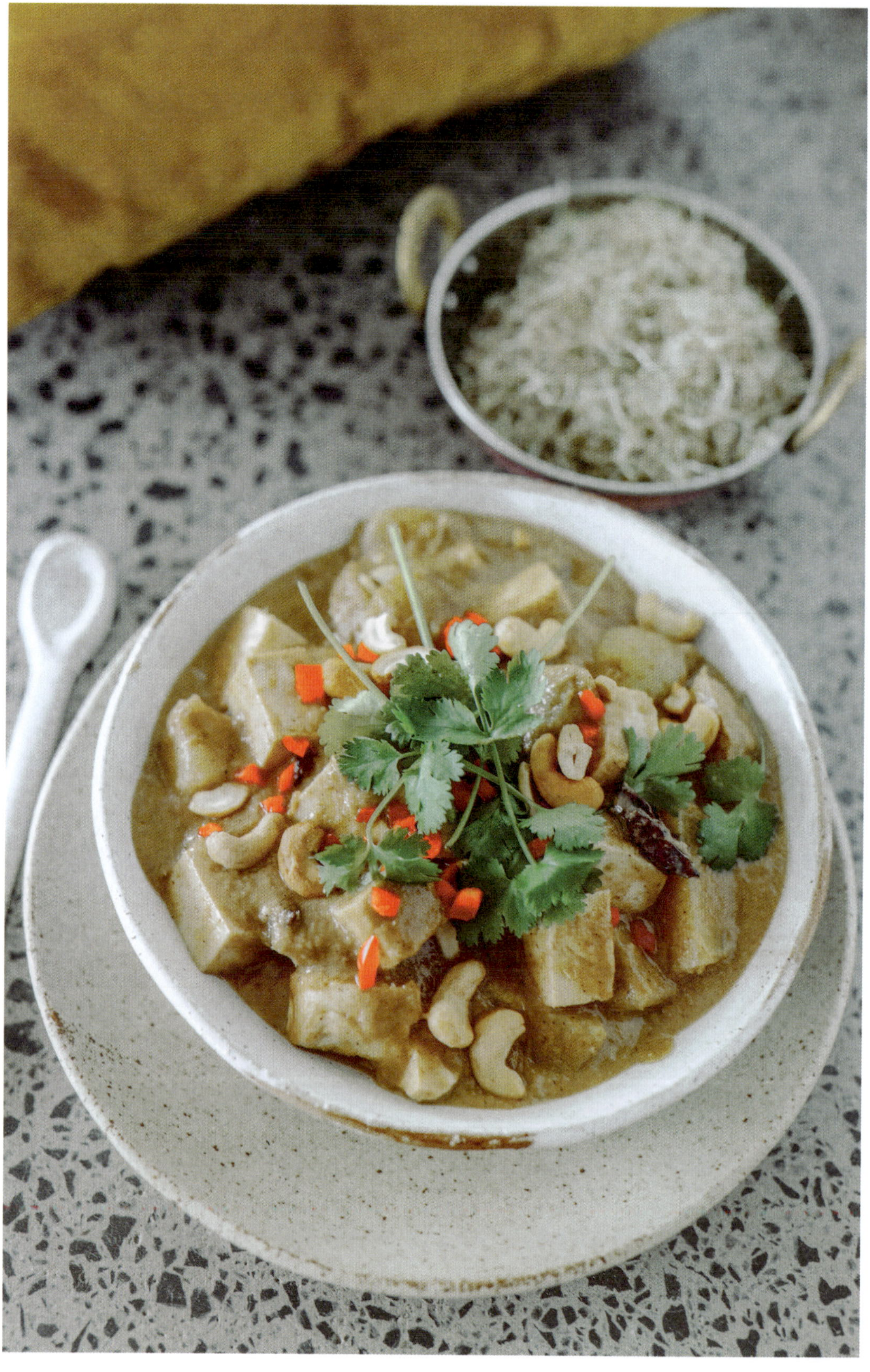

Spicy Massaman Curry

Serves 2 • 40 minutes

This Thai curry is one of my absolute favourites. I like to use tofu but you can really add anything you like, such as carrot, sweet potato or jackfruit.

Paste
1 stalk lemongrass, chopped
2 large chillies, deseeded
1 shallot, quartered
5 cloves garlic
2 cm piece of ginger, chopped
1 tsp ground coriander
1 tsp ground cumin
½ tsp ground cinnamon
½ tsp ground nutmeg
1 Tbsp peanut butter
⅓ cup water

Curry
400 ml can coconut milk
2 star anise
2 potatoes, peeled and cubed
300g firm tofu, cut into cubes
1 Tbsp soy sauce or tamari
1 Tbsp coconut sugar
1 Tbsp tamarind paste

To Serve
1 cup basmati rice
Fresh coriander, cashew nuts and chilli, to garnish

Precook rice (see p. 98).

In a food processor, blend all of the curry paste ingredients together. Add the paste to a pan and stir over medium heat for around 5 minutes until fragrant.

Add coconut milk, star anise and potatoes, cover and leave to cook for 15 minutes.

Add the tofu, soy sauce or tamari, coconut sugar and tamarind paste; stir through until combined. Cover and cook for a further 10 minutes.

Serve with rice, fresh coriander, cashew nuts and fresh chilli.

• • • • • • •

Hot Tip: If you don't like it too spicy add fewer chillies to the curry paste.

• • • • • • •

(GF)

Mouth-watering Mains

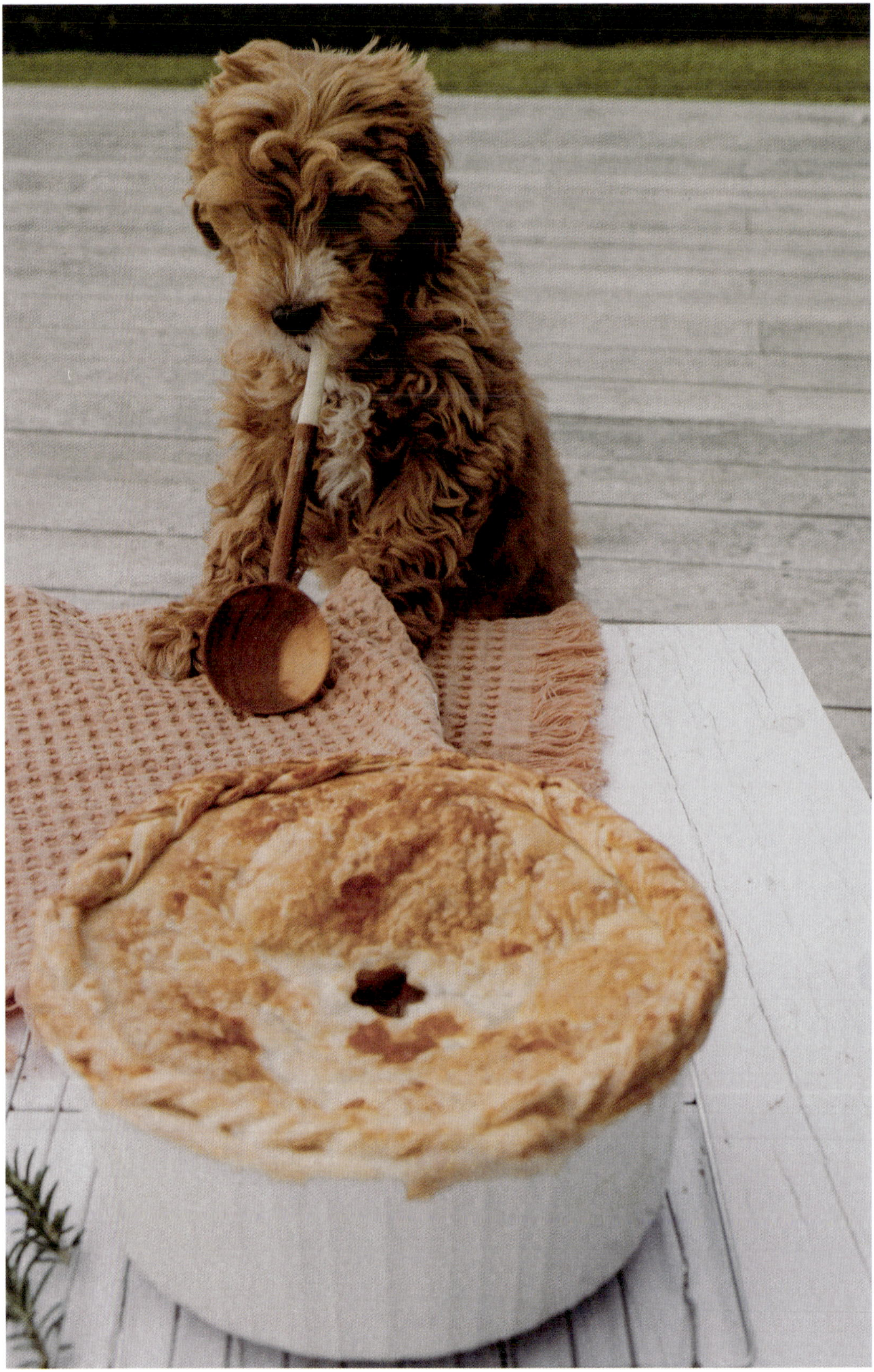

Creamy Mushroom Pot Pie

Serves 6 • 75 minutes

Everyone who's eaten this pie has absolutely adored it. The recipe is one of my favourites to whip up and is beyond creamy. It makes for the perfect family dinner or dish to bring to a gathering. There's lots of puff pastry options out there — some a lot healthier than others, so be sure to read the labels.

3 cloves garlic, finely chopped
1 onion, diced
1 Tbsp olive oil
2 sticks celery, diced
2 carrots, diced
2 zucchini, diced
500 g white button or portobello mushrooms, sliced
1 Tbsp dried thyme
1 cup plant milk
½ cup white wine
2 Tbsp coconut yoghurt or cream
2 Tbsp tapioca flour
1 sheet puff pastry (vegan/GF option)

Preheat oven to 180°C.

Add garlic, onion and olive oil to a medium-sized heated pan. Once onion is translucent, add celery, carrots and zucchini. Once carrots have softened slightly add mushrooms and thyme.

Finally, add plant milk, white wine, coconut yoghurt or cream, and mix through. Once mushroom filling is boiling, add tapioca flour and remove from heat.

Tip mixture into a 30 cm casserole dish and prepare pastry for your pie top. Place pastry on top of pie filling and trim edges to fit neatly on dish. If you want a braided pie crust, slice a sheet of pastry into 2 cm strips, braid together and circle round the edge of the pie.

With a fork, poke a few holes into the pastry and brush with plant milk. Cook in the oven for around 45 minutes until golden and bubbling.

Hot Tip: If you don't want to make a pie, the filling ingredients taste great with pasta!

GFO NF

Cheesy Potato Gratin

Serves 6 • 20 minutes

Can you imagine a cheese sauce created from vegetables? The sauce is unbelievably cheesy and tastes great with Mexican dishes, pasta and baked potatoes and even works as a salad dressing.

Cheese Sauce

1 potato, roughly chopped
1 large carrot, roughly chopped
½ onion, chopped
1 tsp garlic powder
¼ cup nutritional yeast
½ tsp mustard
1 cup soy milk

Gratin

600 g agria potatoes, peeled and finely sliced
2 cups baby spinach
2 Tbsp Sunflower Parmesan (see p. 211)

Preheat oven to 180°C.

To make the sauce: Steam potato and carrot until soft. Add all sauce ingredients to a blender and blend until smooth.

Add half the sliced potatoes to a medium-sized baking dish, top with half the spinach and half the cheese sauce. Layer remaining potatoes into the baking dish and top with the rest of the spinach and cheese sauce.

Top the dish with Sunflower Parmesan. Cover with foil and place in the oven for 40–45 minutes, then remove the foil and cook for a further 5–10 minutes until golden.

GF NF

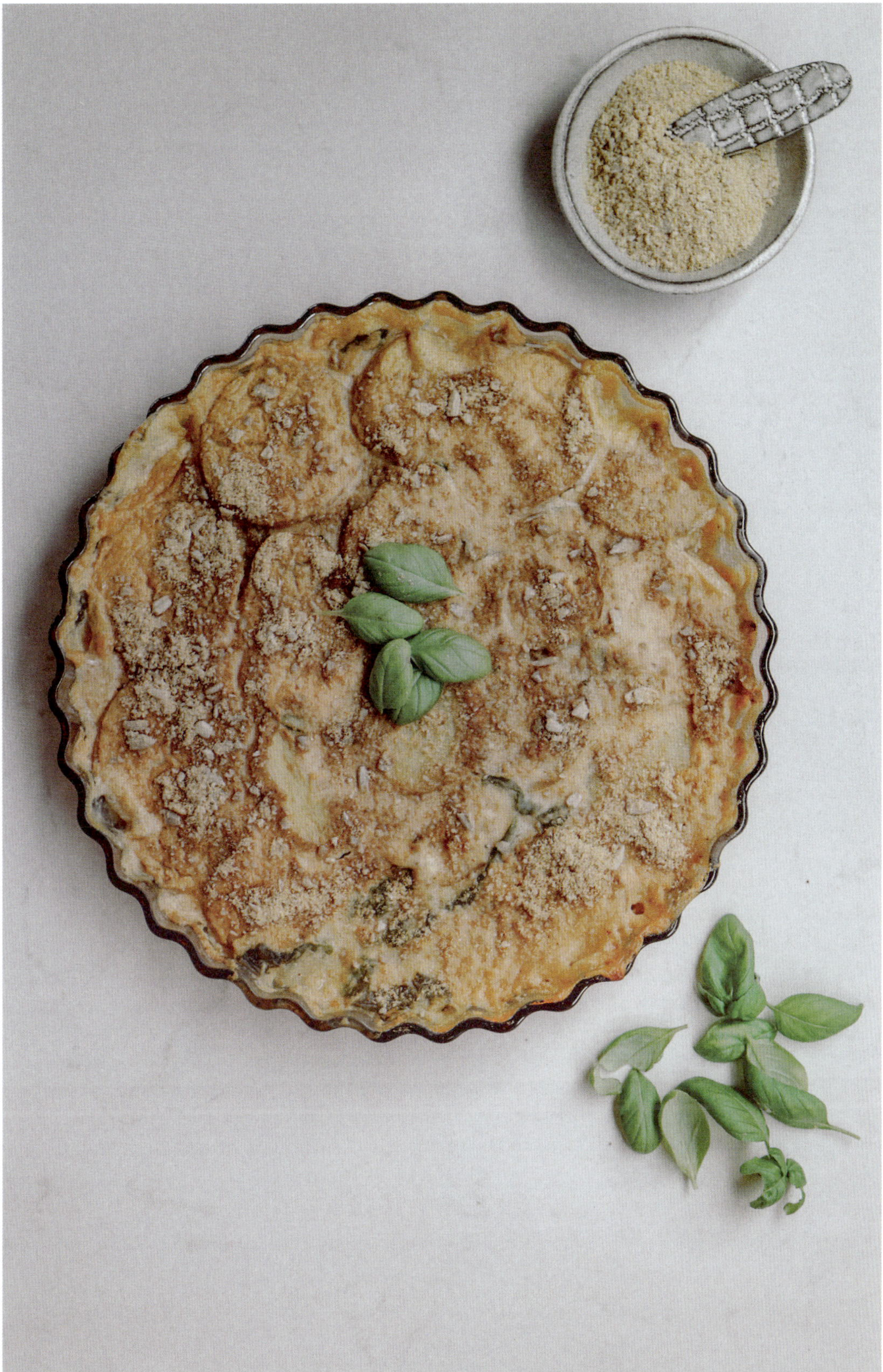

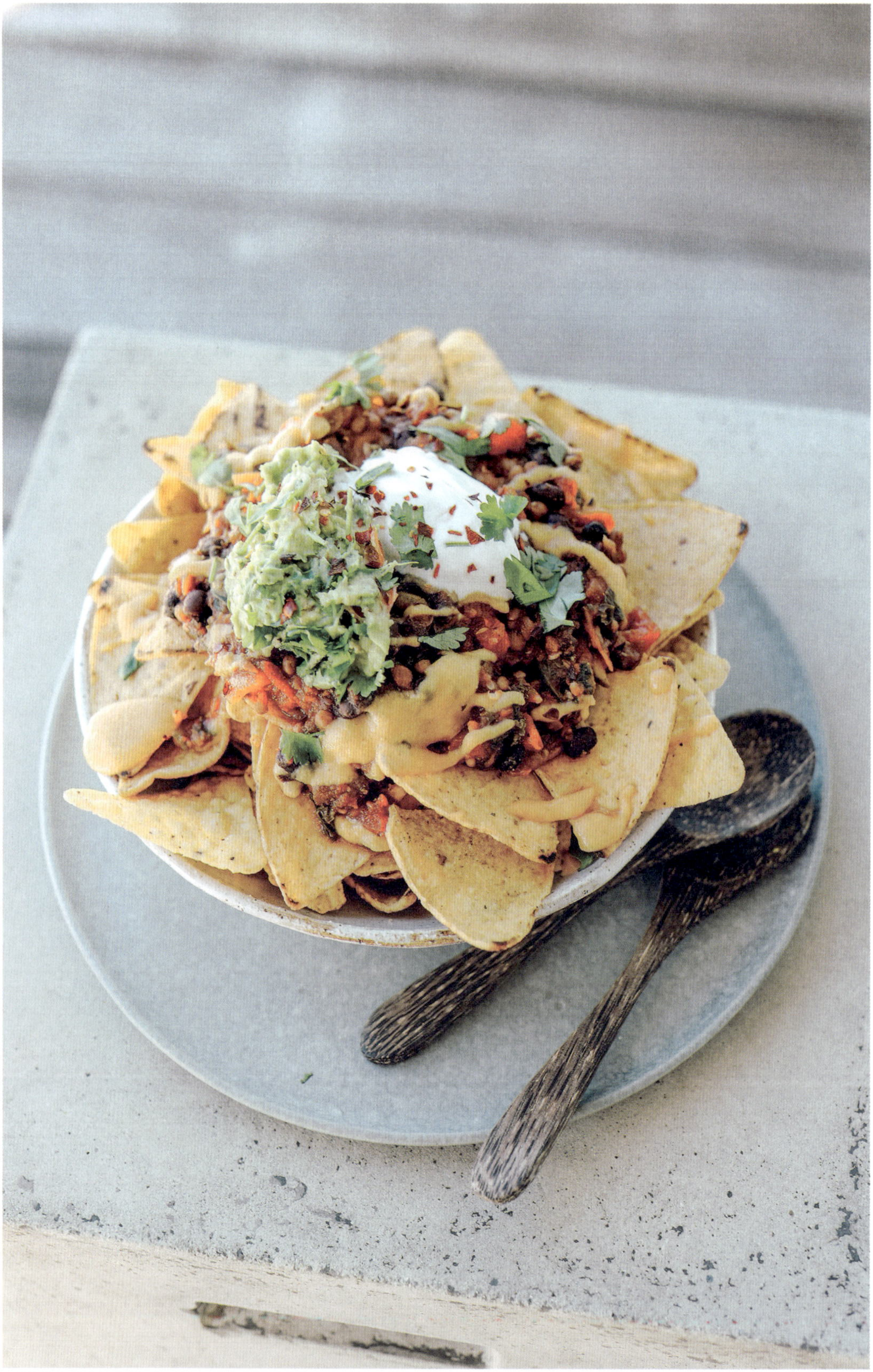

Wholesome Black Bean Nachos with Cashew Cheese

Serves 2 • 45 minutes

Who doesn't love nachos? I like to make my own chips by baking plain corn tortillas until they go crispy. Feel free to double this recipe for a large family dinner.

Corn Chips
12 medium-sized corn tortillas

Beans
1 red onion, finely chopped
1 Tbsp tomato paste
1 tsp ground cumin
1 tsp ground coriander
1 tsp smoked paprika
400 g can black beans, drained
400 g can chopped tomatoes

Cashew Cheese
1 cup cashews
¼ cup nutritional yeast
1 clove garlic
½ tsp ground turmeric
½ tsp paprika
1 cup water

To Serve
2 Tbsp Easy Guacamole (see p. 84)
Plain coconut yoghurt
Fresh coriander leaves

To make the corn chips: Preheat oven to 200°C and line a baking tray with baking paper. Slice tortillas into triangles and place them on baking tray in the oven for 15–20 minutes until crispy.

To make the beans: Add red onion, tomato paste, cumin, coriander and paprika to a hot frying pan and cook until fragrant (add a little oil or water if necessary to stop it from sticking). Add beans and chopped tomatoes. Cover pan and leave it to simmer.

To make cashew cheese: Combine all ingredients in a blender and blend until smooth. If you don't have a high-powered blender, soak cashews prior to making the cheese sauce.

Load a large plate with corn chips, followed by beans, Easy Guacamole and cashew cheese. Top with plain coconut yoghurt and fresh coriander.

GF

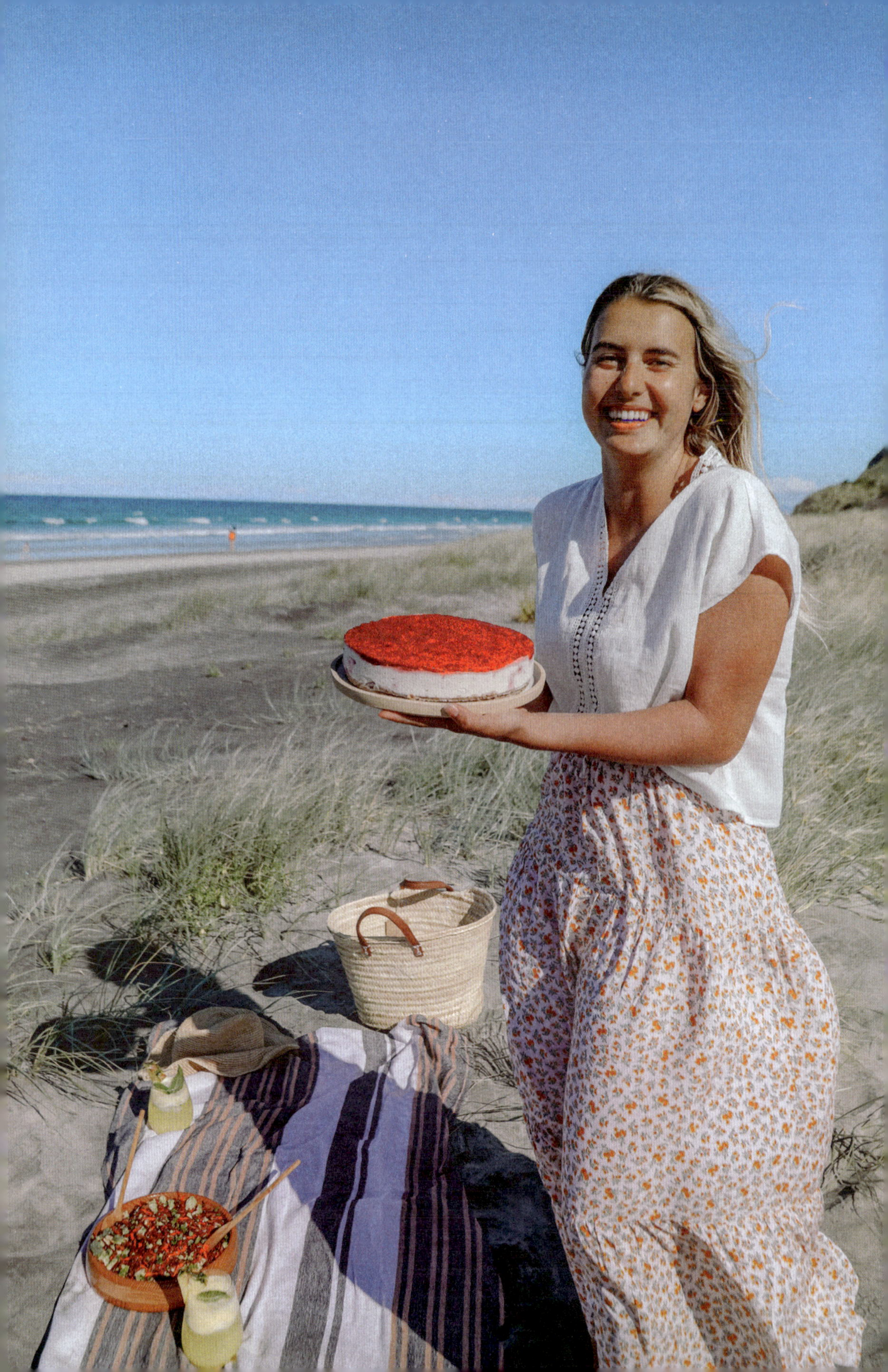

Sweet Treats

Okay, when I said breakfast was my favourite meal of the day, I obviously completely forgot about dessert. I have a massive sweet tooth, which is why I love to make slightly healthier and more nutritious versions of all the best sugary treats. One of my favourite things to make for friends and family are raw slices. The Miso Caramel Slice (see p. 189) and the After Dinner Mint Slice (see p. 193) are seriously addictive!

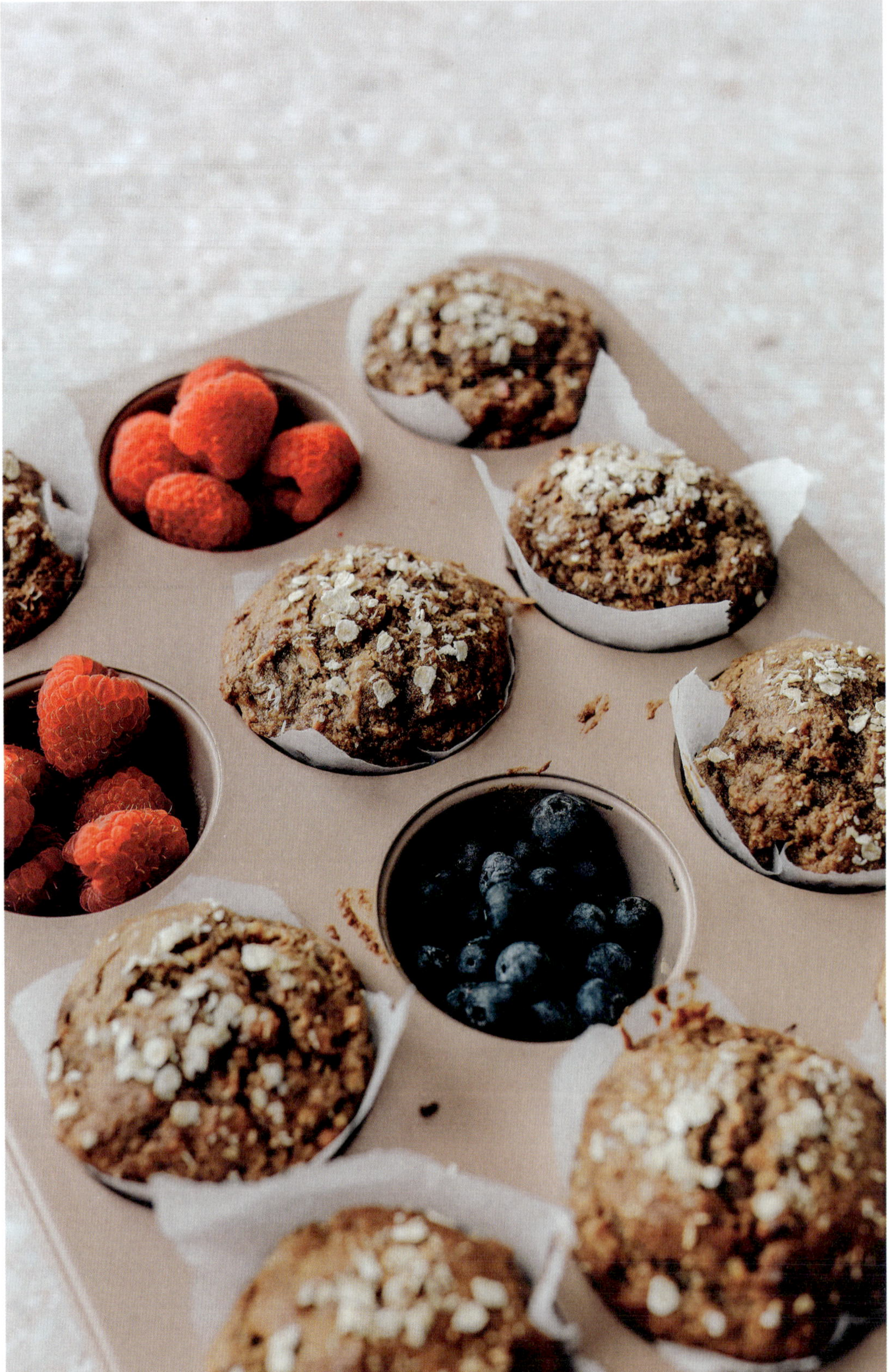

Banana Muffins

Serves 10 • 50 minutes

I love using banana muffins as a base then adding whatever filling my heart desires. As far as muffins go, these are super moist and spongy. Try adding coconut yoghurt to the top once they've cooled for a creamy texture.

4 ripe bananas
½ cup coconut sugar
2 Tbsp almond butter
¼ cup plant milk
1 tsp vanilla extract
1 Tbsp apple cider vinegar
½ cup spelt flour
  (or gluten-free flour)
1 cup almond meal
1 tsp baking powder
1 tsp baking soda
Pinch of salt

Preheat oven to 180°C and line 10 holes of a muffin tray with baking paper or grease lightly with coconut oil.

In a medium-sized bowl, mash bananas and add coconut sugar, almond butter, milk, vanilla and apple cider vinegar. Mix well to combine.

Add spelt flour, almond meal, baking powder, baking soda and salt and fold through to combine. Scoop the mixture into the prepared muffin tray. Bake in the oven for 25 minutes until golden and cooked through.

. . . .

Hot Tip: There are so many flavour combinations for these muffins. One of my favourites is 2 tablespoons peanut butter swirled through the batter with ½ cup strawberries for a PB&J flavour. You can also try adding 1 cup blueberries and top each muffin with a sprinkle of oats and cinnamon.

. . . .

GFO

Sweet Treats

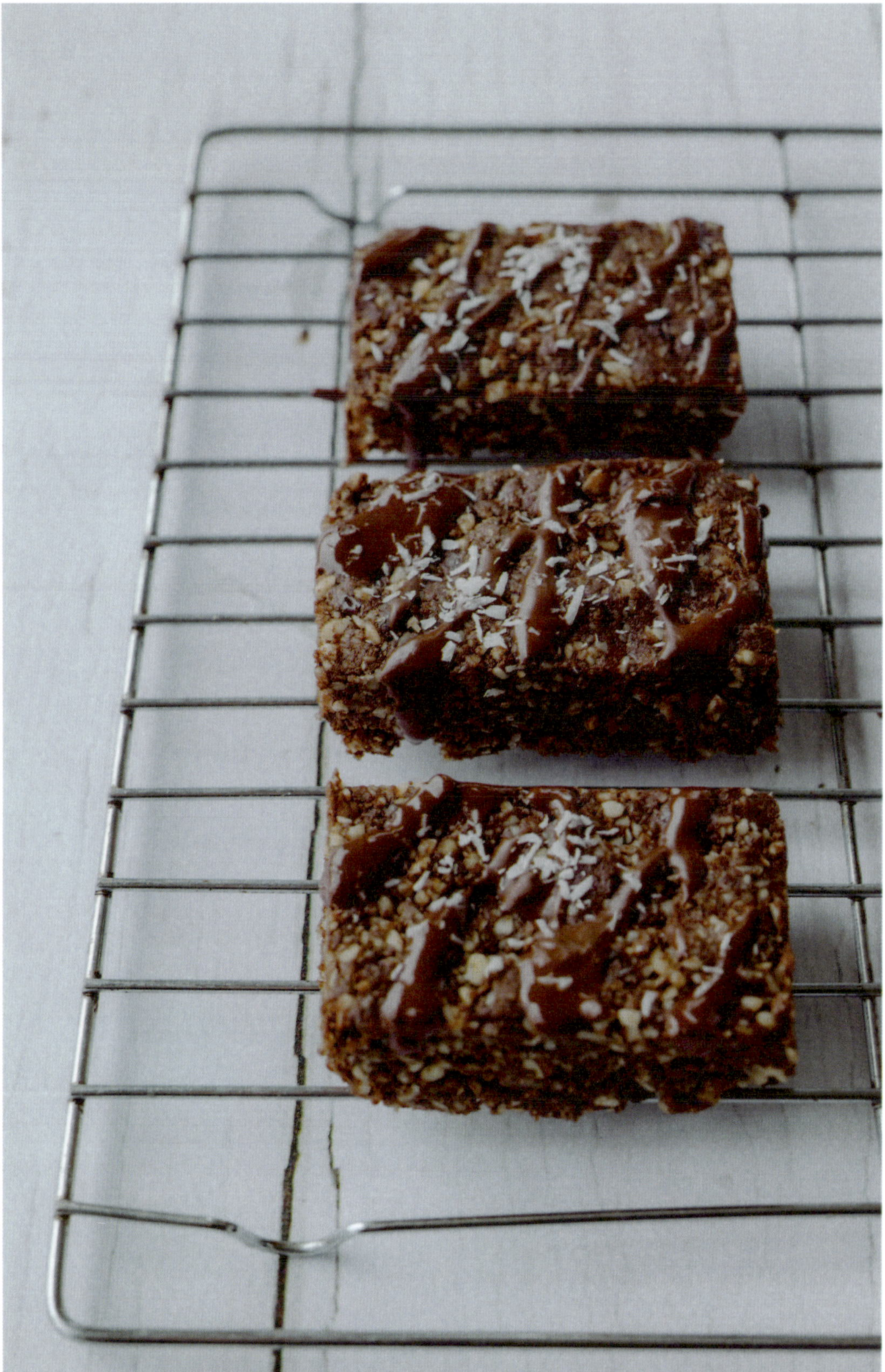

Rawtella Brownies

Makes 8 • 20 minutes + 2 hours for setting

I don't know a single person who doesn't love hazelnuts in desserts. This is a really delicious raw brownie made with only a few simple ingredients. I like to top the brownies with a drizzle of melted chocolate and coconut.

2 cups hazelnuts

1 cup almond meal

½ cup cacao powder

15 dates, pitted and soaked in boiling water for 10 minutes

½ cup coconut thread

⅓ cup maple syrup

Pinch of salt

40 g dark chocolate for coating, optional

1 Tbsp coconut oil

Line a 20 x 30 cm slice tin with baking paper.

Place all ingredients (excluding chocolate and coconut oil) in a high-powered blender or food processor. Blend until it forms a sticky paste.

Tip mixture into slice tin and press down firmly. Leave in the freezer to set for 2 hours.

Remove from freezer and slice the brownie into bars. Melt the chocolate with the coconut oil in a heatproof bowl over a pot of boiling water. Drizzle chocolate over brownies and store in the fridge for up to a week.

· · · · · · ·

Hot Tip: You can also store these in the freezer. Just remove them 10 minutes before eating to thaw.

· · · · · · ·

GF

Double Chocolate Chip Cookies

Serves 12 • 30 minutes

Soft and chewy on the inside with slightly crunchy edges — these cookies are smooth, rich, chocolatey and deeply satisfying. You might find it hard to stop eating them!

1 cup wholemeal flour or plain GF flour
⅓ cup cacao powder
1 tsp baking powder
¼ tsp baking soda
Pinch of salt
⅓ cup coconut oil, melted
¼ cup soy milk
½ tsp vanilla essence
¼ cup Apple Sauce (see page 212)
1 cup coconut sugar
½ cup dark chocolate chips

Preheat oven to 180°C and line a baking tray with baking paper.

In a large bowl, place flour, cacao, baking powder, baking soda and salt.

To a separate bowl, add coconut oil, soy milk, vanilla, apple sauce and coconut sugar. Blend together using a stick blender for around 30 seconds.

Add wet ingredients to the dry and fold through. Stir through chocolate chips then take around 1–2 tablespoons of cookie dough and roll into a ball. Place on baking tray. Repeat with remaining mixture.

Cook for 12–15 minutes. Leave to cool before eating.

GFO NF

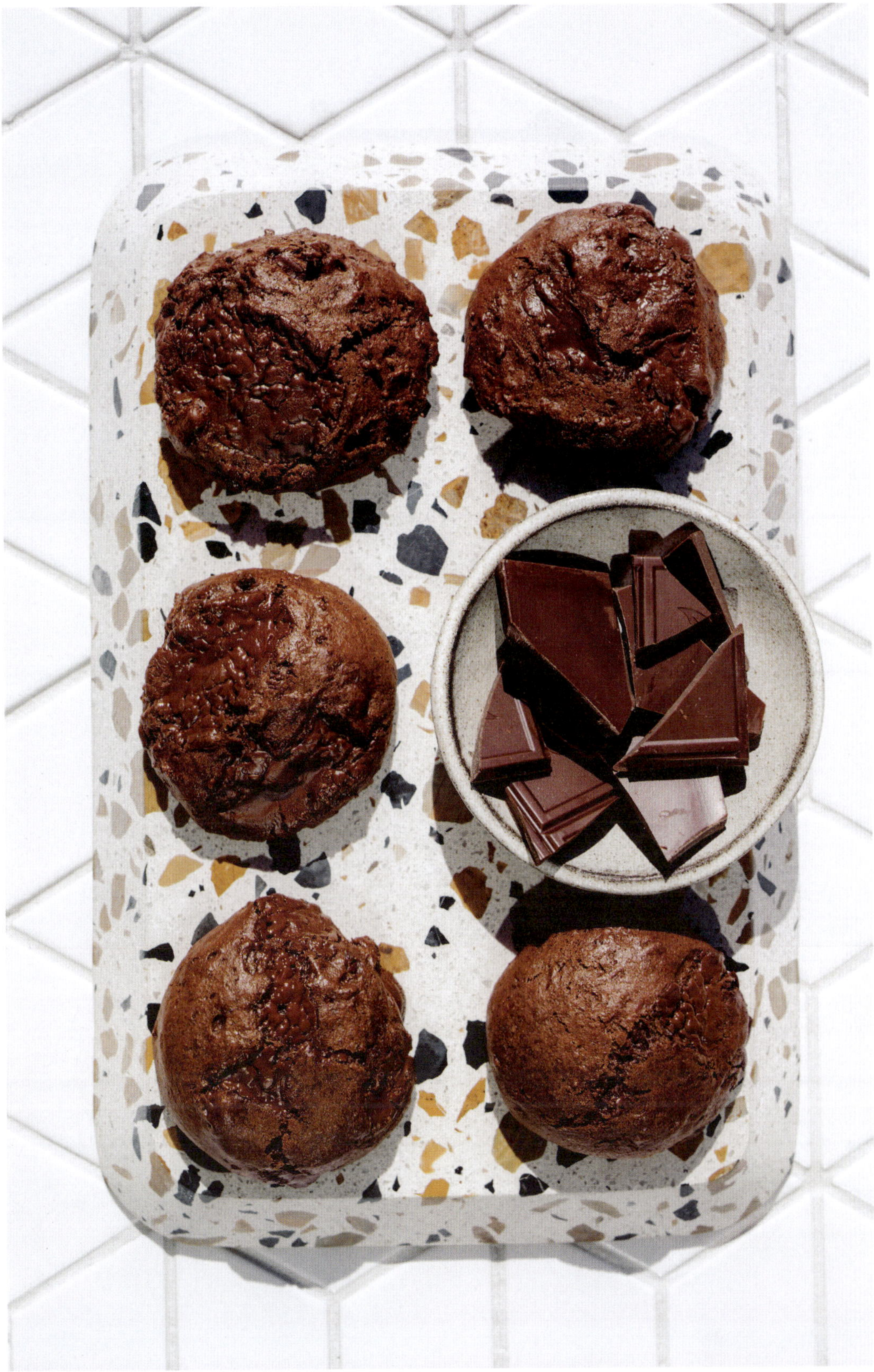

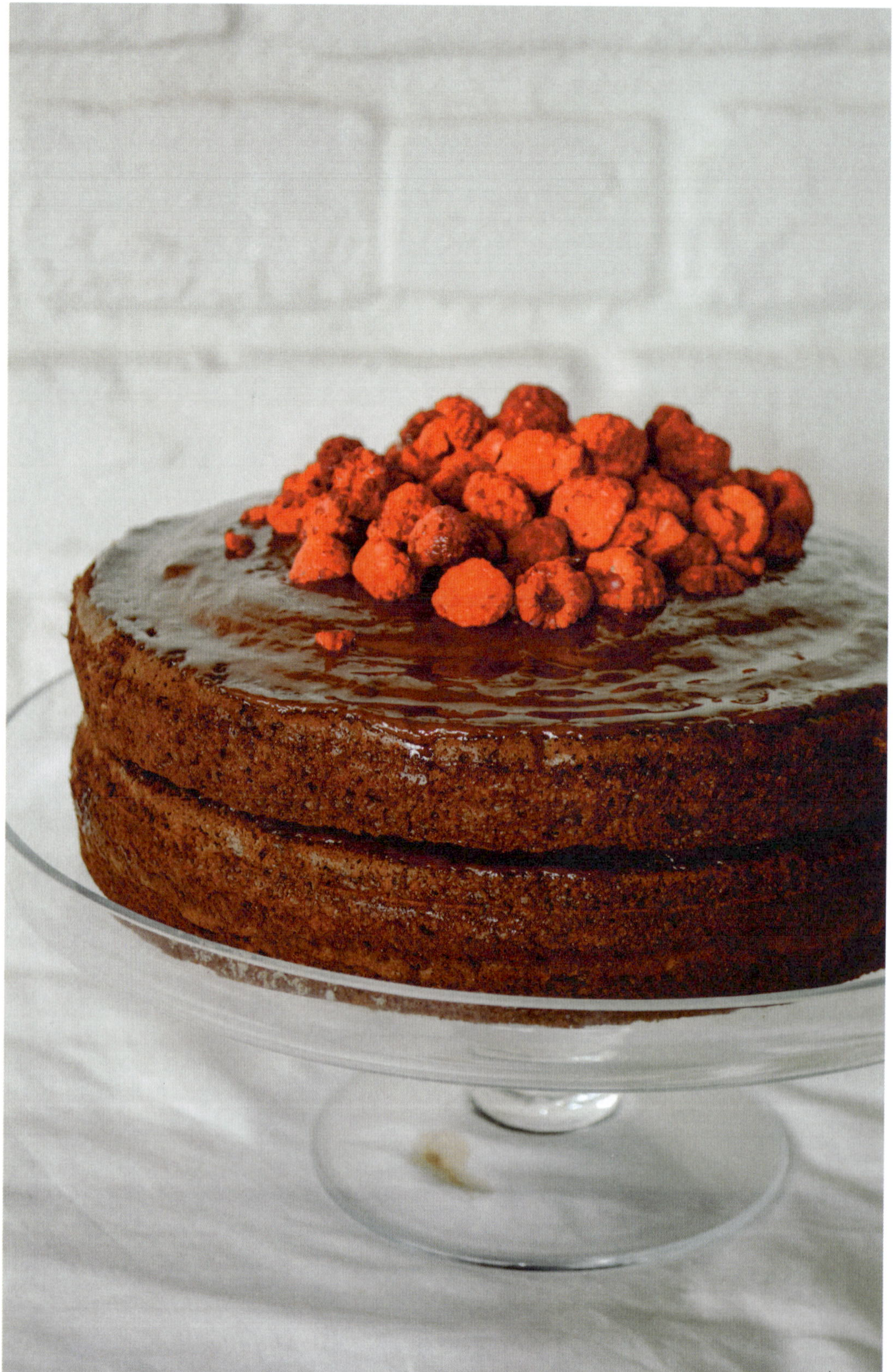

My All-time Favourite Chocolate Cake

Serves 10 • 45 minutes

Just in case you haven't realised by now, I'm a big chocolate fan. This cake is my go-to for birthdays and it always goes down an absolute treat. The coffee enhances the chocolate flavour beautifully! I love to top this cake with fresh or freeze-dried berries.

3 cups wholemeal flour (for GF, use 2 cups GF flour and 1 cup almond meal)
1½ tsp baking soda
½ tsp baking powder
Pinch of salt
1 tsp ground cinnamon
⅓ cup cacao powder
2 cups coconut sugar
½ cup coconut yoghurt
¼ cup Apple Sauce (see p. 212)
2 tsp vanilla extract
2 cups warm water
2 Tbsp apple cider vinegar
1 Tbsp coffee

. . . ingredients continued overleaf

Preheat oven to 180°C and line two 23 cm cake tins with baking paper or grease with a little coconut oil.

Into a large bowl, sift flour, baking soda, baking powder, salt, cinnamon and cacao powder. Then add coconut sugar and mix through to combine.

In a separate bowl, combine coconut yoghurt, apple sauce, vanilla, warm water, apple cider vinegar and coffee. Make sure coffee has fully dissolved, mixing well to combine.

Slowly add wet mixture to dry and mix through, making sure there are no lumps. The batter will foam up a bit due to combining baking soda and coffee.

. . . recipe continued overleaf

GFO NFO

Chocolate Ganache

100g dark chocolate

¼ cup coconut oil

¼ cup coconut milk

Fresh or freeze-dried berries to garnish, optional

Divide mixture evenly between cake tins and cook for around 25 minutes.

Remove from oven and set aside to cool.

To make chocolate ganache: Place the chocolate, coconut oil and coconut milk in a heatproof bowl set over a small pot of boiling water and stir until melted.

Put the bowl in the fridge for 20 minutes, giving it a stir every 5 minutes until it reaches a spreadable consistency.

Once ganache has thickened up and cake is cool, place one cake on a plate and spread half the ganache on top. Place the second cake on top and cover with the remaining chocolate ganache. Top with fresh or freeze-dried berries.

GFO NFO

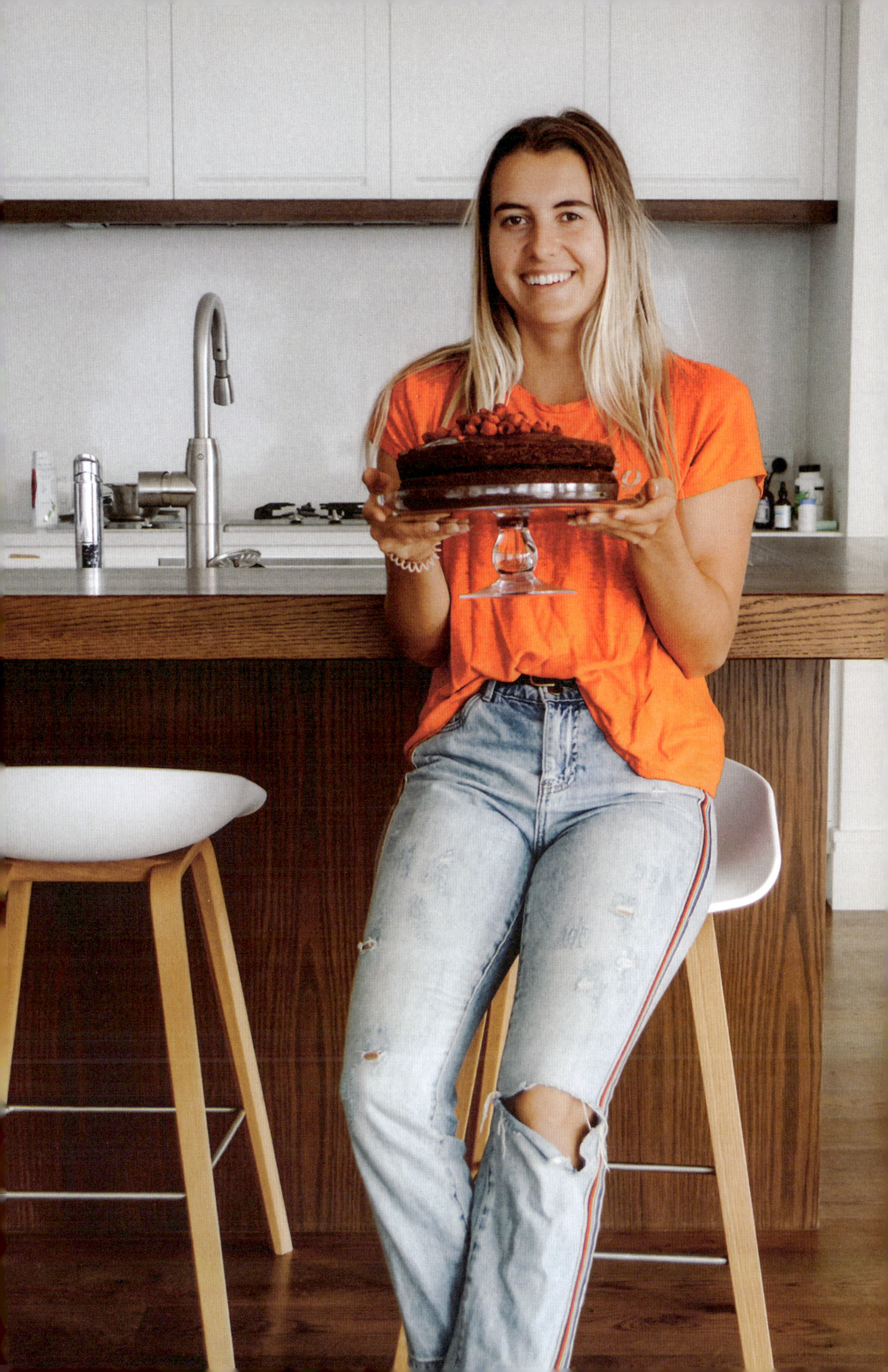

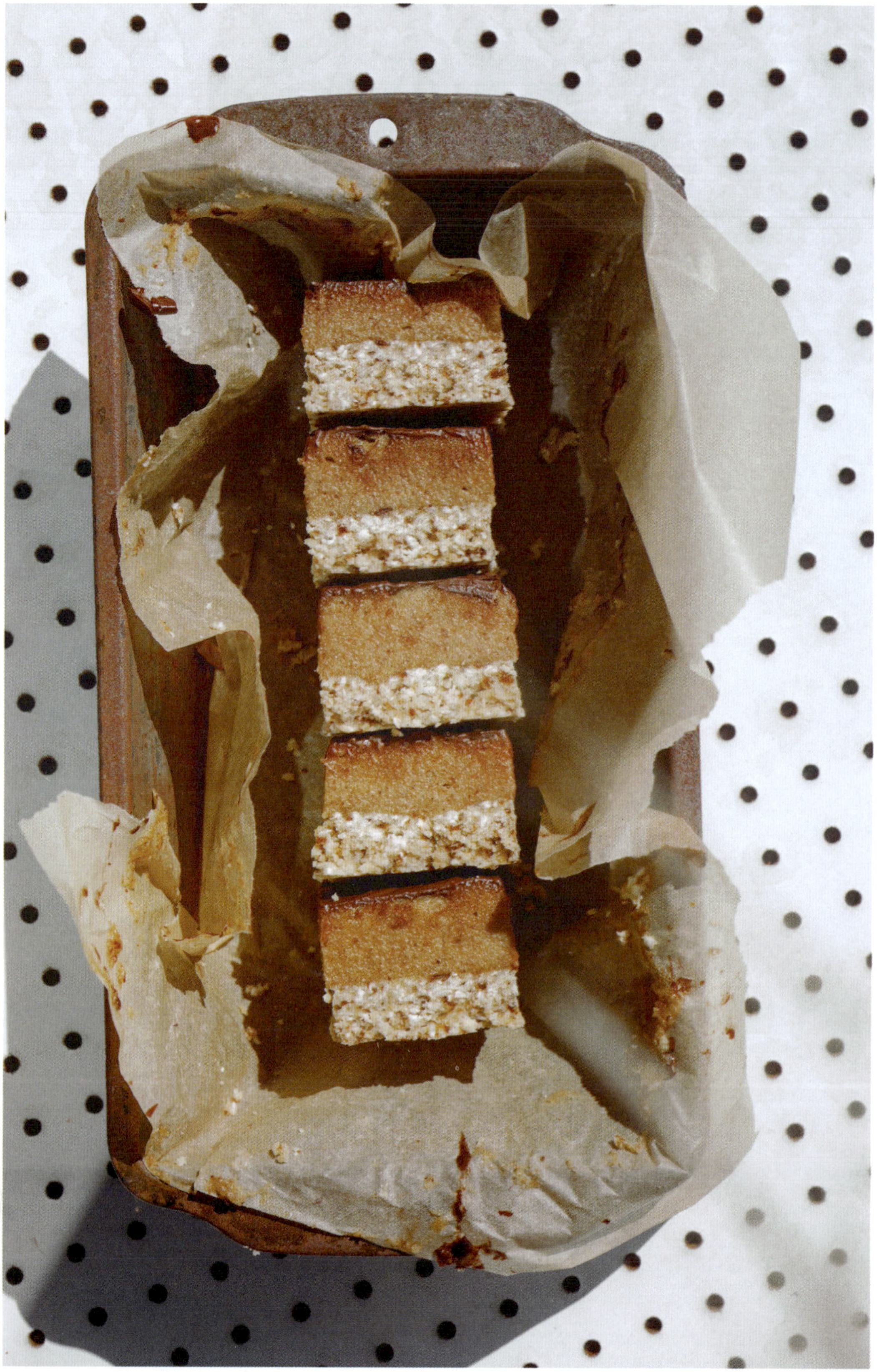

Miso Caramel Slice

Serves 12 • 60 minutes + 2 hours for setting

This may well be the best caramel slice you've ever eaten. The saltiness from the miso marries perfectly with the sweet dates. If you haven't eaten it all on the day, you can freeze it, too.

Base
1 cup gluten-free oats
1 cup desiccated coconut
10 fresh medjool dates, pitted
1 Tbsp vanilla extract
2 Tbsp melted coconut oil
1 cup buckwheat

Caramel
14 fresh medjool dates, pitted
½ cup boiling water
1 Tbsp miso paste
2 cups cashews, soaked in hot water for 20 minutes
2 Tbsp almond butter
¼ cup maple syrup

Topping
100 g dark chocolate
1 Tbsp coconut oil

For the base: Line a 20 x 30 cm slice tin with baking paper. Blend the oats, desiccated coconut, dates, vanilla and coconut oil in a food processor until fully blended. Add buckwheat and pulse until combined (don't blend too much as you want the buckwheat to retain some crunch).

Press base into lined tin, flattening with a spatula or your fingers. Place in freezer to set while making the caramel.

To make the caramel: Add dates and water to a pot over high heat and cook until all the water has evaporated. Place cooked dates in blender, along with miso paste, cashews, almond butter and maple syrup and blend until smooth. Pour over the base and place back in freezer.

To make the topping: Melt chocolate and coconut oil in a heatproof bowl set over a pot of boiling water. Once melted, pour over slice and place back in freezer for at least 2 hours. Slice into squares with a hot knife.

GF

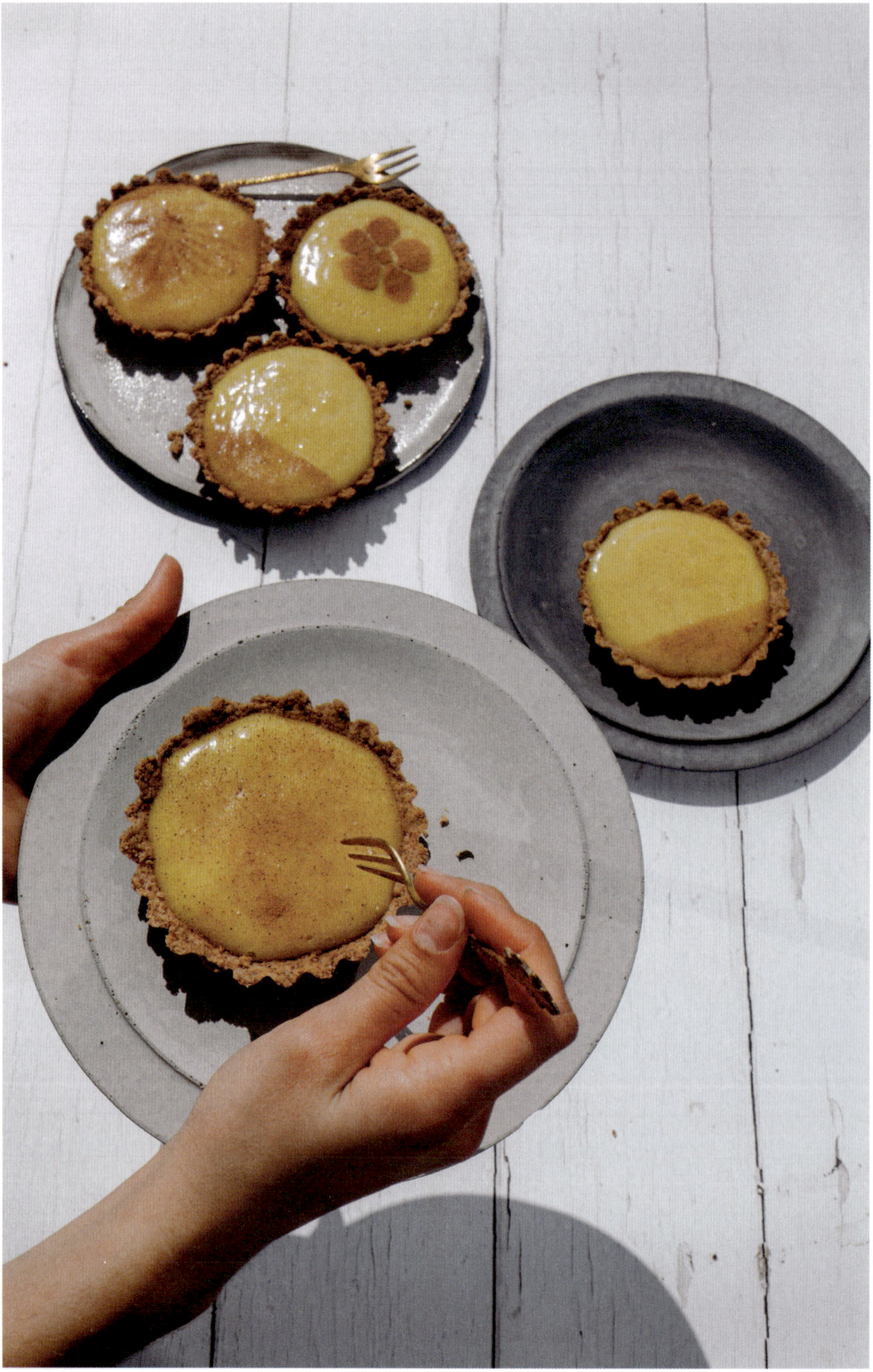

Custard Tarts

Makes 4–5 small tarts • 60 minutes

When we were kids, Dad would sometimes let us get a treat from the bakery, and custard tarts were my pick every time. When I first made them, none of my friends could believe they were vegan! The almond meal crust is perfect for any filling — you can also turn this into one large custard tart.

Bases

2 cups almond meal (use oat flour for NF)
½ cup tapioca flour
3 Tbsp coconut oil, not melted
2 Tbsp maple syrup

Custard

2 cups soy milk
2 Tbsp cornflour
½ cup rice malt syrup
1 tsp vanilla extract
Pinch of ground turmeric
1 tsp ground nutmeg

Hot Tip: If you don't want to make the full tart, the vanilla custard on its own makes a great accompaniment to a crumble or stewed fruit.

Preheat oven to 180°C and prepare five 10 cm tart cases by greasing them with a little coconut oil.

To make the bases: Place almond meal, flour, oil and maple syrup in a food processor and pulse until combined (when pressed the mixture should stick together). Tip mixture into tart cases and press down firmly. Bake in the oven for 20 minutes until golden. Once removed from the oven you may need to press down on the crust again if they've risen. Place the crust in the fridge to cool.

To make the custard: Place soy milk, cornflour, rice malt syrup, vanilla and turmeric in a medium-sized pot off the heat and whisk until smooth. Place pot over medium heat and stir regularly. As the mixture thickens, turn down the heat and continue to mix until it becomes a custard consistency (it will also thicken as it cools).

Divide the mixture evenly between tart cases. Sprinkle nutmeg on top. Place in fridge for 1–2 hours until set.

GF NFO

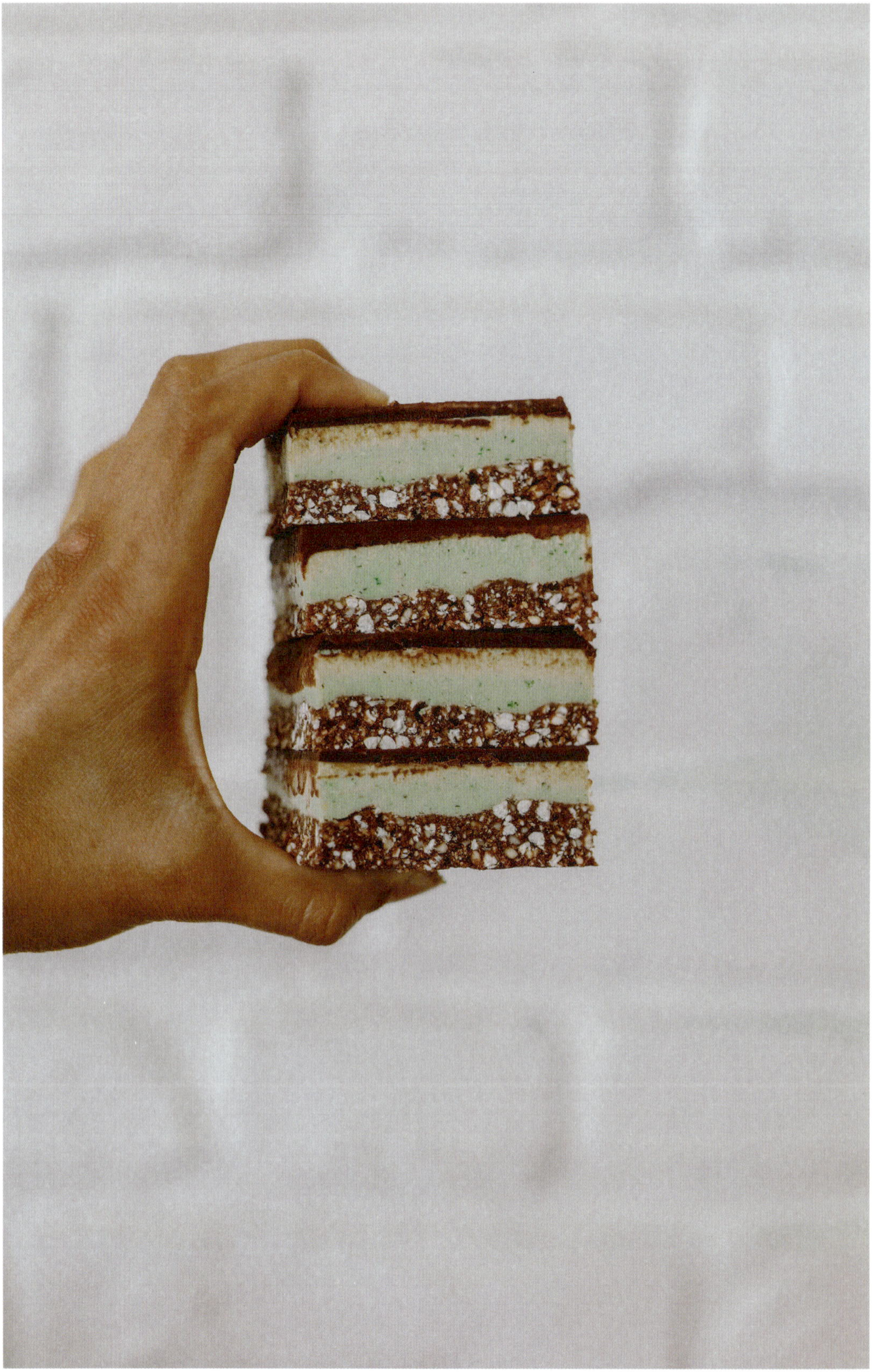

After Dinner Mint Slice

Serves 12 • 70 minutes + 2 hours for setting

Mint and chocolate could be one of the best combos out there. I decided to add mint leaves to the filling which adds a freshness that's unbeatable. The crunchy buckwheat in the base pairs perfectly with the soft chocolate topping.

Base

1 cup buckwheat

8 dates, pitted and soaked in hot water for 5 minutes

⅔ cup almonds

¼ cup cacao powder

2 Tbsp date syrup or honey

Filling

1 cup cashews, soaked in hot water for 20 minutes (or overnight)

½ cup thick coconut cream

Large handful of mint leaves

2 Tbsp maple syrup

¼ cup coconut oil, melted

½ tsp peppermint extract

Topping

100 g dark chocolate

2 Tbsp coconut oil

Line a 20–25 cm slice tin with baking paper.

To make the base: Combine buckwheat, dates, almonds, cacao and date syrup or honey in a food processor and blend until sticky, but still a little crunchy. Pour into slice tin and press down with wet fingers. Place in freezer to set.

To make the filling: Blend together the soaked cashews, coconut cream and mint to make a smooth paste. Add maple syrup, coconut oil and peppermint extract and blend until smooth. Spread on top of the base layer and return to freezer to set for 1 hour.

To make the topping: Melt chocolate with coconut oil in heatproof bowl set over a pot of boiling water. Once melted, pour chocolate over the filling. Return to freezer for 1 hour. Slice with a hot knife.

....

Hot Tip: To make the filling extra green, add some matcha powder. For an extra minty flavour, use mint-flavoured chocolate.

....

GF

Sweet Treats • 193

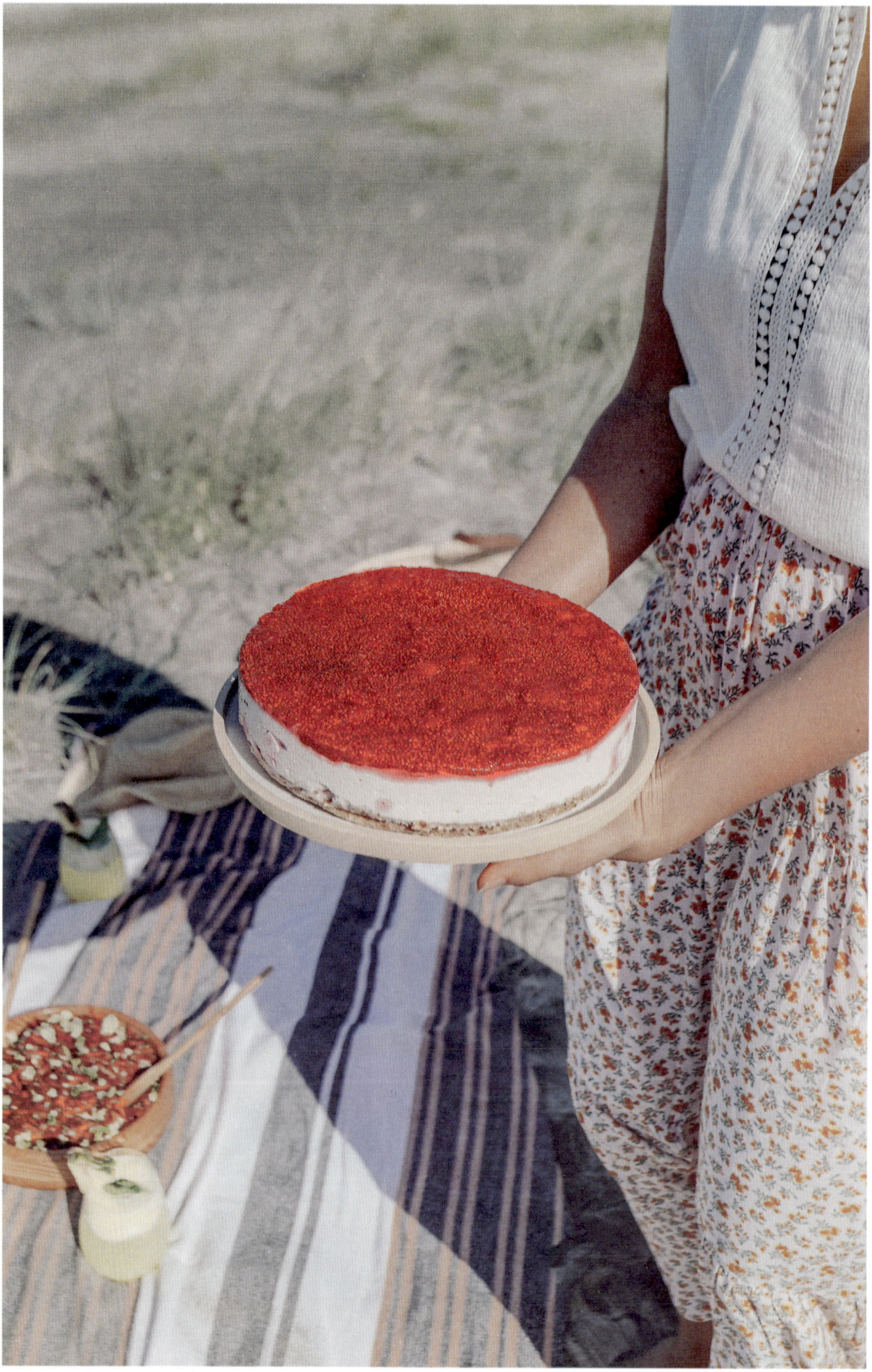

Raspberry and Lime Raw Cheesecake

Serves 6 • 40 minutes (plus setting time)

Made with wholesome, decadent ingredients, this cheesecake is the perfect treat for any occasion. It's super creamy, tangy and bound to impress. I like to make it the day before and leave it to set overnight.

Base
1 cup oat flour
1 cup almond meal
10 medjool dates, pitted and soaked in boiling water for 10 minutes

Filling
3 cups cashews, soaked overnight
½ cup maple syrup
Juice from 4 limes
1 cup coconut cream
1 cup fresh or frozen raspberries

Chia Jam
2 cups raspberries
2 Tbsp chia seeds
2 Tbsp water

Line a 23 cm springform cake tin with baking paper.

To make the base: Place all ingredients in food processor and pulse until combined. Tip into cake tin and press down firmly. Place in the freezer while you make the filling.

To make the filling: Add cashews, maple syrup, lime juice and coconut cream to a blender or food processor and blend on high speed until smooth. Add raspberries to the mixture and use a spoon to mix through. Pour on top of base layer and place in freezer to set.

To make the chia jam: Add all ingredients to a pot over a medium heat and stir until it reaches a jam-like consistency. Remove from heat and leave in the fridge to cool down.

Spread the cooled chia jam evenly on top of filling layer. Place in the fridge to set for at least 4 hours.

GF

Strawberries and Cream Ice Creams

Makes 4 ice creams • 10 minutes (and overnight)

I'll always remember making homemade ice creams and ice blocks growing up — strawberries and cream was always a favourite flavour of mine. Perfect for a hot summer's day!

2 frozen bananas
400 g fresh or frozen strawberries
2 Tbsp maple syrup
½ cup coconut milk
¼ cup melted coconut oil
80 g white chocolate, optional
Freeze-dried raspberry powder
Ice-pop sticks

In a food processor or high-powered blender, blend bananas, strawberries, maple syrup, coconut milk and coconut oil together until smooth. Pour into ice cream moulds, insert ice-pop sticks, and leave in the freezer to set overnight. If you don't have ice cream moulds, use an ice-cube tray or ramekins instead.

Melt the chocolate in a heatproof bowl set over a pot of boiling water. Coat ice cream blocks in the melted white chocolate, if wished, and sprinkle with freeze-dried raspberry powder. Store in the freezer for up to 7 days.

GF NF

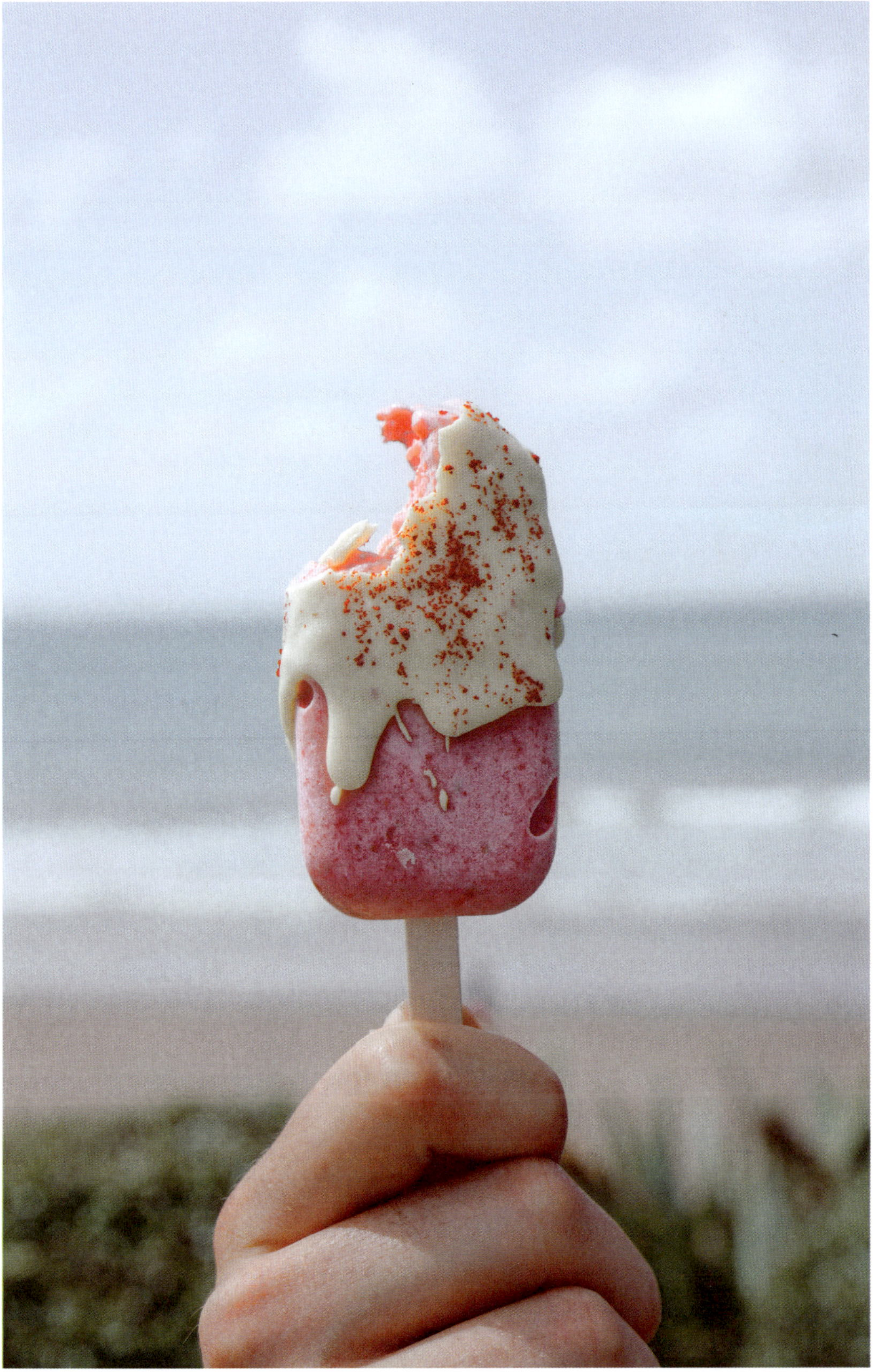

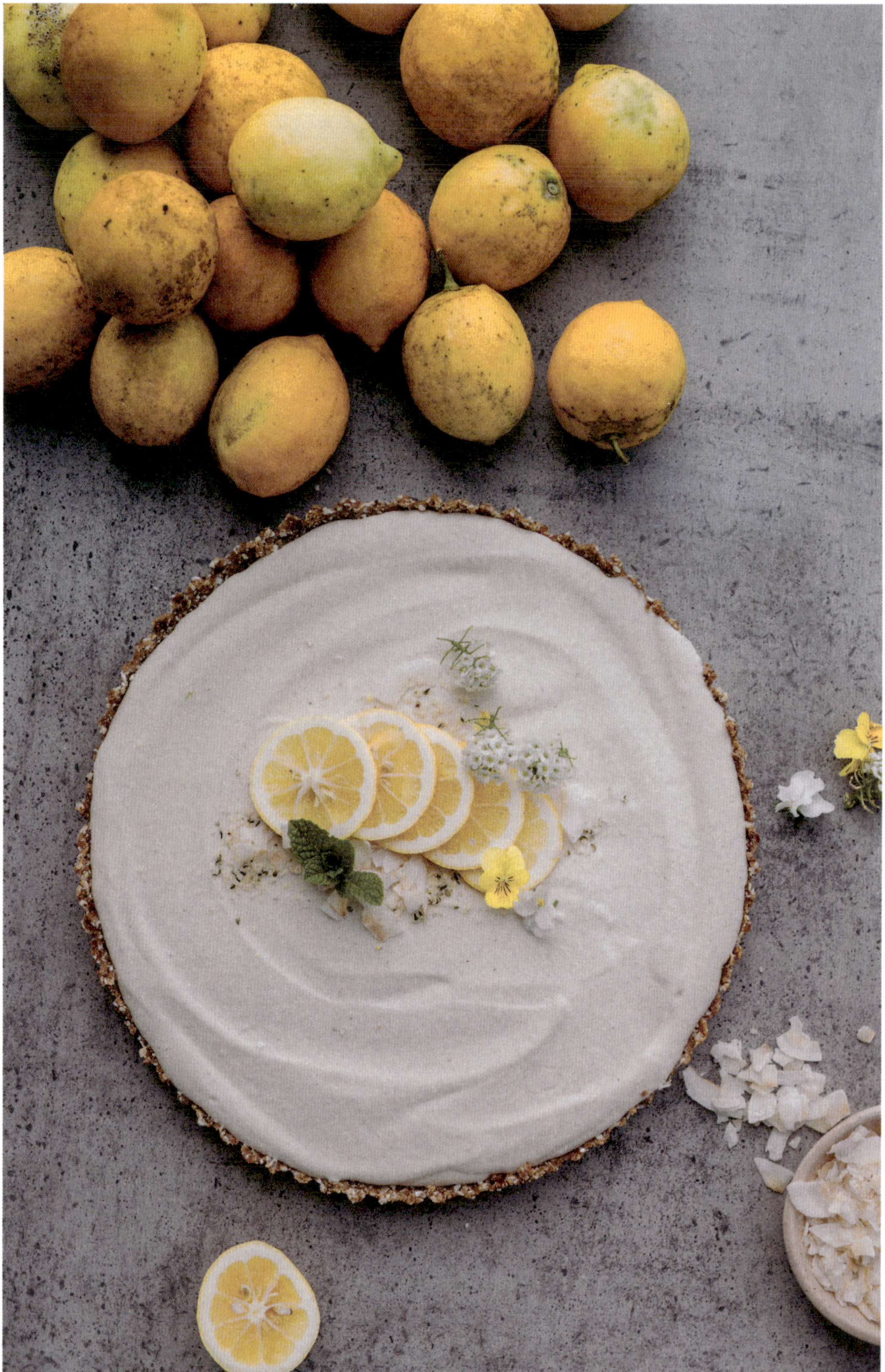

Raw Lemon and Coconut Pie

Serves 12 • 45 minutes (plus setting time)

My family and I absolutely love this raw dessert. The filling is so creamy it reminds me of a lemon cheesecake. This pie is a fantastic balance of sweet and zesty, countered beautifully by the sticky buckwheat crust.

Base
- 1 Tbsp coconut oil
- 1 cup ground almonds
- 1 cup desiccated coconut
- ½ cup buckwheat
- 12 medjool dates, pitted
- Zest from 3 small lemons
- 1 tsp vanilla essence
- 1 Tbsp maple syrup

Filling
- 2 cups cashews, soaked for at least 3 hours (or overnight)
- 1½ cups coconut yoghurt
- Zest from 2 lemons
- Juice from 3 lemons
- ¼ cup maple syrup
- 1 Tbsp melted coconut oil

To Serve
Sliced lemons, shredded coconut and edible flowers

Grease a 20–25 cm tart tin with coconut oil.

To make the base: Place all ingredients together in a food processor and blend to a semi-fine texture. Tip mixture into tart tin and press down firmly with your fingers, creating a raised edge around the edge of the tin. Place in the freezer to set while making the filling.

To make the filling: In a food processor or high-powered blender, blend all ingredients together until smooth. Pour on top of base and spread evenly. Place back in the freezer for at least 2 hours to set.

Remove pie from tart tin and serve topped with sliced lemons, shredded coconut and edible flowers.

GF

Sweet Treats

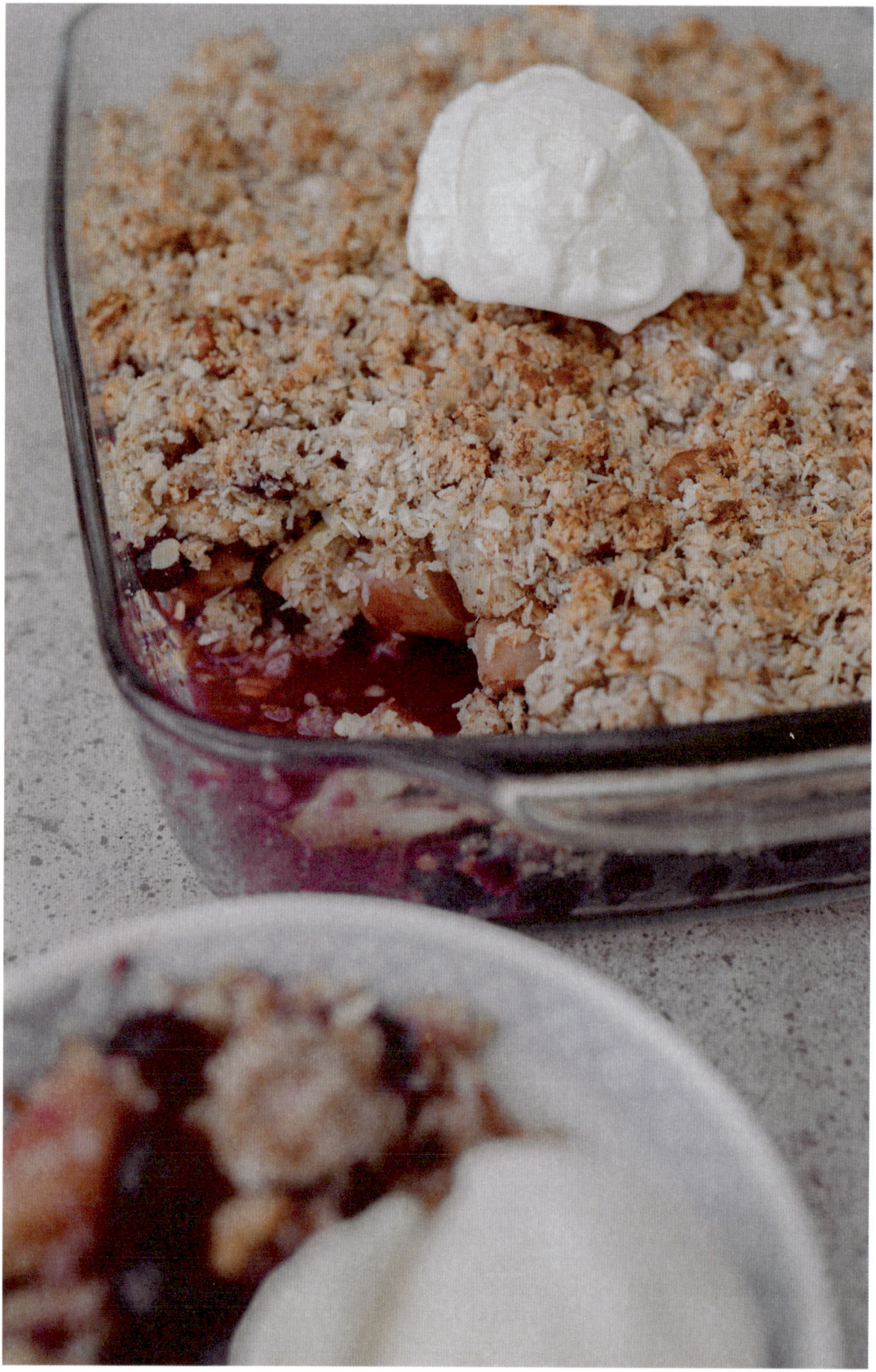

Maple-spiced Pecan and Pear Crumble

Serves 8 • 50 minutes

Crumbles were our staple dessert growing up — nothing beats the smell of a crumble in the oven. The ginger-spiced pears create a light yet intense flavour, which is why I pair them with something creamy like ice cream or yoghurt. I recommend preparing this before dinner then cooking it straight after your meal for a fresh-out-of-the-oven dessert.

Stewed Fruit

4 pears, peeled, cored and chopped
2 apples, peeled, cored and chopped
1 tsp ground ginger
1 tsp ground cinnamon
1 cup frozen blueberries

Crumble Topping

⅔ cup chopped pecans
1 tsp finely grated fresh ginger
1 tsp ground cinnamon
1 cup gluten-free rolled oats
1 cup desiccated coconut
1 cup almond meal
Pinch of salt
2 Tbsp olive oil
2 Tbsp plant milk
⅓ cup maple syrup

Preheat oven to 180°C.

To make the stewed fruit: Place pears and apples in a large pot with ginger, cinnamon and bit of water to stop from sticking. Cook for 10 minutes or until the fruit is relatively soft.

To make the crumble topping: Combine pecans, ginger, cinnamon, rolled oats, coconut, almond meal and salt in a large bowl, then slowly add olive oil, plant milk and maple syrup.

Place stewed fruit in a baking dish, along with frozen blueberries. Tip crumble mixture on top of the fruit and bake for 30 minutes, or until golden.

GF

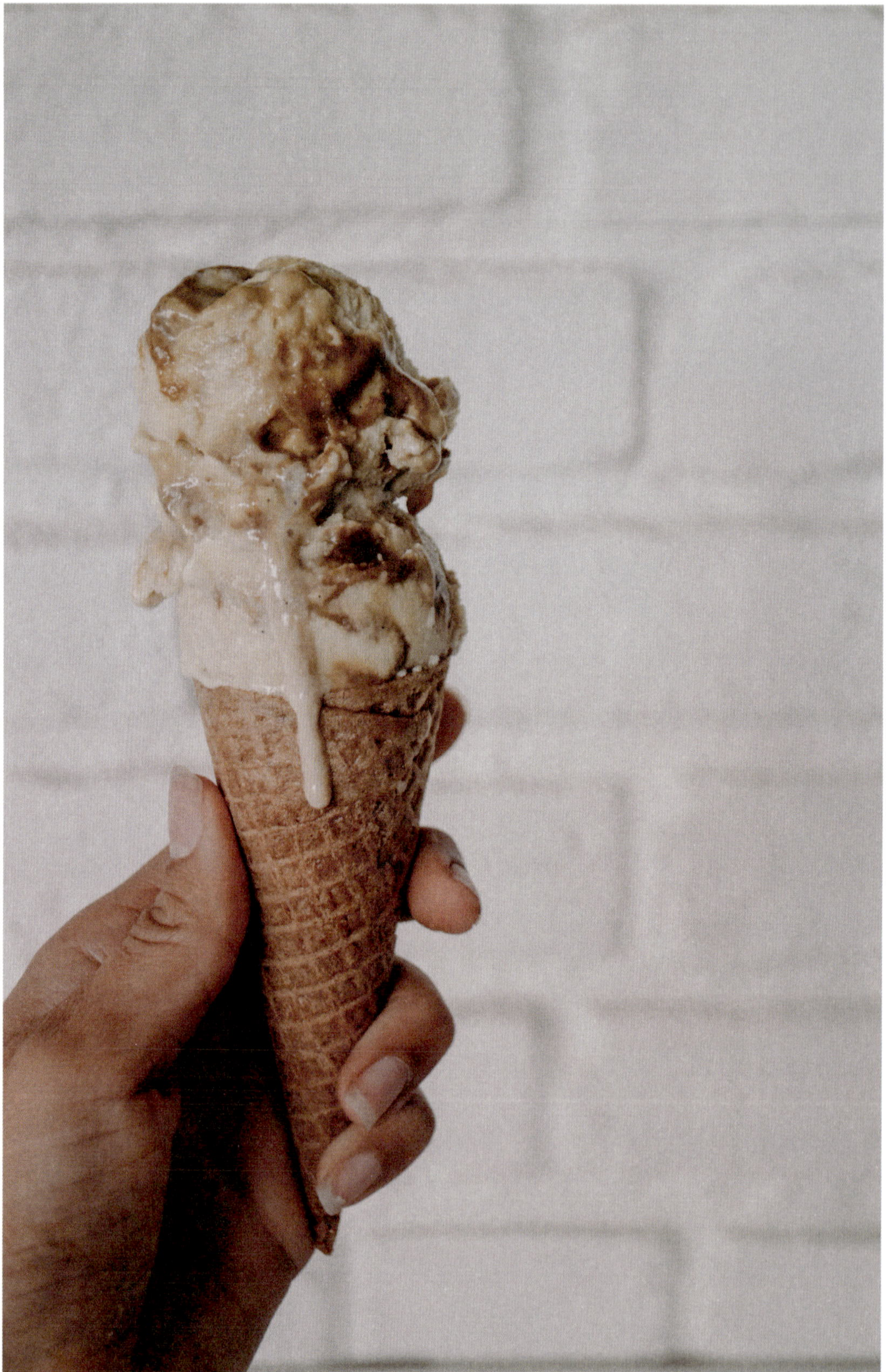

Coconut Salted Caramel Ice Cream

Serves 6 • 10 minutes (plus setting time)

If you've ever wanted to make your own ice cream, now is the time! This recipe delivers maximum taste with minimum effort. You can also make this a basic coconut ice cream by leaving out the caramel sauce. You'll need to start making this two days beforehand, as the coconut cream needs to sit in the fridge overnight.

1 cup cashews, soaked overnight

2 x 400 ml cans coconut cream, refrigerated overnight and water drained

⅓ cup maple syrup

1 tsp vanilla extract

3–4 Tbsp Salted Caramel Sauce (see p. 212)

In a high-powered blender, place cashews, coconut cream, maple syrup and vanilla, and blend until soft and creamy.

Pour mixture into a 20 x 10 cm loaf tin, adding around 3–4 tablespoons Salted Caramel Sauce and mixing through with a spoon. Leave in the freezer to set overnight. Remove ice cream from freezer 5–10 minutes before serving.

GF

Self-saucing Sticky Date Pudding

Serves 6 • 40 minutes

Sweet, sticky deliciousness is the best way to describe this pudding. Dates are an amazing source of vitamins and minerals, energy and fibre.

2 cups wholemeal flour (or 1 cup GF flour and ½ cup almond meal)
1 cup coconut sugar
1 tsp baking powder
1 tsp baking soda
1 tsp ground cinnamon
½ tsp ground nutmeg
Pinch of salt
1 cup soy milk
10 medjool dates, pitted and chopped

Sauce
½ cup boiling water
¼ cup coconut sugar
½ cup soy milk

To Serve
Dairy-free ice cream
Salted Caramel Sauce (see p. 212)

Preheat oven to 180°C.

Mix together flour, coconut sugar, baking powder, baking soda, cinnamon, nutmeg and salt in a large bowl. Add soy milk and dates and fold through mixture. Tip into a baking dish.

To make the sauce: In a small pot over high heat, combine water, coconut sugar and soy milk and stir until dissolved.

Pour sauce over the sticky date pudding mixture and do not stir it in. Bake in the oven for around 20 minutes or until bubbling on the edges.

Serve with dairy-free ice cream and Salted Caramel Sauce.

GFO NFO

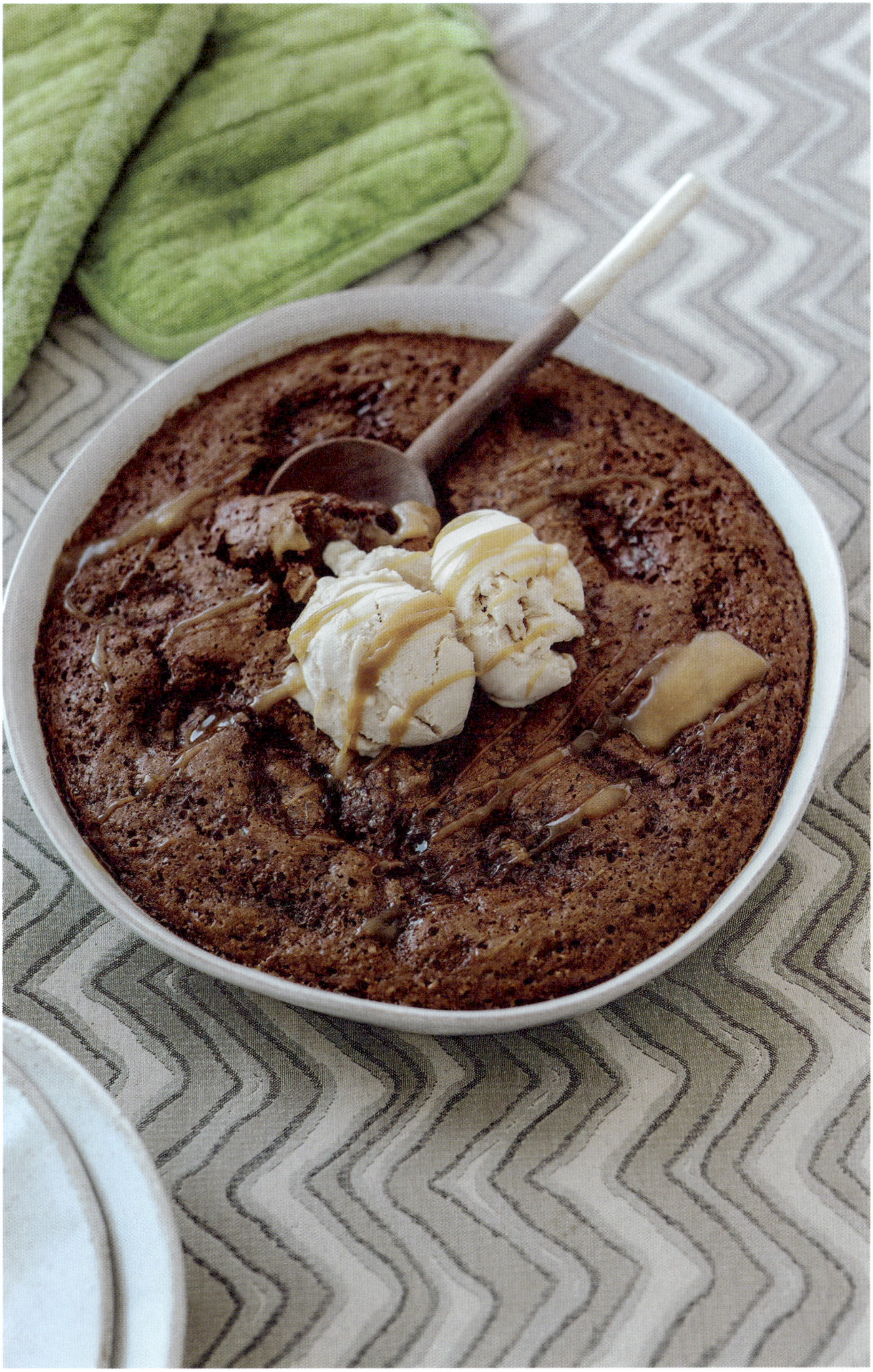

Probiotic Mango Bites

Makes 12 bites • 10 minutes (and 2 hours)

These are homemade ice blocks, but in perfect bite-sized pieces. I adore mangos and this recipe is great for an afternoon summer snack.

2 cups frozen or fresh mango

300 ml plant-based yoghurt (I use coconut)

¼ tsp vanilla paste

Blend all ingredients together in a high-powered blender. Pour into small silicon moulds or ice-cube trays and freeze for at least 2 hours.

. . . .

Hot Tip: You can freeze these for up to a week — be sure to thaw 5 minutes before eating.

. . . .

GF NF

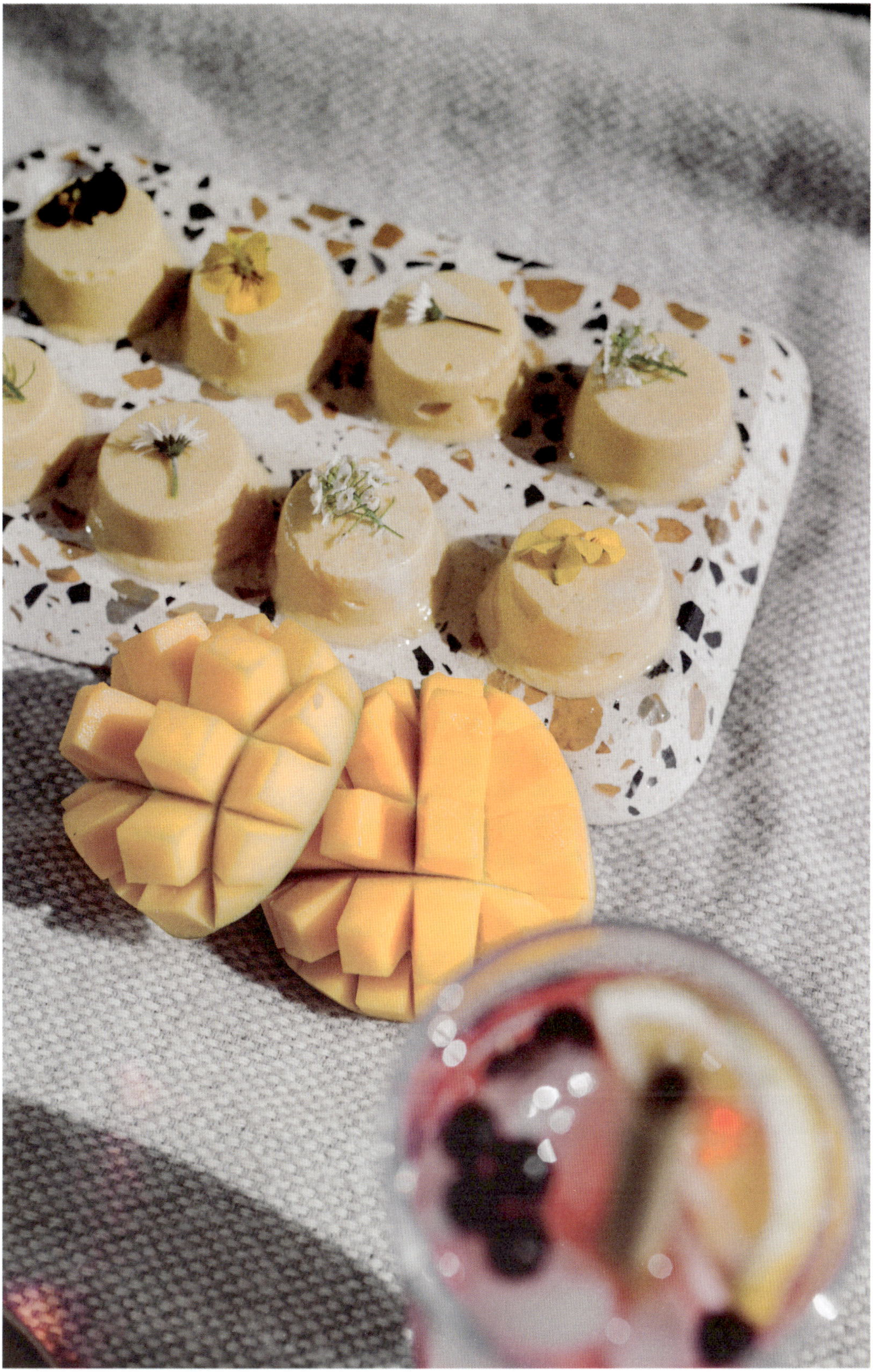

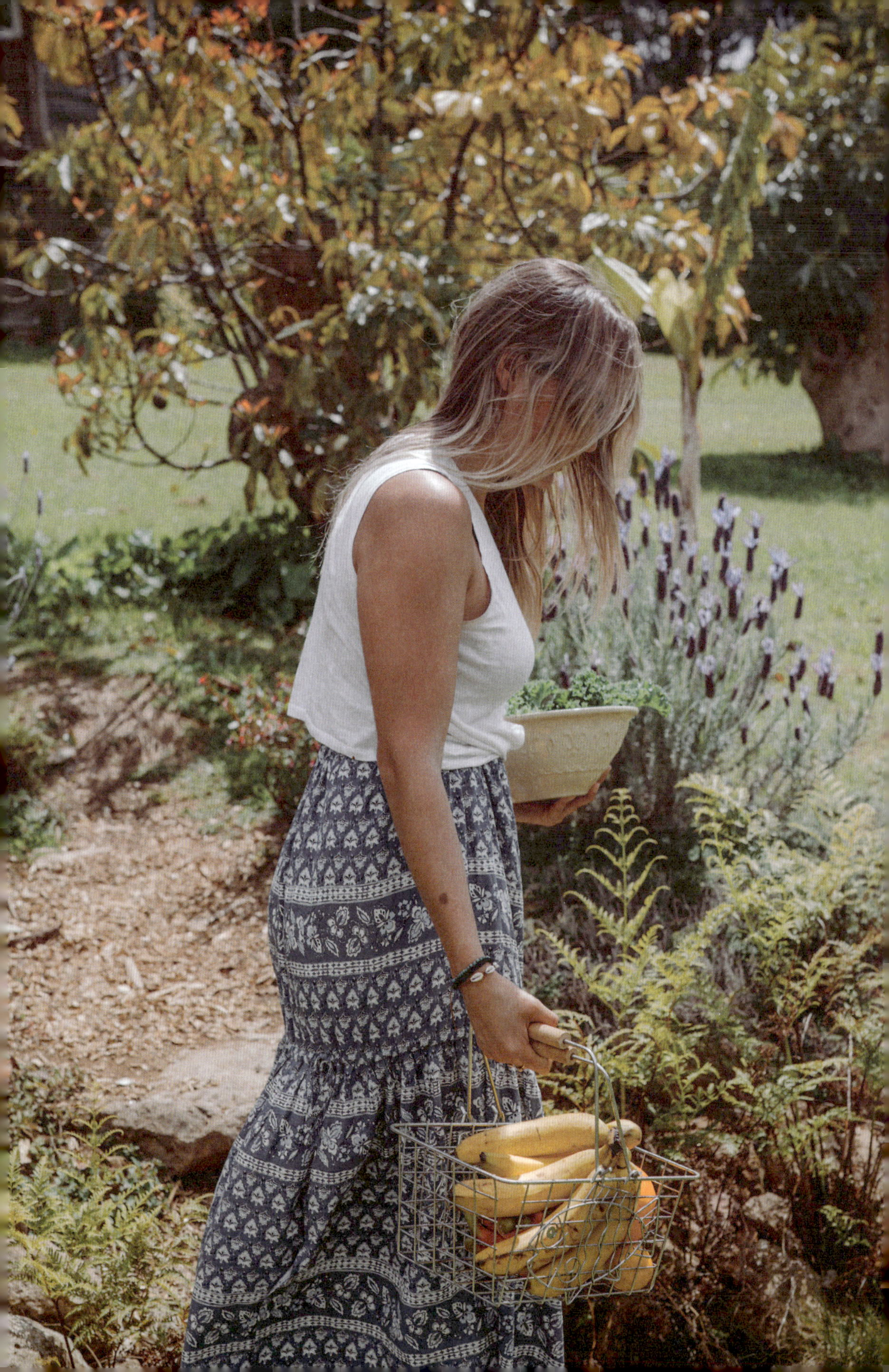

Back to Basics

In this section you'll find a bunch of my favourite sauces, salad dressings and nut butters to add to those delicious meals you'll be making. I honestly think a good basic can transform a dish from average to extraordinary, and once you start making them from scratch you'll never go back to store-bought. The Salted Caramel Sauce (see p. 212) is a personal favourite of mine as well as the Satay Sauce (see p. 214).

Salad Dressings

Everyone knows how to make a salad but making a dressing changes the salad game completely. It will take your bowl of vegetables to the next level.

GF, NF

Lemon Caesar
2 Tbsp vegan aioli
1 Tbsp nutritional yeast
1 tsp wholegrain mustard
1 clove garlic, crushed
Juice from ½ lemon
1 tsp maple syrup

Lemon Mustard
1 Tbsp olive oil
1 Tbsp wholegrain mustard
Juice from 1 lemon

ACV Tahini
1 Tbsp tahini
1 Tbsp apple cider vinegar
1 tsp honey or maple syrup

Sweet and Tangy
1 clove garlic, crushed
1 Tbsp rice wine vinegar
1 Tbsp maple syrup
Juice from ½ lemon
½ chilli, deseeded and finely chopped

Ginger Sesame
1 Tbsp rice wine vinegar
1 Tbsp soy sauce or tamari
1 Tbsp sesame oil
1 clove garlic, crushed
1 cm fresh ginger, grated
1 tsp maple syrup
1 chilli, deseeded and finely chopped

Curried Yoghurt
¼ cup coconut yoghurt
1 Tbsp curry powder
1 tsp cumin
Juice from ½ lemon

Honey Mustard
1 Tbsp Dijon mustard
1 tsp honey
1 Tbsp apple cider vinegar
1 Tbsp olive oil
Pinch of salt

Balsamic Vinaigrette
1 Tbsp balsamic vinegar
1 tsp maple syrup
1 Tbsp olive oil
1 clove garlic, crushed
Pinch of salt

Choose your dressing. Place all ingredients in a small bowl and whisk to combine. Alternatively, place ingredients in a jar with a lid and shake to combine.

Sunflower Parmesan

5 minutes • GF, NF

¾ cup sunflower seeds
¼ cup nutritional yeast
½ tsp salt
½ tsp garlic powder

Add all ingredients to a food processor and process to make fine crumbs. Store in the fridge for up to 3 weeks.

Homemade Dukkah

10 minutes • GF

⅓ cup almonds
⅓ cup hazelnuts
2 Tbsp sesame seeds
1 Tbsp ground coriander
1 Tbsp ground cumin
¼ tsp salt

Add all ingredients to a food processor and pulse to a fine crumb. Store in the fridge in an airtight container for up to 6 months.

Homemade Curry Powder

20 minutes • GF, NF

1 Tbsp coriander seeds
2 Tbsp fennel seeds
2 Tbsp cumin seeds
20 curry leaves
1 Tbsp fenugreek seeds
1 tsp ground turmeric

Place all ingredients (excluding turmeric) into a pan and dry roast over low heat for around 10 minutes.

Remove from pan and add turmeric. Leave to cool then, using a mortar and pestle or food processor, grind spices until they become a fine powder. This mix can last up to a year so I like to make it in big batches.

Rich Chocolate Sauce

10 minutes • GF

2 Tbsp peanut butter
⅓ cup cacao powder
⅓ cup maple syrup
¾ cup plant milk
Pinch of salt

Combine all ingredients in a pot over medium heat. Cook for 5 minutes using a whisk to mix well.

Use immediately or store in the fridge for up to 5 days. The sauce will thicken as it cools, so if you want a thinner sauce add a little extra plant milk.

Apple Sauce

20 minutes • GF, NF

4 apples, peeled, cored and sliced into cubes
⅓ cup water
Juice from ½ lemon
½ tsp ground cinnamon

Combine all ingredients in a pot over medium heat. Cover and cook for around 15 minutes until soft. Remove from heat and pour into a blender. Blend until smooth. Use immediately or store in the fridge for up to 7 days.

Salted Caramel Sauce

30 minutes • GF, NF

400 g can coconut milk
¾ cup coconut sugar
Pinch of salt

Add coconut milk, coconut sugar and salt to a pot and stir constantly over medium heat. Once mixture begins to boil, turn down heat and continue to stir until it thickens (this can take up to 30 minutes).

Salted Maca Almond Butter

25 minutes • GF

1 cup almonds
1 cup macadamia nuts
¼ tsp salt

Preheat oven to 180°C. Line a baking tray with baking paper. Spread nuts over baking tray and bake for 5–10 minutes until fragrant.

Place nuts and salt in a food processor or blender and blend until smooth. This will take 5–10 minutes. You'll have to stop a few times to scrape down the sides with a spatula. You'll know it's ready when the oils start to be released.

Berry Chia Jam

15 minutes • GF, NF

2 cups frozen raspberries
¼ cup water
2 Tbsp chia seeds
1 Tbsp maple syrup

Combine raspberries and water in a small pot over a medium heat and cook, stirring, for 5 minutes. Add chia seeds and maple syrup and stir over heat until thick (this should only take a couple of minutes).

Keep in an airtight container in the fridge for up to 2 weeks.

Harissa Paste

5 minutes • GF, NF

10 medium-sized dried red chillies
3 cloves garlic
Pinch of salt
1 tsp ground cumin
1 Tbsp olive oil
Juice from ½ lemon

Cover dried chillies with boiling water and leave to soak for 1 hour. Strain chillies and roughly chop.

Smash chillies in a mortar and pestle, along with the rest of the ingredients, until a thick paste has formed. You can also use a food processor if you're short on time.

Satay Sauce

5 minutes • GF

3 Tbsp peanut butter
½ cup coconut milk
1 tsp maple syrup
2 cm piece of ginger
1 Tbsp soy sauce or tamari
1 clove garlic

Add all of the ingredients to a blender and blend until smooth. Use immediately or store in the fridge for up to 5 days.

Cashew Aioli

20 minutes • GF

1 cup cashews, soaked in boiling water for 20 minutes (or overnight)
⅓ cup cold water
1 Tbsp apple cider vinegar
¼ tsp Dijon mustard
½ tsp salt

Add all ingredients to a blender and blend until smooth. Place in an airtight container and keep in the fridge for up to a week.

Plant Milk 3 Ways

20 minutes • GF, NF

Hemp Milk

1 cup hemp seeds

3 cups water

1 Tbsp vanilla extract

1 date, pitted

Put all ingredients in a blender and blend for 1 minute until smooth.

Pour liquid into a bottle and use within 3 days.

Oat Milk

1 cup gluten-free rolled oats

3 cups cold water

2 dates, pitted

Put all ingredients in a blender and blend for 1 minute until smooth. Transfer the milk into a nut bag, or you can use a muslin cloth by placing it over a bowl with the edges over the sides, and pour in the mixture. Gather up the corners, twist and lift the bag to release the liquid.

Pour the liquid into a bottle and use within 3 days.

Sunflower Seed Milk

1 cup sunflower seeds, soaked overnight

3 cups water

2 dates, pitted

Place all ingredients in a blender and blend on high until smooth. Transfer the milk into a nut bag, or use a muslin cloth by placing it over a bowl with the edges over the sides, and pour in the mixture. Gather up the corners, twist and lift the bag to release the liquid.

Pour the liquid into a bottle and use within 3 days.

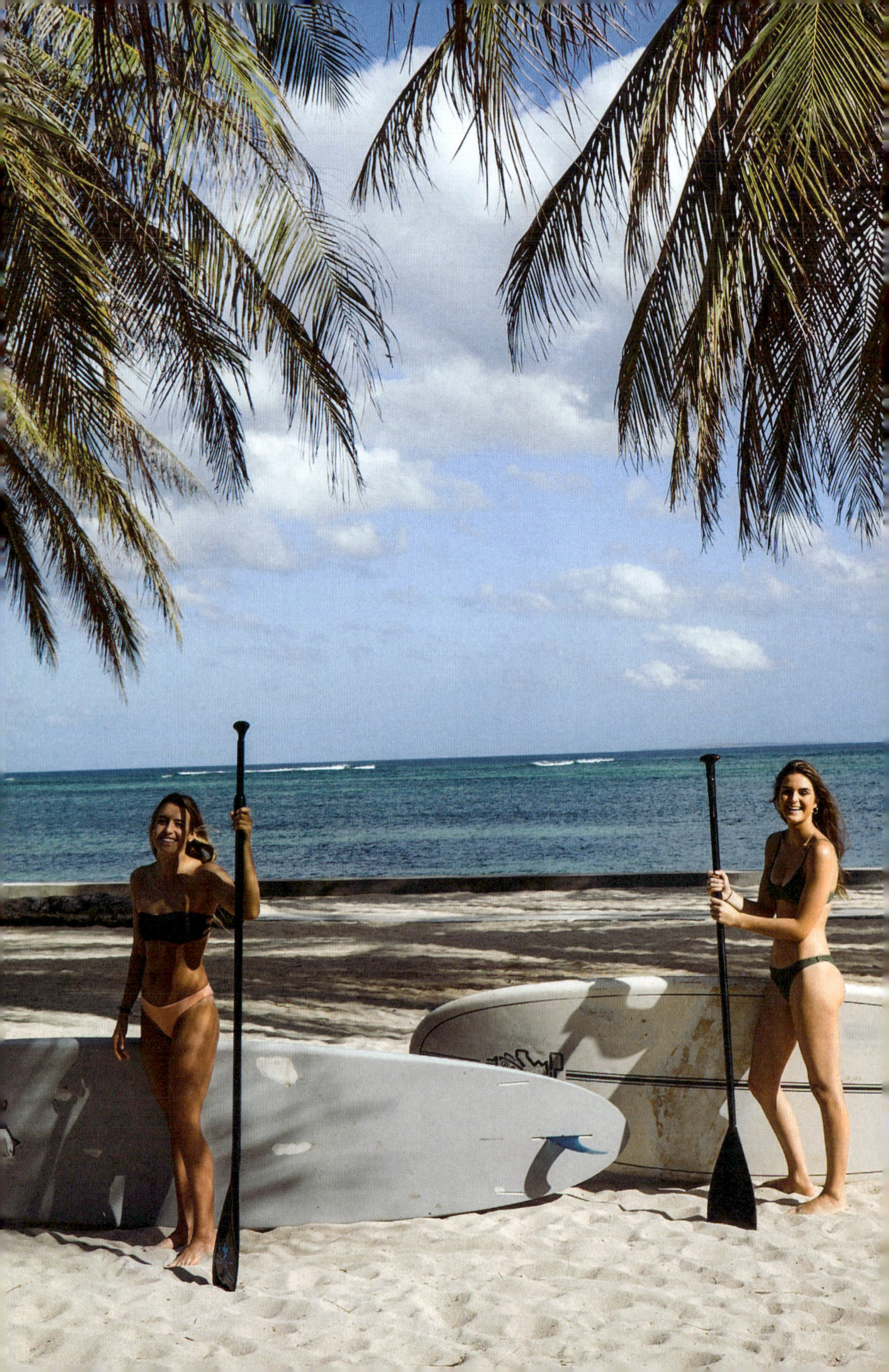

Conversion Charts

DRY MEASURES

METRIC	IMPERIAL
15 g	½ oz
30 g	1 oz
60 g	2 oz
100 g	3½ oz
125 g	4 oz
185 g	6 oz (¼ lb)
200 g	7 oz
250 g	8 oz (½ lb)
375 g	12 oz
500 g	16 oz (1 lb)

LENGTH

METRIC	IMPERIAL
2.5 cm	1 in
5 cm	2 in
10 cm	4 in
13 cm	5 in
15 cm	6 in
20 cm	8 in
23 cm	9 in
25 cm	10 in
30 cm	12 in

LIQUID MEASURES

CUPS	METRIC	IMPERIAL
¼ cup	60 ml	2 fl oz
⅓ cup	80 ml	2½ fl oz
½ cup	125 ml	4 fl oz
⅔ cup	160 ml	5 fl oz
¾ cup	180 ml	6 fl oz
1 cup	250 ml	8 fl oz
2 cups	500 ml	16 fl oz
4 cups	1 ltr	32 fl oz

SPOONS

¼ tsp	1.25 ml
½ tsp	2.5 ml
1 tsp	5 ml
2 tsps	10 ml
1 Tbsp	15 ml

OVEN CONVERSIONS

CELSIUS	FAHRENHEIT
120°C	250°F
150°C	300°F
160°C	320°F
180°C	350°F
200°C	400°F
220°C	428°F

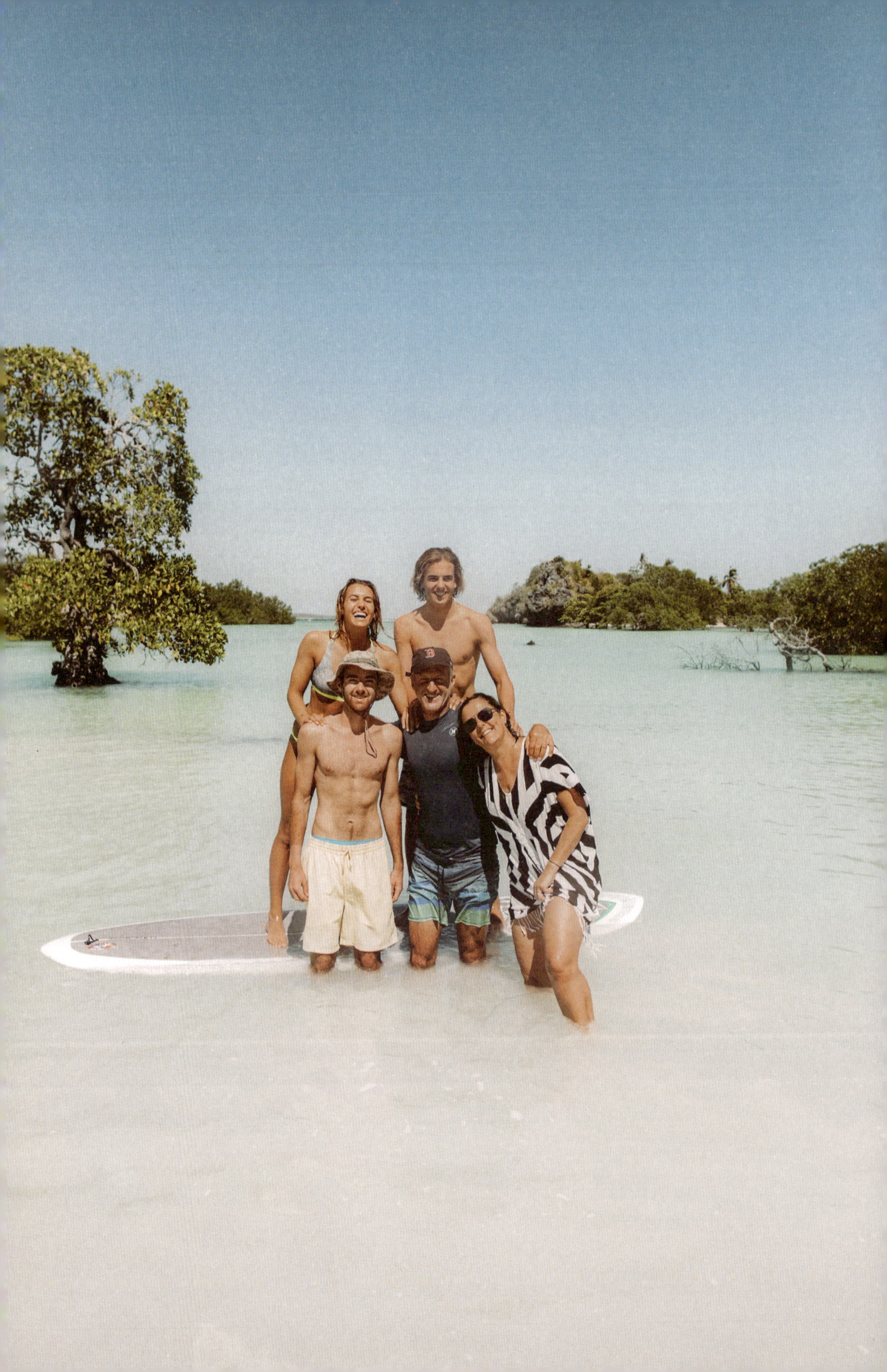

Thank Yous

Firstly, I want to thank my amazing parents, Rose and Paul, for inspiring me every single day to live a life full of fun and adventure. You've always pushed me to pursue my passion and I feel so lucky to have you as my parents. A big thank you to my brothers Leroy and Max — I genuinely couldn't have asked for a better family!

To Andrew, my best bud and one pretty incredible human. Thank you for inspiring me to be the best version of myself I can be. I love how you push and encourage me, not only in work but in my day-to-day life (as well as being the best taste tester I know!). I couldn't have completed this project without you.

Thank you to my nana, who has been my number one supporter my entire life, and to my whole extended family, who I love to death. I could genuinely write a whole book about how much you guys mean to me, and whether you know it or not you have contributed to this book in so many ways.

Thank you to Brad and Sarah for letting me photograph your extraordinary garden as well as Ora and Itay for not only growing the tastiest mushrooms but also letting me photograph them.

To Jane from Fume Ceramics, who makes such beautiful plates and bowls — thank you for allowing me to photograph my recipes with them.

Thank you to my wonderful friends, including Courtney and Sarah, who have been great recipe testers/impromptu photographers, and Poppy, who is always keen to lend a hand as well as being one of my biggest supporters from day one. To the rest of my friends (I could list so many people), thank you for all of the adventures we've shared over the years. I wouldn't be the person I am today without you all.

To my publishers — the team at Batemans — you guys believed in me from the very beginning and I can't thank you enough for helping me bring this book to the world.

To all of the Healthy Kelsi followers, I started my social media account because I wanted to share my love for food with people. I can't thank you enough for being on this journey with me.

Index

After Dinner Mint Slice 193
aioli
    Cashew Aioli 214
almond
    Salted Maca Almond Butter 213
Andrew's 'World-Famous' Pesto Pasta 127
Apple Sauce 212
apricot
    Apricot and Coconut Rice Bubble Muesli 25
avocado
    Easy Guacamole 84
    Simple Kale and Avocado Salad 108

Balsamic Vinaigrette 210
banana
    Banana Bread Bliss Balls 88
    Banana Muffins 179
    Banoffee Pie Rawnola Bowl 31
    Chocolate Banana Shake 69
Béchamel Sauce 165
beetroot
    Beetroot Dahl with Coconut Raita 162
    Beetroot Falafels 100
    Beetroot Hummus 81
    Berry and Beet Smoothie Bowl 67
Berry Chia Jam 213
Bircher Bowls 26
biscuits
    Date and Carrot Cookies 95
    Double Chocolate Chip Cookies 182
    Walnut Breakfast Cookies 59
black bean
    Wholesome Black Bean Nachos with Cashew Cheese 175
Bliss Balls 88
blueberry
    Blueberry and Coconut Bliss Balls 88
    Blueberry Muffin Smoothie 73
    Blueberry Vinaigrette 117
    Lemon and Blueberry Fizz 64
    Lemon Blueberry Loaf 97
bread
    Herbed Pizza Dough 141
    Omega-3 French Toast 46
    Seedy Buckwheat Bread 44
Breakfast Tacos 53
Broccoli Slaw 107
brownies
    Rawtella Brownies 181

buckwheat
    Buckwheat Crêpes with Creamy Mushrooms 51
    Seedy Buckwheat Bread 44
burger
    Carrot and Quinoa Burgers 137
Burrito Bowls 123
butter
    Salted Maca Almond Butter 213
butterbeans
    Miso Mushrooms with Kale and Butterbeans 113
butternut
    Quick and Easy Butternut Risotto 143

cake
    Gingerbread Breakfast Loaf 43
    Lemon Blueberry Loaf 97
    My All-time Favourite Chocolate Cake 185
caramel
    Coconut Salted Caramel Ice Cream 203
    Miso Caramel Slice 189
    Salted Caramel Sauce 212
carrot
    Carrot and Quinoa Burgers 137
    Date and Carrot Cookies 95
cashew
    Cashew Aioli 214
    Cashew Cheese 175
    Cashew Dressing 121
cauliflower
    Roast Cauliflower, Chickpeas and Mango 118
Cheese Sauce 172
cheesecake
    Raspberry and Lime Raw Cheesecake 195
Cheesy Potato Gratin 172
cherry
    Spiced Cherry Biryani 159
chia
    Berry Chia Jam 213
    Sunrise Chia Pudding 39
chickpea
    Chickpea Herb Crackers 87
    Hummus 3 Ways 81
    Roast Cauliflower, Chickpeas and Mango 118
Chimichurri Sauce 103
chocolate
    Chocolate Banana Shake 69
    Chocolate Ganache 186
    Chocolate Orange Bliss Balls 88
    Chocolate Porridge 29

Double Chocolate Chip Cookies 182
My All-time Favourite Chocolate Cake 185
Oat and Nutty Chocolate Granola 33
Plant-powered Hot Chocolate 75
Rich Chocolate Sauce 212
Chunky Monkey Granola Bars 93
Chunky Monkey Smoothie Bowl 67
coconut
    Apricot and Coconut Rice Bubble Muesli 25
    Blueberry and Coconut Bliss Balls 88
    Coconut Cakes 37
    Coconut Corn Fritters 49
    Coconut Raita 162
    Coconut Salted Caramel Ice Cream 203
    Raw Lemon and Coconut Pie 199
cookies *see* biscuits
corn
    Coconut Corn Fritters 49
crackers
    Chickpea Herb Crackers 87
Creamy Garlic Hummus 81
Creamy Mushroom Pot Pie 171
crêpes *see* pancakes
curry
    Beetroot Dahl with Coconut Raita 162
    Curried Eggplant 157
    Curried Potato Salad with Cashew Dressing 121
    Curried Yoghurt Dressing 210
    Homemade Curry Powder 211
    Spicy Massaman Curry 169
    Sri Lankan Pulled Jackfruit Curry 149
Custard Tarts 191

date
    Date and Carrot Cookies 95
    Self-saucing Sticky Date Pudding 204
Double Chocolate Chip Cookies 182
dressing
    ACV Tahini 210
    Balsamic Vinaigrette 210
    Blueberry Vinaigrette 117
    Cashew Dressing 121
    Curried Yoghurt 210
    Ginger Sesame 210
    Honey Mustard 210
    Lemon Caesar 210
    Lemon Mustard 210
    Sweet and Tangy 210
drinks *see also* smoothies
    Frozen Pineapple Mojitos 71
    Golden Hour Latte 75
    Lemon and Blueberry Fizz 64
    Orange Spritzer 64
    Plant-powered Hot Chocolate 75
    Smashed Strawberry Margarita 77

dukkah
    Homemade Dukkah 211

Easy Guacamole 84
eggplant
    Curried Eggplant 157
    Soba Noodles and Sticky Eggplant 128

falafel
    Beetroot Falafels 100
Fig and Tahini Bliss Balls 88
fritters
    Coconut Corn Fritters 49
Frozen Pineapple Mojitos 71
Fruit Salad Breakfast Muffins 34

garlic
    Creamy Garlic Hummus 81
ginger
    Ginger Sesame Dressing 210
    Gingerbread Breakfast Loaf 43
granola *see* muesli
Green Goodness 63
guacamole
    Easy Guacamole 84

Harissa Paste 214
hazelnut
    Strawberry and Hazelnut Salad 117
hemp
    Hemp Milk 215
    Hempy Tropical Vibes 63
Herbed Pizza Dough 141
Homemade Curry Powder 211
Homemade Dukkah 211
Honey Mustard Dressing 210
Hummus 3 Ways 81

ice cream
    Coconut Salted Caramel Ice Cream 203
    Strawberries and Cream Ice Creams 196

jackfruit
    Sri Lankan Pulled Jackfruit Curry 149
jam
    Berry Chia Jam 213

kale
    Miso Mushrooms with Kale and Butterbeans 113
    Simple Kale and Avocado Salad 108
Kumara Pancake Stack 54

lemon
    Lemon and Blueberry Fizz 64
    Lemon Blueberry Loaf 97

Lemon Caesar Dressing 210
Lemon Mustard Dressing 210
Raw Lemon and Coconut Pie 199
lentil
    Lentil Bolognese 165
lime
    Raspberry and Lime Raw Cheesecake 195

macadamia
    Salted Maca Almond Butter 213
mango
    Probiotic Mango Bites 206
    Roast Cauliflower, Chickpeas and Mango 118
Maple-spiced Pecan and Pear Crumble 201
Marinara Sauce 154
Meatless Meatballs with a Marinara Sauce 153
milk
    Plant Milk 3 Ways 215
milkshake *see* smoothies
mint
    After Dinner Mint Slice 193
miso
    Miso Caramel Slice 189
    Miso Mushrooms with Kale and Butterbeans 113
    Miso Smashed Pumpkin with Herbs and Dukkah 57
muesli
    Apricot and Coconut Rice Bubble Muesli 25
    Banoffee Pie Rawnola Bowl 31
    Bircher Bowls 26
    Chunky Monkey Granola Bars 93
    Oat and Nutty Chocolate Granola 33
muffin
    Banana Muffins 179
    Fruit Salad Breakfast Muffins 34
Mum's Brown Rice Salad 131
mushroom
    Buckwheat Crêpes with Creamy Mushrooms 51
    Creamy Mushroom Pot Pie 171
    Miso Mushrooms with Kale and Butterbeans 113
    Mushroom Arancini Balls with Homemade Parmesan 98
mustard
    Honey Mustard Dressing 210
My All-time Favourite Chocolate Cake 185

nacho
    Wholesome Black Bean Nachos with Cashew Cheese 175
Nasi Goreng 161
noodle
    Peanut Butter Noodle Stir-fry 138
    Soba Noodles and Sticky Eggplant 128
    Vegetable Pho 135

oat
    Banoffee Pie Rawnola Bowl 31
    Bircher Bowls 26
    Chocolate Porridge 29
    Oat and Nutty Chocolate Granola 33
    Oat Milk 215
Omega-3 French Toast 46
orange
    Chocolate Orange Bliss Balls 88
    Orange Spritzer 64

pancake
    Buckwheat Crêpes with Creamy Mushrooms 51
    Coconut Cakes 37
    Kumara Pancake Stack 54
papaya
    Rainbow Papaya Salad 111
parmesan
    Sunflower Parmesan 211
pasta
    Andrew's 'World-Famous' Pesto Pasta 127
    Meatless Meatballs with a Marinara Sauce 153
    Rainbow Lasagne 165
peanut butter
    Peanut Butter Freak Shake 73
    Peanut Butter Noodle Stir-fry 138
pear
    Maple-spiced Pecan and Pear Crumble 201
pesto
    Andrew's 'World-Famous' Pesto Pasta 127
    Pumpkin Seed Pesto 83
pho
    Vegetable Pho 135
pie
    Creamy Mushroom Pot Pie 171
    Raw Lemon and Coconut Pie 199
pineapple
    Frozen Pineapple Mojitos 71
    Pineapple Fried Rice 144
pizza *see* bread
Plant Milk 3 Ways 215
Plant-powered Hot Chocolate 75
poke
    Tofu Poke Bowl 114
potato
    Cheesy Potato Gratin 172
    Curried Potato Salad with Cashew Dressing 121
Probiotic Mango Bites 206
pudding
    Maple-spiced Pecan and Pear Crumble 201
    Self-saucing Sticky Date Pudding 204
    Sunrise Chia Pudding 39
pumpkin
    Miso Smashed Pumpkin with Herbs and Dukkah 57

Roast Pumpkin Hummus 81
Pumpkin Seed Pesto 83

Quick and Easy Butternut Risotto 143
quinoa
    Carrot and Quinoa Burgers 137

Rainbow Lasagne 165
Rainbow Papaya Salad 111
raita
    Coconut Raita 162
Raspberry and Lime Raw Cheesecake 195
Raw Lemon and Coconut Pie 199
Rawtella Brownies 181
rice
    Mum's Brown Rice Salad 131
    Mushroom Arancini Balls with Homemade
        Parmesan 98
    Nasi Goreng 161
    Pineapple Fried Rice 144
    Quick and Easy Butternut Risotto 143
    Spiced Cherry Biryani 159
Rich Chocolate Sauce 212
Roast Cauliflower, Chickpeas and Mango 118
Roast Pumpkin Hummus 81

salad
    Andrew's 'World-Famous' Pesto Pasta 127
    Broccoli Slaw 107
    Burrito Bowls 123
    Curried Potato Salad with Cashew Dressing 121
    Miso Mushrooms with kale and Butterbeans 113
    Mum's Brown Rice Salad 131
    Rainbow Papaya Salad 111
    Roast Cauliflower, Chickpeas and Mango 118
    Simple Kale and Avocado Salad 108
    Soba Noodles and Sticky Eggplant 128
    Strawberry and Hazelnut Salad 117
    Tofu Poke Bowl 114
Salad Dressings 210
Salted Caramel Blend 69
Salted Maca Almond Butter 213
sauce
    Apple Sauce 212
    Béchamel Sauce 165
    Cheese Sauce 172
    Chimichurri Sauce 103
    Coconut Raita 162
    Marinara Sauce 154
    Rich Chocolate Sauce 212
    Salted Caramel Sauce 212
    Satay Sauce 214
Seedy Buckwheat Bread 44
Self-saucing Sticky Date Pudding 204

sesame
    Ginger Sesame Dressing 210
Simple Kale and Avocado Salad 108
slice
    After Dinner Mint Slice 193
    Miso Caramel Slice 189
Smashed Strawberry Margarita 77
Smoothie Bowl 3 Ways 67
smoothies
    Blueberry Muffin Smoothie 73
    Chocolate Banana Shake 69
    Green Goodness 63
    Hempy Tropical Vibes 63
    Peanut Butter Freak Shake 73
    Salted Caramel Blend 69
Soba Noodles and Sticky Eggplant 128
Spiced Cherry Biryani 159
Spicy Massaman Curry 169
Sri Lankan Pulled Jackfruit Curry 149
stir-fry
    Peanut Butter Noodle Stir-fry 138
strawberry
    Smashed Strawberry Margarita 77
    Strawberries and Cream Ice Creams 196
    Strawberry and Hazelnut Salad 117
sunflower seed
    Sunflower Parmesan 211
    Sunflower Seed Milk 215
Sunrise Chia Pudding 39
Sunshine Smoothie Bowl 67

taco
    Breakfast Tacos 53
tahini
    ACV Tahini 210
    Fig and Tahini Bliss Balls 88
tart
    Custard Tarts 191
    Raw Lemon and Coconut Pie 199
tofu
    Tofu Poke Bowl 114
    Tofu Scramble 53
turmeric
    Golden Hour Latte 75

Vegetable Pho 135
Veggie Skewers with Chimichurri Sauce 103

Walnut Breakfast Cookies 59
Wholesome Black Bean Nachos with Cashew
    Cheese 175

yoghurt
    Curried Yoghurt Dressing 210

Text and photography: © Kelsi Boocock, 2021
Photos © Claire Murphy, pages 1, 10, 20 (top),
21 (bottom right), 65 (top and bottom right),
72 (top right, bottom left and right),
90–91, 155, 216, 218.

The moral rights of the author have been asserted.

Typographical design © David Bateman Ltd, 2021

Published in 2021 by David Bateman Ltd,
Unit 2/5 Workspace Drive, Hobsonville,
Auckland 0618, New Zealand

Reprinted 2021

www.batemanbooks.co.nz

ISBN: 978-1-98-853881-5

This book is copyright. Except for the purposes of fair review, no part may be stored or transmitted in any form or by any means, electronic or mechanical, including recording or storage in any information retrieval systems, without permission in writing from the publisher. No reproduction may be made, whether by photocopying or any other means, unless a licence has been obtained from the publisher or its agent.

A catalogue record for this book is available from the National Library of New Zealand.

Book design: Katrina Duncan
Printed in China by Everbest Printing Co. Ltd